Critical S

Levi Isaac C

Production by eBookPro Publishing
www.ebook-pro.com

Critical State
Levi Isaac Cohen

Translation from Hebrew: Simon Spungin
Editing: Raz Barnoach

Contact: ywrmlk@gmail.com

ISBN 9798291391983

Critical State

The History of Israel and the Future of the Jewish State

LEVI ISAAC COHEN

Contents

Introduction

I am not a historian, but I have been fascinated by history—and especially by understanding historical processes—since I was a young boy. Throughout my entire life, I have read and studied history. Historical events and historical developments, in particular, have always held a certain fascination for me. I was fascinated by and always felt I was 'blessed' with an ability to recognize historical trends. I was born, raised, educated, and worked my whole life in the State of Israel. My late mother immigrated to Israel from Vienna at the age of nine-and-a-half, an only child who had the good fortune to be spirited out of Austria by her parents just a week before the outbreak of World War II. After a tortuous four-month journey organized by the Jewish Agency, she arrived in Palestine in December 1939.

I received a European-style education at home, and by the time I finished university, it was clear to me that Israel's occupation of the West Bank might eventually lead to the destruction of the state, would ruin Israeli society, and would turn it into a violent and lawless country. I thought about continuing my education abroad. Even though I was accepted into overseas universities, my mother beseeched me not to leave Israel and, at the last minute, I decided to stay. I have never looked back. I had the privilege of interning at the High Court of Justice. At the Hebrew University of Jerusalem, I was a teaching assistant for Prof. Aharon Barak—who would also be appointed as a Supreme Court justice and, later, as president of the Supreme Court.

Throughout my extensive and strenuous career, I have kept close tabs on events in the State of Israel. I have now reached the conclusion that I can share my views on Israel and the processes unfolding here. This book does not try to paint a rosy picture and is not written to please anyone. It does not glorify Israel, is not an exercise in public relations, and does not relay any false sense of optimism. It reflects a genuine and unbiased view of reality—while adhering strictly to the facts and the historical truth—to the best of my understanding.

David Ben Gurion, who is rightly considered the father of the nation, wrote that the State of Israel will not survive unless it is a country in which law, justice, morality, and equality are its founding principles.[1] He was right. Unlike many countries, Israel is subject to existential threats from its neighbors, which seek to bring about its (physical) demise. Under these circumstances, the absence of these principles would mean that Israel will not survive.

This book details the accomplishments of the State of Israel, from its establishment and consolidation—which, in many respects, are extraordinary achievements, human and social wonders. But it also addresses the severe problems Israel faces, including the growing phenomena of corruption, immorality, lack of social solidarity, polarization between different groups in society, intolerance of other opinions, violence, religious messianism, growing nationalism, and politicians who are cynical, corrupt, and manipulative. All of these endanger Israel's image in the world, its economy, its solid foundations, and its very future.

This book is not designed to be a history of Israel; rather, it provides an overview of the dynamics that preceded its establishment and the most significant events since then. These will form the basis for a discussion of the most critical issues facing Israel and will allow the reader to understand the background to the current dramatic events in Israeli society—events that could defeat the country from within unless there is a major change in direction.

---

1. "A State at Any Cost: The Life of David Ben Gurion," by Tom Segev.

One more point: the analyses provided herein reflect my best judgment and understanding of reality and the unfolding of events. I refrained, as far as possible, from making any predictions, since no mortal can unequivocally see the future. There were some cases, however, where that was unavoidable. I would be happy if some of these predictions did not come true. Readers are invited to draw their own conclusions.

Chapter 1

The Jews and the State of Israel

The story of the establishment of the State of Israel is an incredible, fascinating, and inspiring one. It is the impossible realization of a 2,000-year-old dream. It was against all the odds. No right-thinking person would have given it any chance of success. In the history of human civilization, there has been nothing like it. Never before had a people that were scattered to all four corners of the earth for 2,000 years risen again. Slowly, and with incredible human fortitude, led by people with rare courage, vision, leadership, and determination, they returned to their indigenous homeland. They built the social, organizational, economic, scientific, and later military infrastructure needed to establish the Jewish State from scratch. They made something out of nothing. A truly unique wonder of human society.

Our story, however, begins with the events leading up to the destruction of the Second Jewish Temple. These events are in the very DNA of every Israeli and every Jew with an awareness and knowledge of history—and Jewish history in particular. We will use these events throughout the book to show the threads connecting the Jewish people's past in the Land of Israel to what is happening in the State of Israel today. The similarities that exist between the Second Temple-era zealots and the religious-messianic Jewish extremists of today are highly concerning, extremely threatening, and pose a grave danger to the future of the modern State of Israel. They raise a fundamental question: Are Jews capable of establishing and running an independent country for a long period of time? Do the Jewish people—who have been blessed with a rich history, with incredible accomplishments in every sphere of life and with individuals who have become global cultural icons over a 3,000-year period, and whose contribution to the world of spirituality, culture, science and technology that far exceeds their numbers[2]—have the communal characteristics needed to have an independent, sovereign state over a significant length of time?

We will start, therefore, with the Second Temple. The First Temple existed for some 280 years, from around 1000 BCE. It was built by the Kings of Israel—Saul, David, and Solomon. It was during the reign of Rehoboam, Solomon's son, that the first Jewish Civil War began. The outcome was the division of the unified Kingdom of Israel into the kingdoms of Judah and Israel. The latter survived until 721 BCE, when it was conquered by the ancient kingdom of Assyria. The Kingdom of Judah, which is mentioned extensively in the Bible and from which many impressive archaeological artifacts have been found, enjoyed fluctuating fortunes and survived until 586 BCE, when it was conquered by the Babylonians. This came about because the leaders of Judah made a dramatic error of judgment by forging an alliance with the Kingdom of Egypt, which was seen as an enemy of the Babylonians. As a result, Hezekiah, the king of Judah, was captured, and most of the Jewish population was exiled—most of them to Aram-Naharaim, in modern-day Iraq.

The years passed, and the Persian Empire was led by Cyrus the Great, a powerful and visionary monarch. One of his policies was to allow the Jews to return to the Land of Israel and resettle it. As a result, in 458 BCE, Ezra and Nehemiah, two religious officials in Babylon, migrated from Iraq to the Land of Israel with tens of thousands of their followers to Jerusalem. That was around 120 years after the destruction of the First Temple. Over time, they were joined by more Jews from across the region. By 166 BCE,

---

2. Around 22 percent of Nobel laureates are Jewish, while Jews make up less than 0.2 percent of the world's population.

there were already half a million Jews living in the Land of Israel, an impressive number for that time in history. At that time, the Land of Israel, Syria, and Lebanon were ruled by the Seleucid dynasty, which was founded by a general and successor of Alexander III of Macedon, better known as Alexander the Great, who defeated the Persian Empire and occupied its lands. Alexander divided up his spoils between his ministers and commanders. The Seleucids were given the Land of Israel, Lebanon, and Syria. In 166 BCE, the Jews launched a rebellion against their Seleucid occupiers. The revolt lasted several years and was led by the Hasmoneans, who lived in the Modi'in region. These were the Maccabees, after whom the revolt is now named. The head of the Hasmoneans was Mattathias, who had five sons. Two of his sons were killed during the revolt, but his third son, Judas Maccabeus, proved himself to be a courageous, daring leader who showed impressive leadership and tactical acumen. He took charge of the rebel forces and eventually secured victory.[3] By 161 BCE, the Seleucids had been defeated, and the Land of Israel was once again controlled by Jews, led by Judas Maccabeus, who is now viewed as a wise, responsible, and honest leader. That was the beginning of the Second Temple period. When Judas Maccabeus died at the Battle of Elasa in 160 BCE, he was succeeded by his brother, Jonathan Apphus. In practice, the Maccabee family ruled the Land of Israel, but even then, its rule involved many internecine arguments, which often led to physical violence and many murders. As a result of these disputes and requests to Roman General Pompey, in 63 BCE, Roman Empire troops marched into the Land of Israel and conquered it. The Hasmonean kingdom, therefore, remained independent for around 100 years. Thereafter, the Land of Israel was under the control of the Romans, the dominant global empire at the time. Roman rule lasted decades. In 66 CE, around 130 years after the start of the Roman occupation, the Jewish population began to rise up against the occupiers. These revolts erupted in

---

3. The Jewish holiday of Hanukkah commemorates this victory.

various places throughout the Land of Israel. At around that time, Herod Agrippa II, one of the leaders of the Jewish people, gave an address to the people of Jerusalem, which Jewish historian Flavius Josephus (Yosef ben Matityahu) documented in his book *The History of the Jewish War against the Romans*.

In his address, Agrippa tells the people of Jerusalem about the might and strength of the Roman Empire and warns them that they have no chance of launching a successful revolt against it. This was, of course, sage advice. At that time, the Roman Empire was at the height of its power. Anyone rebelling against it had no chance of success. Nonetheless, a revolt did indeed break out and, because of Jewish zealots, it intensified. These zealots were characterized by a messianic fervor and a refusal to listen to logical considerations or sober analyses of the situation.[4] In 68 CE, the Romans quashed the rebellion, although groups of radical Jewish zealots entered Jerusalem, took control of the city, murdered the leaders of the local community, who were more moderate, and continued to revolt against Rome, committing acts of violence, including murder, against their own people. In the end, the Romans captured Jerusalem in 70 CE and sacked the Temple. To this day, Jews mourn the day on which the Temple was destroyed.

Even after the revolt was put down, most Jews remained in the Land of Israel. Only the leaders of the rebellion were captured and taken to Rome. There was still a Jewish majority in the Land of Israel, however. Around 60 years later, in 132 CE, another revolt was launched against the Roman Empire. This revolt lasted for three years and was led by Simon Bar Kochba (Bar Kokhba) and had the support of the greatest living Jewish sage, Rabbi Akiva.[5]

---

4. Sadly, even at this stage, the modern State of Israel also contains significant elements which are characterized by the same hostility toward foreigners, disdain for considerations based on political logic, denial of the importance of a broad education and openness to the outside world, and an unfounded sense of superiority to others – as well as a messianic-religious belief that God will lead Israel to endless victories.

5. Once again, the inescapable conclusion is that great Torah sages can be utterly clueless when it comes to political matters.

This revolt against the mighty Roman Empire was also hopeless from the outset. At that time, Rome was at the height of its power, under Emperor Hadrian, considered one of the most successful emperors of the Roman Empire. This time, the revolt ended not only with the conquest of Jerusalem, not only with the deaths of hundreds of thousands of Jews—but with the full exile of all the Jews from the Land of Israel. This was, in fact, the second destruction. In order to eradicate any memory of the Kingdom of Judah, Hadrian ordered that the province be renamed Syria Palaestina (the term Palestine comes from the Greek). The move was intended to sever the connection of the Jews to their historical homeland.

The Jews were sent into exile and were scattered across the world. The exile lasted almost 2,000 years. Before we go back to the Jews' return to the Land of Israel, however, it is important to stress: the whole Second Temple incident, the Great Jewish Revolt and the Bar Kokhba Revolt, were characterized by extremist elements, people who believed unwaveringly in the righteousness of their cause, who ignored facts, reality, and reasoned arguments because they were unwilling and unable to listen to them. They were all filled with the belief that they were in the right and did not allow logical and realistic considerations to penetrate and influence their worldview. It is important to stress this because right now, in the modern-day State of Israel, people with extremist religious and messianic worldviews wield massive influence over the conduct of the new state. Anyone who is aware of historical processes must draw a link between these phenomena.

Let us return to the historical sequence of events. The exile. This is a complex period of Jewish history. For centuries, Jews were not a sovereign nation and were not called upon to make decisions as a people in control of their own destiny or politically and governmentally responsible for the ramifications of their choices and conduct. The Jewish people lost the experience and the ability to govern, with all the compromises, decisions, and mechanisms of government and order that are needed to run a state. This dramatic fact would have equally dramatic ramifications for the Jewish state that would be established for a third time in the 20th century.

It was during the 19th century that the Western world underwent processes of nationalism. New countries were "born" in Europe in the aftermath of countless wars, including those waged by Napoleon Bonaparte, who brought about social revolution and new human rights. These developments also sparked new movements within European Jewry. There was an ever-increasing phenomenon of Jews integrating into local society, in a process known as emancipation. These newfound freedoms were opposed by groups of religious Jews. Thus, European Jewry was split between those who advocated assimilation into local societies, including in the areas of education and study, and those who aspired to isolation from the locals, insularity, and efforts to maintain the practices of their faith. The Haskalah, also known as the Jewish Enlightenment, meant that Jews were becoming closer to new worldviews of nationalism. Between 1818 and 1870, there was a massive outbreak of nationalism across Europe. These developments also brought with them harbingers of increasing antisemitism—a phenomenon that existed even in enlightened Europe, including in Austria and France. The man who is considered the founder of the Zionist vision—that is, the return of the Jewish people to the Land of Israel to establish a Jewish state—is Theodor (Binyamin Ze'ev) Herzl, a journalist and talented playwright who was born in Hungary in 1860 and lived in Vienna. At the time, Vienna was the cultural capital of Europe and Herzl wrote for the Neue Freie Presse newspaper. It was as a correspondent for the newspaper that he covered the trial of Captain Alfred Dreyfus, who was accused of treason for communicating French military secrets to the German Embassy in Paris.

The Dreyfus Trial sent shockwaves through France. Famed writer Émile Zola penned J'Accuse, an open letter in the newspaper L'Aurore, in which he accused the French army of antisemitism and of fabricating evidence against the Jewish officer. Herzl, who covered the trial as a reporter, was shocked by the levels of antisemitism. This dramatic incident spurred him on to new and exciting activities. He dedicated himself to Zionism, to encouraging Jews in the Diaspora to return to the Land of Israel. He effectively launched the Zionist movement. Herzl was suddenly seen as an oddball in Vienna, where he was mocked (including by Stefan Zweig in his book *The World of Yesterday*). But elsewhere, especially in parts of Poland and Russia, Herzl and his ideas were warmly welcomed. The Zionist movement was officially established in 1897, at the First Zionist Congress, in Basel, Switzerland. From that moment, the reverberations of Zionism and Herzl's work resonated mainly with Jews in Eastern Europe—in Russia and Poland. One of the people swept up in this new movement was David Grün, later to become David Ben-Gurion.

Grün was a young man when Herzl visited the town he was living in, but he left a lasting impression on him. Slowly but surely, the Zionist movement began to win supporters, especially in Eastern Europe, where economic hardship and antisemitism were prevalent. The first large wave of Jewish immigration to the Land of Israel was in 1882. These pioneers set up agricultural communities in Rishon LeZion and Petah Tikvah.[6] Later, more settlers arrived, including Ben-Gurion.

At that time, the Land of Israel was under the control of the Ottoman Empire, which made it hard for Jews to settle the land. By 1914, there were around 75,000 Jews in the Land of Israel, most of them living in moshavim and agricultural communities. World War I brought a temporary halt to Jewish immigration. Ben-Gurion and his close friend, Zalman Shazar, who would go on to become the second president of the State of Israel, traveled together to Turkey to continue their legal studies. From there, they traveled to the United States to try and recruit the support of American Jews. Their visit to the United States was not a success,

---

6. Approximately 40% of them left Palestine and 90% of the youngsters; see Yehoshua Kaniel, "The figures of immigration from Palestine in the 1st and 2nd Immigration," Katedra 73, September 1994.

but one of the people they did manage to recruit was Golda Meir, at the time Golda Meyerson, who was living in Cleveland.[7] At the end of World War I, Ben-Gurion and Shazar returned to the Land of Israel, which by that time was under British control. In a complex move, Zionist leaders in the United Kingdom, spearheaded by world-renowned chemist Dr. Chaim Weizmann, managed to get the British foreign secretary to sign a declaration recognizing the rights of the Jewish people to a national homeland in the Land of Israel. That was the Balfour Declaration, and it gave the Zionist movement and its goals—the foremost of which was the establishment of a Jewish state in the Land of Israel—its first official international recognition. At that time, there were in Palestine 75,000 Jews and 675,000 Palestinians. The next few years, up to the outbreak of World War II in 1939, were years of institutional building by the Jewish settlement, including the Jewish Agency. The Histadrut's mission was to look after workers' rights, build medical institutions to provide healthcare to the community, and establish schools, colleges, and universities, including the Hebrew University of Jerusalem in 1928. The university, which was co-founded by Dr. Albert Einstein, the Technion, and the Bezalel Academy of Art and Design; the Habima and Cameri theaters; and other cultural and educational institutions. They also set up paramilitary organizations to provide training, some of which were known to the British authorities, while others—the Haganah, the Palmach, and the Irgun, which was an offshoot of the Haganah—were clandestine, leading to the development of an underground weapons industry. The rise to power of the Nazis in 1933 led to a significant wave of immigration from Germany. These new arrivals contributed greatly to the economy and industry of the Land of Israel. At the outbreak of World War II, the Jewish population of the Land of Israel was 450,000, and there were around 1.1 million Arabs. It is important to note that, when their Mandate in Palestine began, the British conducted a

---

7. Later to become Israel's foreign minister and (so far) only female prime minister.

census, which found that the population of the Land of Israel (the territory to the west of the Jordan River) was 757,182. Of them, 591,000 were Muslims, around 84,000 were Jewish, and 73,000 were Christians. By 1948, on the eve of the outbreak of the War of Independence, there were 1.2 million Arab residents (Muslims and Christians).[8] There had already been violent clashes between the Jewish and Arab residents. The battle for the Land of Israel was well underway. There were sporadic riots and attacks, the worst of them coming in 1921, 1929, and 1936-1939. The British were called upon to restore law and order under extremely testing conditions. There were British judges in the highest positions in the Mandatory legal system, with only a handful of Jews and Arabs occupying positions lower down the ladder. This legal system is one of the greatest gifts that the State of Israel, when it was established, would inherit from the British Mandate. The Jewish community in the Land of Israel waited out World War II in trepidation. In 1942, there was genuine concern that the German army would invade. The Jews in Palestine prepared for the worst. That danger abated when the British won the Battle of El-Alamein in their Egypt campaign. When the war ended, the horrific reality of what had happened in Europe became apparent to the Jews in the Land of Israel. Ben-Gurion had seen European Jewry as a vast and valuable resource for the State of Israel. Then the scale of the unspeakable tragedy that had befallen the Jewish people became clear. The Holocaust. Six million Jews—men, women, and children—were murdered. A systematic attempt to wipe out a race—starting with execution by shooting and then in the industrialized slaughter of the concentration camps and gas chambers (see Saul Friedländer's exceptional book *The Years of Extermination: Nazi Germany and the Jews, 1939-1945*, which meticulously details the Nazi efforts to eradicate European Jewry). A vast reservoir of humanity was wiped out with such unspeakable cruelty. And

8. A large proportion of growth in the Arab-Muslim population after 1922 can be ascribed to mass migration from Egypt. Brawer, "The Geography of the Land of Israel and the Middle East," 1975, Pages 72-81.

yet, after the tragedy, it was clear to everyone, not just the Jews, that the establishment of a state for the Jewish people was vital. The rest of the world saw it, too. And so, the idea of a Jewish state gained widespread support. The Jewish settlement, under the leadership of Ben-Gurion, prepared for the critical moment when they would declare the establishment of the State of Israel and the inevitable war that would follow. On November 29, 1947, the General Assembly of the United Nations passed Resolution 181, supporting the establishment of a Jewish state, alongside a Palestinian state. The resolution was international recognition of a Jewish state—all that remained was for decisive steps to be taken. The Jewish settlement was blessed with a great leader of historic proportions, David Ben-Gurion, who surrounded himself with excellent people, driven by the mission and their faith in it. On May 14, 1948, Ben-Gurion pronounced the establishment of the State of Israel and read the Declaration of Independence, the founding document of the new state. The Declaration of Independence, which played a similar role to that of the American document from 1776, was also based on UN Resolution 181. This is what it says:

Eretz-Israel [the Land of Israel] was the birthplace of the Jewish people. Here their spiritual, religious, and political identity was shaped. Here they first attained statehood, created cultural values of national and universal significance, and gave to the world the eternal Book of Books (The Bible).

After being forcibly exiled from their land, the people remained faithful to it throughout their Dispersion and never ceased to pray and hope for their return to it and for the restoration of their political freedom in it.

Impelled by this historic and traditional attachment, Jews strove in every successive generation to re-establish themselves in their ancient homeland. In recent decades, they returned in masses. Pioneers, illegal immigrants, and defenders, they made deserts bloom, revived the Hebrew language, built villages and towns, and created a thriving community controlling its own economy and culture, loving peace but knowing how to defend itself, bringing the blessings of progress to all the country's inhabitants, and aspiring towards independent nationhood.

In the year 5657 (1897), at the summons of the spiritual father of the Jewish State, Theodor Herzl, the First Zionist Congress convened and proclaimed the right of the Jewish people to national rebirth in its own country.

This right was recognized in the Balfour Declaration of the 2nd of November, 1917, and reaffirmed in the Mandate of the League of Nations, which, in particular, gave international sanction to the historic connection between the Jewish people and Eretz-Israel and to the right of the Jewish people to rebuild its National Home.

The catastrophe which recently befell the Jewish people— the massacre of millions of Jews in Europe—was another clear demonstration of the urgency of solving the problem of their homelessness by re-establishing in Eretz-Israel the Jewish State, which would open the gates of the homeland wide to every Jew and confer upon the Jewish people the status of a fully privileged member of the comity of nations.

Survivors of the Nazi Holocaust in Europe, as well as Jews from other parts of the world, continued to migrate to Eretz-Israel, undaunted by difficulties, restrictions, and dangers, and never ceased to assert their right to a life of dignity, freedom, and honest toil in their national homeland.

In the Second World War, the Jewish community of this country contributed its full share to the struggle of the freedom- and peace-loving nations against the forces of Nazi wickedness and, by the blood of its soldiers and its war effort, gained the right to be reckoned among the peoples who founded the United Nations.

On the 29th of November, 1947, the United Nations General Assembly passed a resolution calling for the establishment of a Jewish State in Eretz-Israel; the General Assembly required the inhabitants of Eretz-Israel to take such steps as were necessary on their part for the implementation of that resolution. This recognition by the United Nations of the right of the Jewish people to establish their State is irrevocable.

This right is the natural right of the Jewish people to be masters of their own fate, like all other nations, in their own sovereign State.

ACCORDINGLY, WE, MEMBERS OF THE PEOPLE'S COUNCIL, REPRESENTATIVES OF THE JEWISH COMMUNITY OF ERETZ-ISRAEL AND OF THE ZIONIST MOVEMENT, ARE HERE ASSEMBLED ON THE DAY OF THE TERMINATION OF THE BRITISH MANDATE OVER ERETZ-ISRAEL AND, BY VIRTUE OF OUR NATURAL AND HISTORIC RIGHT AND ON THE STRENGTH OF THE RESOLUTION OF THE UNITED NATIONS GENERAL ASSEMBLY, HEREBY DECLARE THE ESTABLISHMENT OF A JEWISH STATE IN ERETZ-ISRAEL, TO BE KNOWN AS THE STATE OF ISRAEL.

WE DECLARE that, with effect from the moment of the termination of the Mandate beginning tonight, the eve of the Sabbath, the 6th of Iyar, 5708 (15th of May, 1948), until the establishment of the elected, regular authorities of the State in accordance with the Constitution which shall be adopted by the Elected Constituent Assembly not later than October 1, 1948, the People's Council shall act as a Provisional Council of State, and its executive organ, the People's Administration, shall be the Provisional Government of the Jewish State, to be called "Israel."

THE STATE OF ISRAEL will be open for Jewish immigration and for the Ingathering of the Exiles; it will foster the development of the country for the benefit of all its inhabitants; it will be based on freedom, justice, and peace as envisaged by the prophets of Israel; it will ensure complete equality of social and political rights to all its inhabitants, irrespective of religion, race, or sex; it will guarantee freedom of religion, conscience, language, education, and culture; it will safeguard the Holy Places of all religions; and it will be faithful to the principles of the Charter of the United Nations.

THE STATE OF ISRAEL is prepared to cooperate with the agencies and representatives of the United Nations in implementing the resolution of the General Assembly of the 29th of November, 1947, and will take steps to bring about the economic union of the whole of ERETZ-ISRAEL.

WE APPEAL to the United Nations to assist the Jewish people in the building-up of its State and to receive the State of Israel into the comity of nations.

WE APPEAL—in the very midst of the onslaught launched against us now for months—to the Arab inhabitants of the State of Israel to preserve peace and participate in the upbuilding of the State on the basis of full and equal citizenship and due representation in all its provisional and permanent institutions.

WE EXTEND our hand to all neighboring states and their peoples in an offer of peace and good neighborliness, and appeal to them to establish bonds of cooperation and mutual help with the sovereign Jewish people settled in its own land. The State of Israel is prepared to do its share in a common effort for the advancement of the entire Middle East.

WE APPEAL to the Jewish people throughout the Diaspora to rally around the Jews of ERETZ-ISRAEL in the tasks of immigration and upbuilding and to stand by them in the great struggle for the realization of the age-old dream—the redemption of Israel.

PLACING OUR TRUST IN THE ALMIGHTY, WE AFFIX OUR SIGNATURES TO THIS PROCLAMATION AT THIS SESSION OF THE PROVISIONAL COUNCIL OF STATE, ON THE SOIL OF THE HOMELAND, IN THE CITY OF TEL-AVIV, ON THIS SABBATH EVE, THE 5TH DAY OF IYAR, 5708 (14TH OF MAY, 1948).

The day after Ben-Gurion declared independence, the neighboring Arab countries—Egypt, Syria, and Jordan—declared war. The newly born and impoverished State of Israel needed luck, effective organization, a courageous population, and mobilization for the military cause. We shall not spend time describing the battles. Rather, there are three important facts that the reader should be aware of since they will shed light on issues raised later in this book. Of the 600,000 Jews living in Israel at the time of its establishment, 6,000 were killed in the War of Independence. In percentage terms, based on today's U.S. population, that would be akin to a war in which 3.3 million Americans were killed. Of the Arab population, around half fled from the nascent state and became refugees. Some of them moved to the West Bank, Jordan, Lebanon, and the Gaza Strip. During the final stages of the war, when it was clear that Israel had the upper hand, the IDF had the opportunity to capture the West Bank from the Jordanians. The matter was brought before Ben-Gurion for a decision,[9] but he was vehemently opposed to the idea, saying that a clear Jewish majority in the State of Israel was essential in order for it to be a Jewish and democratic regime. This issue would trouble the State of Israel for many years to come and would lead to, under different circumstances following the Six-Day War, dramatic and potentially disastrous threats to its society, as well as to the emergence of religious, nationalist, racist, and messianic streams.

After the War of Independence, Israel was a poor state. It was almost penniless. For three years, the government implemented a strict austerity policy, including controls on many foodstuffs. As a result, there was a thriving black market in basic goods. In 1952, three years into Konrad Adenauer's term as German chancellor, negotiations began between Germany and the Israeli government, headed by Ben-Gurion. The talks ended with a generous package of reparations for Jewish victims of the Holocaust, their children, and their heirs. Although many people in Israel objected to the agreement on ideological grounds, the reparations were a significant boost for the Israeli economy. At the same time as facing a dire economic situation—almost on the brink of bankruptcy—the State of Israel was also struggling to fulfill its main function, namely, to be a safe haven for Jews everywhere, somewhere they

---

9. See Ya'akov Tzur's book "From the Sea to the Desert," pages141-150.

could live without fear of harassment or antisemitism. However, as mentioned, the primary potential source for citizens of the State of Israel was wiped out in the Holocaust. On the other hand, in the Arab countries adjacent to Israel and further afield, and especially after the War of Independence and the State of Israel's victory, there were acts of violence against local Jewish communities. This, in turn, intensified the desire of Jews in these countries to join up with the 2,000-year-old dream and to return to the Land of Israel. Ben-Gurion, exhibiting his usual exceptional leadership, decided to make this a national mission. The result was the immigration to Israel of hundreds of thousands of Jews from various Arab countries, including Syria, Morocco, Tunisia, Libya, Iraq, and Egypt. Proportionally, it was as if the United States decided to allow 500 million migrants (!) into the country in the space of three to four years. Of course, it was an almost impossible mission, which required Israel to address many outstanding issues—among them accommodation, schools, clinics, kindergartens, infrastructure for housing, roads, and sewage. All this happened at a time when the economic situation was dire, and the new country lacked financial resources. And that is without even mentioning the social challenges that the move would involve (for more on this, see Chapter 2). In 1956, Israel found itself under threat from Egypt. President Gamal Abdel Nasser, a retired colonel, was trying to acquire massive quantities of arms from European countries and then nationalized the Suez Canal. This was a dramatic move that also threatened Israel and damaged the interests of the United Kingdom and France. The three countries gradually devised a plan to capture the Sinai Peninsula and take control of the Suez Canal. In 1956, the IDF launched a blitz offensive and, with the help of the British and French air forces, captured the Gaza Strip[10] and the Sinai within

10. During the withdrawal from the Sinai, Ben-Gurion was worried about the Gaza Strip remaining in Israeli hands since that would leave Israel with responsibility for the welfare of 250,000 people (as it was in 1956; the current population of Gaza is 2 million) and would expose Israel to a security threat "like

seven days, with the loss of just 170 soldiers. It was a stunning military achievement. However, within just a few days, the Soviet Union issued an ultimatum, demanding a complete withdrawal from the Sinai. A similar ultimatum came from the United States, which also threatened to impose an arms embargo. Ben-Gurion, who was still prime minister at the time, with his considerable leadership skills and decision-making experience, recognized the severity of these threats and that it had been a mistake to join forces with the French and the British. He took the decision, as leader, to withdraw from the Sinai. Within three months, the IDF had completely withdrawn from the peninsula.[11]

While all of this was going on, the State of Israel was progressing under the leadership of Ben-Gurion and was expanding its educational institutions and building hospitals (13 were built between 1948 and 1962, compared to just one between 2009 and 2023). During those years, up until 1964, Arab society in Israel lived under military rule. As a result, the activities of Israel's Arab citizens were limited in terms of movement—as well as, of course, in terms of employment. Because of this, it was impossible for them to integrate into Israeli society during that period. They were all viewed—and there is some justification for this suspicion—as collaborators with enemy states. When Ben-Gurion's time as prime minister ended and Levy Eshkol took over, military rule was lifted for the first time. This created a historic opportunity to integrate Israeli Arabs into Israeli society. This is a process that continues even today and, even though there have been some accomplishments, there could have been more and

---

the more dangerous explosives." Incidentally, Benjamin Netanyahu's father, Prof. Benzion Netanyahu, approached Ben-Gurion and tried to persuade him to remain in Gaza and, at the same time, to achieve this goal, to set up a propaganda mechanism in the United States, to be operated by the State of Israel but without any official ties to the government. He offered himself as head of the project and suggested that his real activity could be concealed by getting him a lecturing job at an American university. *See footnote 11, Page 553.*

11. See Tom Segev, "A State at Any Cost: The Life of David Ben-Gurion," Pages 530-550.

should have been more—given that, in practice, this process of integration was hugely beneficial.[12] 1967 found the State of Israel in repeated confrontations with Egypt.

The 1967 war, known as the Six-Day War, was a dramatic turning point in the history of the State of Israel. On the one hand, it proved to the Arab world that Israel was an impressive military power. It bolstered Israel's image in the world, and global sympathy for Israel grew. The Jewish world was proud of its accomplishments, and immigration increased significantly. Israel captured the Sinai from Egypt, the Golan Heights from Syria, and the West Bank from Jordan. Taking the Egyptian Sinai quickly led to land battles along the defensive line on the Nile. There were constant artillery and commando attacks. During those years, the State of Israel made economic progress. In the West Bank, however, Jewish settlements suddenly started appearing. The first of them was established on the eve of the Passover holiday in Hebron in 1968. A number of families settled there. That was the starting point for a Jewish settlement movement, a religious-nationalist movement created by the National Religious Party-Hapoel Hamizrachi, which also included disciples of the ideology of Rabbi Zvi Yehuda Kook. We will return to this group, which continued to grow in size and strength and which brought about the roots of the greatest disaster to the State of Israel: a group of national-religious, messianic fanatics who believe in the start of redemption (*Atchalta De'Geulah* in Aramaic) and the supremacy of Jews over Palestinian Arabs. While the Jewish settlement of the West Bank was progressing gradually, on the Egyptian front there were already talks over an agreement in the Sinai. U.S. Secretary of State William Rogers tried to mediate between Egypt and Israel, with proposals for interim agreements, including an Israeli withdrawal up to 20 kilometers from the Suez Canal, as well as other

---

12. More than 35 percent of medical professionals in Israel are Arabs and Arab-Israelis are integrated in many walks of life, often in senior positions, including in the High Court of Justice. The extent of this integration is less than optimal.

suggestions. The Israeli government, under the leadership of Golda Meir, rejected all these offers. Meir, who was raised in the United States, dedicated her life to Israel and later worked alongside Ben-Gurion—but on this issue, she was unwisely stubborn and obstinate. Warnings from Egyptian President Anwar Sadat, who said that he would be willing to sacrifice a million Egyptian soldiers to liberate the Sinai, fell on deaf ears. Meir rejected every interim proposal. She had absolute faith in the strength of the IDF to rebuff any Egyptian attempt to liberate or capture the Sinai. However, her faith was baseless. On October 6, 1973, at 2 o'clock p.m., Egyptian and Syrian forces launched joint attacks on Israel, which was taken by surprise. The shock was immense. The war broke out on Yom Kippur, the holiest day in the Jewish calendar.

The first two days of the war raised concerns about the very future of the State of Israel. There were genuine concerns that the Syrian army would capture the Golan Heights and infiltrate into northern Israel, including the Galilee. Similar concerns existed on the Egyptian front.

The Egyptians crossed the Suez Canal, captured the Israeli positions on its eastern banks, and there were concerns that they would continue eastwards. The first IDF offensive, on October 8, was a failure. Israel was experiencing shortages of arms and ammunition. The United States came to Israel's assistance and started to airlift munitions. This was a significant contribution to Israel. The war continued with heavy fighting for more than two weeks. By the end of the conflict, the IDF had managed to repel the Egyptians from the Sinai and cross the Suez Canal in a complex operation, reaching within 100 kilometers of the Egyptian capital.

On the northern front, too, Israel managed to push the Syrian army away from the Golan Heights and came within 40 kilometers of Damascus. The Yom Kippur War was the catalyst for a number of profound changes in the Israeli perception. The first was a loss of trust in the Israeli leadership. The second was the understanding that the IDF is not invincible and that more wars could pose an existential threat to the state. Israel can win many wars, but one defeat would spell its end. Third, the understanding that Israel's goal must be to forge peace agreements with its Arab neighbors. In the aftermath of the Yom Kippur War, there were demonstrations against the government calling for a change in leadership. In 1976, an Air France plane that was flying from Paris to Israel was hijacked by Palestinian terrorists and diverted to Entebbe Airport in Uganda. Israel, under the leadership of the late Yitzhak Rabin, took the daring decision to send planes and highly trained commandos to launch a rescue attempt. It was an especially complex operation, thousands of kilometers from Israel's borders—and it succeeded beyond expectations. The commandos managed to rescue all the hostages, apart from one woman. However, Yoni Netanyahu, the commander of the elite Sayeret Matkal commando unit, was killed. Subsequently, Netanyahu's brother, Benjamin, who was living in the United States at the time, launched a campaign to memorialize Yoni, which eventually led to his return to Israel. Benjamin Netanyahu, of course, would go on to become Israel's prime minister, bringing unprecedented destruction and harm in almost every area (see Chapters 6-10 for more). Ironically, it is possible that if Yoni had not died in the Entebbe raid, his brother would have remained a citizen of the United States.

In the 1977 Israeli general election, for the first time in its history, the Likud party—led by Ben-Gurion's long-time rival and former leader of the Irgun, Menachem Begin—was elected to power.

That was a dramatic change in the course of Israel's history. From that moment on, the Mapai Party—the leaders of which were the state's founding fathers—was no longer the ruling party. During the Likud's time in power, between 1977 and 1981, the government empowered the settlement movement in the West Bank. The settlers were given ever-increasing financial support. On the other hand, in 1978, after prolonged and clandestine negotiations, in a dramatic and historic announcement, it was reported that Anwar Sadat, the president of Egypt, who had led his country during the Yom Kippur War, would be coming to Jerusalem. The Israeli public was gripped by indescribable excitement. And the reports turned out to be true. Sadat, one of the greatest Egyptian leaders of all time, flew to Israel and delivered a courageous and historic speech in the Israeli parliament. Two years later—during which there were domestic disagreements in Israel and the Americans provided close and encouraging support, including meetings in the United States with U.S. President Jimmy Carter, the Egyptian president, Israeli Prime Minister Menachem Begin, and members of his cabinet—the Camp David peace accord between Israel and Egypt was finalized. As part of the agreement, Israel returned the entire Sinai Peninsula to Egypt, which became a demilitarized zone. The two sides entered an era of peace, which included the opening of embassies in each other's capital cities. It was an historic achievement for the State of Israel, the government of the late Menachem Begin, President Sadat, and the Egyptian people. Likud also won the 1981 election, and Menachem Begin formed a new government, which now included Ariel Sharon. Sharon—a highly decorated general with an outstanding military record, a courageous and daring character, and exceptional leadership qualities—was appointed defense minister. In 1982, after the attempted assassination of the Israeli ambassador in London, Israel went to war against Lebanon. The war dragged on and ended with Yasser Arafat, the head of the Palestinian Liberation Organization, fleeing Beirut. That was followed by a pathetic and hopeless attempt to get Bachir Gemayel, the leader of the Christian minority in Lebanon, appointed president and to sign a peace deal with him. Gemayel was duly elected president in August 1982, but just a month later, he was killed, along with dozens of members of his party, when a massive bomb was detonated during a party meeting at the Kataeb Party headquarters in Beirut. The Israel-Lebanon "peace accord" lasted just a few days, after which Israel found itself sinking into the Lebanese quagmire for almost two decades. It was only in 2001 that the government of Ehud Barak withdrew Israeli forces from Lebanese soil.

However, the Israeli invasion undermined the internal structure of its neighbor to the north.

A vacuum was created in Lebanon, a fragile country made up of various cultural groups—Druze, Muslims, Sunnis, Shiites, and Christian Arabs—all of which were in conflict with each other. Foreign forces filled the vacuum. To begin with, the Syrians took control of large parts of Lebanese territory, as well as its economy. However, parts of southern Lebanon were taken over by Hezbollah, the Iranian-backed organization. The Lebanese army, which was relatively small, was unable to prevent these foreign forces from taking control. In the meantime, in 2011, disturbances erupted in Syria, leading to over a decade of devastation in that country. One of the results of the Syrian civil war was that Damascus' control of Lebanon was left in ruins. On the other hand, however, Hezbollah's strength continued to grow within Lebanon until it even played a senior role in the Lebanese parliament and, of course, increased its military might and became a significant military power.[13]

In many respects, the (First) Lebanon War that Israel launched not only embroiled Israel in the Lebanese quagmire but also created the infrastructure that allowed Hezbollah, the Iranian proxy, to get a foothold in Lebanon. Another march of Israeli folly. The economic measures enacted by the Likud government in the years after 1984 sent Israel into an inflationary tailspin. In 1984 and 1985, the annual inflation rate rocketed to over 300 percent. Many sectors of the Israeli economy were hurt by this crisis, and the U.S. administration stepped in to help. In 1987, the Israeli government, under Shimon Peres from the Labor Party, launched an economic plan. The plan, which was drawn up by Prof. Michael Bruno—a world-renowned Israeli economist—with the help of the United States, managed to stabilize the Israeli economy within a matter of years, gradually reducing the rate of

---

13. Hezbollah, a Shiite organization in Lebanon, became a proxy for the Shiite regime in Iran. It is funded by Tehran, as well as by growing and selling narcotics.

inflation until it reached around 3 or 4 percent (!) a year. Israeli entrepreneurs and businessmen also contributed to this astonishing achievement. At the same time, the Kibbutz Movement paid a heavy financial price for these years of high levels of inflation. As a result, the communal economic model of many kibbutzim was radically altered. In 1991, under the patronage of the United States and the Soviet Union, the Madrid Conference was convened, and representatives of the Israeli, Egyptian, Syrian, Lebanese, and Jordanian governments were invited to attend. The Palestinians were part of the Jordanian delegation. Although the Madrid Conference did not yield any tangible results, it did produce two important principles. First, for the first time, all the Arab states recognized the existence of the State of Israel. This was an achievement of unparalleled importance. Second, there were the first-ever contacts—albeit unofficial—between the Palestinian delegation and the Israeli government. Having said that, the government of Israel at the time—which was headed by Yitzhak Shamir, the hawkish right-winger whose delegation to Madrid included Benjamin Netanyahu as Deputy Foreign Minister—had no intention of making any progress on the Palestinian issue. The general election of 1992 saw the Labor Party return to power and its leader, Yitzhak Rabin, become prime minister for a second term.

In 1992 and 1993, Israel found itself in a state of diplomatic stalemate. The election saw a handover of power, and the Labor Party, headed by the late Yitzhak Rabin—the IDF chief of staff in the Six-Day War—formed a government. It would eventually come to light that, for around one year, a group of private individuals, along with officials from the Israeli government, senior figures from the PLO, and partners from Norway, had been holding practical talks, which led to a breakthrough in relations between Israel and the Palestinians. The agreement was made public in 1993. The agreement, known as the Oslo Accords, was eventually signed, in an official ceremony at the White House, by Prime Minister Yitzhak Rabin and Foreign Minister Shimon Peres on the Israeli side, Yasser Arafat, the leader of the PLO, on the Palestinian side, and U.S. President Bill Clinton.

The Oslo Accords were a historic breakthrough. For the first time, two of the leading players in the Israeli-Palestinian conflict recognized each other. After hesitation, much suspicion, and concern for the future, the agreement was signed. Under the framework of the deal, Yasser Arafat and his officials, who lived in Tunisia, returned to the West Bank and set up their institutions there. Israel and the Palestinian Authority started to forge relations. A year later, detailed and intricate economic agreements were also signed, allowing the Palestinian Authority to control the economic lives of its people. At the first stage, the PA took control of parts of the West Bank and, over the next five years, more territory was due to be handed over to Palestinian control. During that period, the sides would discuss solutions to issues that were not addressed in the Oslo Accords.

In 1994, meanwhile, the Hashemite Kingdom of Jordan signed a peace accord with Israel, becoming the second Arab state to do so. Once again, significant progress was made toward workable agreements in the Middle East. Israel reaped massive economic benefits from these developments. There was global support for the Oslo Accords, and a wave of optimism swept over Israel. Foreign investors flocked to Israel. International companies, which, because of the Arab boycott, had refrained from opening businesses in Israel, started to do just that. Of course, all of this was a major boost for the Israeli economy. This was a time of optimism, and positive change was in the air.

However, there were (and still are) extremists on both the Palestinian side and the Israeli side who rejected the process. On the Israeli side, groups of right-wingers and messianic religious settlers and their supporters started to protest against the Oslo Accords. There were many demonstrations, which were always raucous and often violent. The Israel Police and the security services, including the Shin Bet, were extremely lenient in their handling of these protests. In 1994, Dr. Baruch Goldstein, a settler from Kiryat Arba, entered the Tomb of the Patriarchs in Hebron and murdered 29 Muslim worshippers. In response to this heinous murder, Palestinian extremists carried out a wave of mass-casualty terror attacks. Hundreds of Israelis were killed. The atmosphere in Israel was tense, violent, and volatile. It would take courage and determination to forge ahead with the Oslo peace process. The Palestinian Authority occasionally created problems and did not act in good faith, but the government of Yitzhak Rabin insisted on going ahead with the process, despite all the opposition. On November 4, 1995—a Saturday night—a mass peace rally was held in one of the main squares in Tel Aviv. Among the participants were Prime Minister Rabin and Foreign Minister Peres. It was a wonderful rally, with more than 150,000 people taking to the streets to show their support for the peace process. At the end of the rally, however, as Rabin was making his way to his car, three shots rang out. A despicable murderer, a member of the far-right settler camp, fired three shots into Rabin's back, killing him. The State of Israel went into a week of official mourning. The paramount significance, however, was that Rabin, the main force driving the peace process forward, had been stopped.

In retrospect, the Rabin assassination was a dramatic landmark in the history of the State of Israel. It changed the very essence of the country. It was a major blow for those people who believed in and aspired to an agreement with the Palestinians and made it clear that there was a large group of Israeli rightists, primarily messianic and religious ultranationalists, for whom handing over any part of the West Bank to a Palestinian entity was a violation of divine instructions. In their view, this gave them the right—indeed, the duty—to do anything to prevent it, including violence and even murder. The assassination of Yitzhak Rabin also changed the future of the State of Israel. An historic opportunity to reach a comprehensive peace agreement with the Palestinians, thereby ending a decades-long and bloody conflict, was missed. As we will see below, it is possible that the historic crisis that Israel is going through at the time of writing will make that historic opportunity feasible once again.

After Rabin's murder, Shimon Peres was appointed prime minister. Peres, a politician with a wealth of experience and endless accomplishments, decided not to call an immediate general election, opting to wait six months. That was a mistake, and the outcome was electoral defeat. During those six months, there were several Palestinian suicide bombings on Israeli buses, killing hundreds of people. In response, Israel launched an offensive in Lebanon. However, an Israeli shell hit a Lebanese village, killing more than 100 civilians. The operation was halted forthwith. That failure and the wave of terror attacks inside Israel were just some of the reasons that—against expectations—the election was won by a young, inexperienced politician who had just become Likud leader: Benjamin Netanyahu. At that time, Netanyahu appeared to be a promising politician. He was blessed with a silver tongue, his demeanor and appearance exuded supreme self-confidence (something that, years later, would turn out to be false; in practice, he is extraordinarily apprehensive and hesitant), he spoke perfect English, he was tall and handsome, and he had served in an elite military unit as a young man. So began the tenure of Benjamin Netanyahu as Israeli prime minister. Very quickly, however, Netanyahu's flaws and his hesitant and weak character became evident. Various incidents showed that Netanyahu suffers from poor judgment, that he easily panics and becomes hysterical, that he systematically prevaricates and puts off decisions, and that he is incapable of creating any vision or carrying out any significant measures. In the first year of Netanyahu's tenure, with the approval of the prime minister and the mayor of Jerusalem, archaeological digs were conducted in the Jerusalem area. Fueled by false rumors that the digs were an excuse for Israel to grab control of the Temple Mount, there was an outbreak of violence in Jerusalem. Seventeen Israeli soldiers and approximately one hundred Palestinians were killed in the subsequent riots, when police opened fire on Palestinian rioters at Prime Minister Netanyahu's behest. In 1997, the Mossad carried out an operation whose goal was to assassinate Khaled Mashal, who was and still is a senior Hamas member. Hamas, an extremist Islamic Palestinian terrorist group, preaches the destruction of the State of Israel and the eradication of the Jewish people. Hamas views Christians as traitors and wants to deny women their fundamental human rights. The operation was a failure. Two of the agents involved were apprehended by the Jordanian security forces. Amman threatened to sever ties with Israel. Netanyahu panicked and ordered the head of the Mossad to travel to Jordan and give authorities there the antidote to the poison that had been injected into Mashal. Later, Netanyahu caved in yet again, freeing dozens of Hamas terrorists—among them one of the group's top leaders, Sheikh Ahmed Yassin—in exchange for the two Mossad agents.[14] Once again, Netanyahu—who likes to boast about his image as "Mr. Security," the counterterror expert—caved.[15]

Later in his tenure, in October 1998, under pressure from the United States, Netanyahu participated in a meeting with Yasser Arafat and U.S. President Bill Clinton. As a result of the agreement that was reached, which was a continuation of the implementation of the Oslo Accords, Israel withdrew from 13 percent of the territory of the West Bank and transferred it to the control of the Palestinian Authority. In return, the PA committed to fight against Palestinian terror and to end incitement in Palestinian schools. The agreement was signed at a festive ceremony in the United States, attended by Netanyahu, Arafat, Clinton, and King Hussein of Jordan. Netanyahu, however, had no intention of moving forward with the agreement with the Palestinians.

---

14. In his second term of office as prime minister, Netanyahu once again showed the same cowardice and panic when, in exchange for a single Israeli soldier, he freed 1,027 Hamas terrorists – including Yahye Sinwar, who would become one of the organization's most important leaders in Gaza and the person behind the October 7 terrorist massacre.

15. After the rescue operation in Entebbe, Netanyahu wrote a book ("Terrorism: How the West Can Win") which he used to try and build a reputation as a terror expert – a claim that has absolutely no basis.

His government carried out the first withdrawal, but thereafter it used fallacious claims against the Palestinians to freeze the process. In practice, the continued implementation of the agreement was frozen during Netanyahu's first term of office. In the 1999 general election, Netanyahu was defeated. He was replaced by Ehud Barak, a highly decorated former IDF chief who had joined the Labor Party. Israel's impressive economic development continued apace. In 2000, the government decided to end the Israeli military presence in Lebanon. Within two days, in a closely guarded operation, the Israeli forces which had been in southern Lebanon since 1983 withdrew entirely from that country. That ended the Israeli military presence in Lebanon and, since then, no part of Lebanon has been under Israeli control.

However, Hezbollah—a Shiite social and military organization supported and funded by Iran—continued to increase its military strength in southern Lebanon and its political strength in Beirut. From that moment, Hezbollah constituted a military threat to Israel on the northern front and it would continue to be instructed and funded by Tehran. Thanks to Hezbollah, Iran had a military foothold in Lebanon. We will return to Shiite Iran later in this book.

Once Israel had withdrawn from Lebanon, Prime Minister Barak turned his attention to the Palestinian front. He continued to implement the Hebron Accords that were signed during the tenure of his predecessor and forged ahead with efforts to reach a full agreement with the Palestinians. To this end, Arafat and Barak were invited to a summit meeting in the United States, under the sponsorship and auspice of President Clinton.

Barak is a courageous and knowledgeable man, but his faith in his own intelligence rendered him incapable of working with a complex team or organization. He arrived at this dramatic summit without having done the requisite preparatory work.[16] Israel offered to withdraw from 90 percent of the West Bank.

16. See Shaul Arieli's book "Israeli myths about the Israeli-Palestinian conflict" (Yedioth Ahronoth publishing).

Still, other issues—such as the status of Jerusalem and the question of compensation for and the return of refugees from the 1948 war—coupled with Arafat's problematic behavior, which was typically underhanded, prevented decisive agreements from being reached, resulting in the summit ending without a deal. There were dramatic ramifications to this failure. On the Israeli side, Barak coined the phrase "there's no partner for peace" with the Palestinians. For their part, the Palestinians, with the encouragement of the PA and Arafat himself, called on the public to launch an uprising. That was the start of the second intifada. It started as violent riots and moved on to violent resistance, including terror attacks, bombs across Israel, on buses, at bus stations, public places, and hotels (including the Passover attack on the Park Hotel in Netanya, in which 27 people were murdered).[17] The second intifada significantly undermined Israel's domestic security. The riots and demonstrations by Israeli Arabs ended with 12 Arab citizens being shot to death by police. In the subsequent elections, Likud, headed by the late Ariel Sharon, was elected back to power. Sharon was a former IDF general who, in the 1950s, established the IDF elite commando units, successfully commanded a division in the Six-Day War (the Battle of Abu-Ageila in the Sinai Peninsula), and was in charge of the Israeli crossing on the Suez Canal in the Yom Kippur War. He became prime minister.

Months before Ariel Sharon took over as prime minister, Israel's domestic security situation was undermined by the start of the second intifada in 2000. There were violent demonstrations across Israel, including in the Arab sector. It was during these riots that Israeli police, who had not been deployed in large enough numbers to contain the disturbances, shot and killed 12 Arab citizens. The incident opened a raw wound in Arab society in Israel. A series of terror attacks by Palestinian organizations—Hamas and the PLO—led to a deterioration in domestic security.

---

17. The Park Hotel attack was carried out by Hamas, in part to sabotage the Saudi peace plan.

As usual, Sharon displayed admirable leadership. Along with then-IDF chief of staff Shaul Mofaz and the rest of the defense establishment, he gradually came up with a complex plan to take control of the centers of Palestinian terror and violence. This included capturing strongholds in the West Bank. It was in the framework of this operation that Israeli forces entered the Jenin refugee camp, where there were hundreds of heavily armed and well-trained terrorists. After fierce battles, Israel retook control of the West Bank towns and cities. The process of reducing the incidence of terror and violence continued for several years, ending in 2005. In 2004, Arafat died and control of the Palestinian Authority was transferred to Mahmoud Abbas (Abu Mazen). Between 2001 and 2005, terror attacks and violence killed 1,100 Israelis and thousands of Palestinians. It was a period of intensive Israeli-Palestinian violence, during which security cooperation between Israel and the PA ceased. In 2005, Sharon decided that Israel would withdraw its military forces from the Gaza Strip and evacuate the civilian settlements there that were home to around 8,000 Israelis. It is worth taking a moment to provide a few explanatory words about Gaza. From 1948, Gaza was under Egyptian control. The bulk of the population was made up of Palestinian refugees who fled during the 1948 war. Between 1948 and 1967, countless terror attacks were launched from Gaza against Israel by fedayeen militia. Israel captured the Gaza Strip during the Six-Day War in 1967 and controlled it until 1979. During those years, Israel began building civilian settlements along a narrow strip of land on the Mediterranean coast.

The issue of Gaza was raised at the 1979 Camp David summit, organized by President Carter, between Egypt's Sadat and Israel's Begin. Israel wanted Egypt to take control of Gaza, but Cairo refused. No country wanted to take responsibility for the 2 million Palestinians living in Gaza. The Camp David negotiations ended with Gaza remaining in Israeli hands. This constituted a huge burden and a massive risk, something we shall return to later. In the meantime, Israeli forces left Gaza in 2005, and some 8,000

Israeli civilians were evacuated. The process was accompanied by demonstrations and violence within Israeli society. Many opposed the evacuation, especially supporters of the West Bank settlements. Their concern was that the evacuation of settlers from Gaza would become a precedent for removing Jews from the West Bank. That was the core of their fierce opposition. It was during this time that Bezalel Smotrich, who would, in 2023, become finance minister in the State of Israel (!), along with other Jewish settlers, was apprehended with 700 liters of gasoline in his possession, on suspicion of planning to use it to commit a terrorist act. They were suspected of planning a sabotage mission in Israel, in the hope of halting the withdrawal from Gaza.[18] At the same time, Ariel Sharon—as usual—displayed leadership and strength. The complex withdrawal was completed. Gaza became a territory with no control. Palestinian forces entered the vacuum that was created—the Palestinian Authority from the West Bank and Hamas.

At first, the Palestinian Authority was in control, but in 2006 there were elections in Gaza (there are serious doubts over how free and fair the elections were). The Gaza public elected Hamas— the radical Islamic movement which advocates the destruction of Israel, opposes equal rights for women, the LGBTQ community, and foreigners—and which sees Christians as enemies who must be destroyed. Hamas started as a popular movement, but when it grabbed power in Gaza in 2006 and 2007, after violent and brutal clashes with the Palestinian Authority forces, its true face was revealed. Hamas is a cruel, violent, and corrupt organization. In 2006, after completing the withdrawal from Gaza, the Israeli prime minister started to withdraw from parts of the West Bank. That was the first in a series of measures planned by Sharon, who was once seen as one of the leaders of the Israeli settlements in the West Bank. Over the years, Sharon recognized that

---

18. The arrests did not lead to indictments since the Shin Bet used kid gloves – unlike its treatment of Palestinian terror suspected. See the testimony of then-deputy Shin Bet chief, the late Yitzhak Ilan.

Israel could face disaster if the situation remained unchanged. In 2006, however, Sharon suffered a stroke and sank into a coma. He died in 2014. When Sharon became incapacitated, an election was called, which was won by the party he had established—Kadima—now led by Ehud Olmert. Benjamin Netanyahu's Likud party sank to an all-time low of 12 seats in the 120-seat Knesset. Olmert, a lawyer and long-time political activist, came from a right-wing background and supported Israeli control of the West Bank. Eventually, however, his views on the issue changed.

Surprisingly, Olmert turned out to be a decent prime minister, with leadership skills and decision-making abilities. These characteristics are essential for any leader, and especially in Israel. However, shortly after he took over as prime minister, Hezbollah carried out a terror attack on the northern front, launching a cross-border raid against IDF forces. They killed several Israeli soldiers and took two of them captive. In response, Israel decided on a series of strong military measures against Hezbollah, which developed into an all-out war—the Second Lebanon War—which lasted for 34 days. During the conflict, the IDF bombed Lebanon, and Hezbollah fired thousands of rockets at Israeli cities. A total of 44 civilians died, and 121 soldiers were killed in combat. On the Lebanese side, there were hundreds of civilian casualties and around 800 soldiers, from Hezbollah and the Lebanese army, killed. Both sides suffered hundreds of thousands of injuries and massive damage to civilian infrastructure. The two abducted soldiers were murdered by Hezbollah. That painful war, however, led to a period of relative quiet on the northern border with Hezbollah, even though the organization continued to build its military strength over the years (according to estimates, it had more than 120,000 missiles of various kinds), set up Iranian-trained commando units (the elite al-Hajj Radwan Force is believed to have some 8,000 fighters), and also became the de facto ruler of Lebanon. When the war ended, Olmert was criticized roundly, but his government remained in power.

In 2007, it became known that Syria, Israel's neighbor to the northeast, had started work on a military nuclear reactor on its soil. In a hugely complex military and intelligence operation, Israel managed to hit the reactor in September 2007 and take it out of commission—even before the reactor had started the enrichment process, since attacking it once there was radioactive material on the site would cause a nuclear blast and untold damage. To manage the process of preparing for such an operation and deciding to execute it required real leadership—and Olmert proved that he had been blessed with it. He also indicated that Israel would disrupt various Arab countries' efforts to achieve military nuclear capability. Nuclear weapons in the Middle East would be an existential danger to all the countries of the region and could pose a grave threat to other nations. Destroying the Syrian nuclear reactor was a supreme military, intelligence, and operational achievement.

In 2008 and 2009, negotiations between Israel and the Palestinian Authority once again picked up steam. The talks progressed, and many issues, mainly territorial questions and issues related to security and counterterrorism in the West Bank, were settled. However, the core issues of the conflict remained unresolved. Moreover, the Palestinian side found it hard to make decisions and lacked determined leadership. As a result, talks continued without ever reaching an agreement. In the meantime, Olmert's standing at home was undermined after he was accused of illegal activities (taking bribes and other favors in various cases). This led to political instability in Israel, which made continued negotiations with the Palestinians impossible and, in the end, led to another general election in Israel. Those elections brought Benjamin Netanyahu back into the spotlight. Netanyahu—whose only concern was taking power and remaining in power and who was willing to promise his potential coalition partners heaven and earth to achieve his goal. And that is exactly what he did this time, too. As a result, he was able to form a coalition with representatives of the ultra-Orthodox groups in

Israel (Shas and Agudat Yisrael) and from the Labor Party. In Chapter 6, we will look at his personal history. Suffice it to say that, just as David Ben-Gurion was a leader of global stature, one of the ten greatest leaders of the 20th century, and Israel has experienced failed prime ministers in its history, it also had leaders who contributed to significant successes, like Menachem Begin (the peace accord with Egypt), Yitzhak Rabin (the Oslo Accords and peace with Jordan), and Ariel Sharon (ending the second intifada, withdrawing from Gaza, and starting the withdrawal from the West Bank). However, many experts and scholars say that Israel has never had a prime minister as disastrous, as unwilling to take responsibility and to make important and tough decisions, and who, in case of conflict, will prefer his interests over the state as Benjamin Netanyahu.

Instead, so they claim, he chases after hollow, bombastic declarations, spreads incitement and division in Israeli society, and attacks the institutions of the state (the State Prosecution, the police, the court, the High Court of Justice, and the free, independent media). At the start of his tenure, Netanyahu decided—in order to avoid the need to deal with the tough decisions that Israeli-Palestinian negotiations and hopefully an agreement would require, including the evacuation of many settlements and a forceful (and probably violent) confrontation with the right-wing settlers and their supporters—to strengthen Hamas in the Gaza Strip and weaken the Palestinian Authority in the West Bank. He hoped to avoid having to make any difficult leadership decisions by claiming that the Palestinian Authority was weak and did not represent the Palestinian people and could therefore not be trusted to enforce its authority; Hamas, on the other hand, was obviously not a partner for negotiations of any kind since its goal, as stated in the organization's charter, is the destruction and annihilation of the State of Israel. So, when Hamas started to get a foothold in the Gaza Strip and when it was relatively weak in military terms—and the IDF was hitting it hard in the West Bank and Gaza and could have destroyed its military capabilities entirely—Netanyahu, as prime minister, ordered the IDF to reduce the military pressure on Hamas.[19] Netanyahu made a strategic error merely to safeguard his grip on power, to avoid confrontations and tough decisions vis-à-vis the right-wing settler bloc in Israel and the Palestinian Authority. The leadership qualities displayed by his immediate predecessors—Ariel Sharon and Ehud Olmert—were utterly absent in Benjamin Netanyahu. As a result, between 2009 and 2015, Israel downgraded its ties with the Palestinian Authority, and the two-state solution was dropped from the Israeli national agenda. In 2009, however, Netanyahu gave a speech at Bar-Ilan University, where he spoke about the need for a two-state solution in the West Bank. But, as usual, his words were empty. It was just lip service.

So, while Netanyahu stopped meeting with Palestinian Authority chairman Mahmoud Abbas in 2011, as of 2016, he allowed Qatar to send money to Hamas. Over the course of 7 years, the Qataris sent at least $1.20 billion (!) to Hamas. Later, he even set up an arrangement whereby Israel would transfer the Qatari money to Hamas itself. Instead of the two-state solution, Netanyahu used those years to put the Iranian nuclear program front and center of the Israeli agenda. Netanyahu, who is blessed with the ability to set the public agenda in Israel and sometimes even abroad and control the public narratives, worked hard to get Iran to the top of the agenda. This is indeed a profoundly worrying issue, not only for Israel but also for Arab moderate states and others in the Middle East and the Persian Gulf, where Iran has aspirations to take control and has become a regional power. However, until Netanyahu's tenure, Israel worked in various and systematic ways—often clandestinely—to thwart the Iranian nuclear program, with much success that caused damage and delays to the program. Netanyahu, whose personality means that he prefers bombastic statements over decisions and determined and daring action, opted to make the issue as public as possible. As far as

---

19. See the testimony of Major General (Ret.) Gadi Shamni, who served as an IDF commander in the West Bank.

Netanyahu was concerned, it was a convenient way out since he had created an issue—albeit a significant one—that he could use for political and public relations gains and which did not obligate him to make any genuine or courageous decisions, unlike previous prime ministers (like Menachem Begin, who, as prime minister in 1981, decided on the operation to destroy an Iraqi nuclear reactor, and Ehud Olmert, who took the decision to destroy the Syrian reactor in 2007). Netanyahu presented himself as the paradigm of a courageous leader and pretended he was the only person capable of dealing with the Iranian threat.

Between 2009 and 2015, the Israeli government was relatively balanced. It was comprised of ultra-Orthodox parties, the right-wing Likud party, under the leadership of Netanyahu, and the centrist Labor Party. This created a kind of balance between the various segments of Israeli society, but the Palestinian arena was completely neglected. Netanyahu invented and sold to the Israeli public the utterly unrealistic doctrine of "conflict management," as if the Israeli-Palestinian conflict were an issue that Israel could unilaterally manage and, in practice, do absolutely nothing. Netanyahu's doctrine boiled down to not deciding and not doing anything significant. Stalemate and stagnation. That is how he hung on to power at the expense of leadership and initiative. But life, as always, is dynamic, and there are some fundamental problems that will not go away just by ignoring them. In 2015, certain facts began to emerge casting a heavy criminal shadow over Netanyahu. To begin with, there were facts raised about favors he had received from Israeli billionaires; that was followed by revelations relating to his efforts to control part of the media (specifically, the *Yedioth Ahronoth* newspaper) and granting regulatory benefits and government approvals to a local tycoon in various transactions (the *Bezeq Affair*). This is how Netanyahu tried to tighten his control over Israeli media outlets. These events led to Netanyahu launching a campaign to avoid criminal charges. And thus began a period, from 2015 to 2024, in the history of the State of Israel.

On the one hand, in the Palestinian arena, Netanyahu's governments ignored the Palestinian Authority, allowed West Bank settlements to grow and expand, and halted any progress toward an agreement with the Palestinians. Within that framework, Netanyahu—who, as already mentioned, explicitly supported the two-state solution in his 2009 speech—bolstered the standing of Hamas in Gaza at a time when Hamas was the Palestinian Authority's main rival and was competing with it for dominance in the Palestinian arena. This support became tangible when Netanyahu's governments reached agreements with Qatar over the transfer of vast sums of money to Hamas (from 2016!). Later, between $15-20 million a month was transferred from Qatar to Hamas—via Israel! Netanyahu believed that this policy would dissuade Hamas from carrying out terror attacks against Israel. In a way, he was paying protection money to a terror organization, based on the foolish belief that one can bribe terrorists to abide by an agreement to maintain the quiet by offering them cash and (partial) work permits for several thousand residents of Gaza to work in Israel. Within Israel, there were rumblings about criminal investigations into Netanyahu. The Israel Police launched probes on several matters. Netanyahu, with the help of his media advisors—including his elder son, Yair, who was gradually incorporated into the propaganda and incitement apparatus that Netanyahu set up—launched a campaign of delegitimization against police investigators! At a later stage, police commissioner Roni Alsheikh—a former senior Shin Bet officer with impeccable right-wing credentials—was subjected to a direct campaign of vilification, threats, and incitement on social media for having voiced his support of the investigators. Smears such as "traitor," "saboteur," and, of course, "liar" became part of the arsenal of abasement that was fired at the police chief. Of course, Alsheikh's term as police commissioner ended after three years and was not extended to a fourth year, as is customary. When Alsheikh stepped down, Netanyahu ensured that the Israel Police did not have a permanent commissioner for more than two years and that the position was filled by temporary appointees, thereby ensuring that he maintained control over the police force. Nonetheless, the police completed their investigations and, as per protocol, recommended that the State Prosecution file three corruption indictments against the prime minister. Netanyahu's violent incitement machine immediately changed direction and set its sights on turning the prosecution, the officials responsible for the cases against Netanyahu, and even the right-wing state prosecutor, portraying them as "enemies of the state." They were all surveilled, harassed, threatened, and smeared with baseless allegations in an insane effort to undermine the public's faith in the prosecution and its top officials.

In the end, the decision was down to the attorney general, Dr. Avichai Mendelblit. A former Military Advocate General who would go on to serve as Netanyahu's cabinet secretary, Mendelblit also happened to be Netanyahu's appointee. He was subservient to Netanyahu. So, he tried to delay handling the investigations against Netanyahu; he downplayed the seriousness and interfered in the investigations. These efforts, however, encountered fierce opposition from the State Prosecution and its top officials, who saw through them. And so, after many months of trying to avoid making a ruling, the attorney general decided to file indictments against Netanyahu in no fewer than three of the cases against him. In some, however, he lowered the threshold of criminality. Of course, the moment that he made his decision, the previously submissive attorney general became a target for incitement and threats on social media by the toxic and menacing machine that Netanyahu's son and media and PR advisors operated on Netanyahu's behalf. The State of Israel entered a four-year period of internal turbulence. The courts were threatened. Violent demonstrations, with physical attacks and threats at the courts where legal proceedings against Netanyahu were held, became commonplace.

When his trial began, Netanyahu brought members of his government with him to the Jerusalem District Court. Inside the court building, just outside the courtroom itself, Netanyahu had the indescribable audacity and disregard for the impartiality and importance of his role as prime minister to set up a podium with the seal of the Prime Minister's Office, from which he proceeded to spend a quarter of an hour lambasting the prosecution and the police—and even threatening the judges. As he did so, standing behind him like speechless mannequins were ministers from his government, lending their support to Netanyahu and his words. Adding to the theatrics was the fact that, because of the coronavirus pandemic, their faces were hidden by masks (see photograph on page 120). It was an insane campaign of incitement by certain parts of the Israeli public against the courts and the legal establishment. Netanyahu launched a de facto war against the institutions of the state and continued to incite against them, intimidate them, and force members of the legal establishment to become subservient and afraid. The prosecution, and especially the attorney general, a weak and ineffective figure, were subjected to a barrage of threats and a violent atmosphere, which Netanyahu encouraged and nurtured.

Incitement among the public intensified on many issues: religion; ethnicity—Ashkenazim against Sephardim and Mizrahim; and the West Bank issue, which pitted the "left" against the "right" and the settlers. Under his rule, Netanyahu turned Israeli society into his plaything, destroying it from within, spreading lies on an "industrial scale" and creating an atmosphere of hate between different segments of society. This divisiveness filtered downward. Members of the public media cooperated with the campaign of incitement being waged by Netanyahu and his family, especially Yair—who has barely ever held a job, apart from helping his father's propaganda efforts. Netanyahu-supporting journalists were embedded in various television stations. They started to brainwash the public with nonsense about the prosecution, the police, the courts, and leftists, and they started to attack the "Ashkenazi elite."

They created a madness in Israeli society and disseminated hatred that tore the Israeli people apart. All of this was accompanied, of course, by an ever-increasing phenomenon of silencing criticism and appointing unfit people to important positions, based solely on their loyalty to Netanyahu and not on their professional qualifications. In 2016, for example, the issue of the next Mossad director was being discussed. Netanyahu, who was ultimately responsible for the decision, prevaricated as usual until the very last minute over who to appoint. He asked the leading candidate whether he would be loyal to Netanyahu, and when the candidate replied that he would be "loyal to the State of Israel," Netanyahu chose the second-favorite candidate to head the Mossad.

The practice of appointing ministers and other senior public officials based on their personal loyalty, irrespective of their experience and professional capabilities, has become the norm in the corridors of power in Israel. The results are self-evident. Slowly but surely, the Israeli public service has declined. Some of the most professional and talented people in the public service decided to leave their posts, making way for incapable, unprofessional, and inexperienced replacements. The current transportation minister is an excellent example. Totally lacking in qualifications for her position, other than absolute loyalty to Netanyahu and his wife, she appointed as director general in her ministry a person with no significant managerial experience or understanding of the world of transport. The chosen candidate was one of her cronies who used to organize political rallies for her campaigns within Likud—Netanyahu's party. These failed appointments led to a deterioration of the public service sector, in terms of its services and the efficiency with which it provided them to the public. But Netanyahu put personal interests and the survival of his regime over the national interest or the good of the people. That is the thread running throughout the whole of Netanyahu's tenure as prime minister.[20]

Between 2015 and 2017, more corruption allegations emerged against Netanyahu—the most serious of which, containing not

---

20. This phenomenon was recognized by many Israeli public figures.

only potentially criminal corruption but also damage to national security, is known as the "submarine affair." This, too, contributed to questions about Netanyahu's ability to continue serving as prime minister. (See Chapter 7 for more on this.) Between 2015 and 2023, Israel held no fewer than six general elections. In 2015, for example, Netanyahu incited against the Arab population of Israel. On Election Day itself, Netanyahu claimed that "the Arabs are going out to vote in droves," with the explicit intention of scaring his supporters into casting their votes, lest Israeli Arabs and other parties that were not part of his loyal coalition win a majority. After winning the election, Netanyahu resorted to his usual manipulations and met with leaders of the Arab community in Israel, trying to appease them with flattery and pleasantries. Repeat elections, coupled with just that kind of play, not only undermined the Israeli democratic system but perpetuated the campaign of denigration, hatred, disputes, and threats that Netanyahu and his people were conducting.

The media and social media platforms were inundated with fake news, downright lies, division, and hatred between sectors of Israeli society. The atmosphere in Israel was tense. Violence between citizens worsened. It became difficult, for example, to publicly express even moderate and conciliatory sentiments on the Palestinian issue without immediately being labeled a "traitor" or an "enemy collaborator." All of this was the bitter fruit of the incitement and propaganda that the Israeli prime minister, Benjamin Netanyahu, had planted. In this respect, Netanyahu may be compared to other figures in history. His character and the nature of his regime combined a lot of rhetoric and bluster; inciting the public against various sectors of society; inventing a domestic enemy that only the leader can defeat; pandering to nationalism and fake patriotism; forging relationships with wealthy tycoons; and emotional speeches, full of pathos and (simulated) self-confidence. That is Benjamin Netanyahu.[21]

---

21. Read the article by prof. S. Ben Ami, "Tyranny past and today," "Haaretz," December 27, 2024.

Thus, in 2018, as part of his campaign to encourage pseudo-patriotism and to curry favor with the right wing of Israeli society—and to manufacture a superfluous and damaging conflict with the Arab and Druze minorities in Israel—Netanyahu signaled the "green light" to pass the Basic Law: Israel as the Nation-State of the Jewish People, informally known as the Nation-State Bill or the Nationality Bill. According to this new law, the state views the development of Jewish settlement as a national value "and will act to encourage and promote its establishment and consolidation." In focusing on "Jewish settlement," the bill ignored the years-long problem faced by Israel's Arab and Druze citizens to plan and build legally in their communities. The Nation-State Bill played on nationalistic sentiment—as is the way of fascist regimes—and severely harmed the Druze and Arab citizens of Israel. It undermined the standing and interests of the State of Israel. But it served those of Prime Minister Benjamin Netanyahu.

Between 2018 and 2021, Israel was ruled by coalitions that Netanyahu formed, mainly with ultra-Orthodox parties and national-religious parties. In these governments, Netanyahu operated a systematic campaign to spread hatred and division between different parts of Israeli society. At that time, his rule relied on a comprehensive campaign of lies and engendering hatred between rightists and leftists; the latter were smeared as "traitors" and "un-Jewish." He nurtured hatred and division between Mizrahim and Ashkenazi, and being a leftist was identified with being an Ashkenazi. Indeed, Israelis whose parents came from Arab countries (Mizrahim) who expressed any opinion even close to the left—that is, calling for peace with the Palestinians and an end to the occupation in the West Bank—were accused of rejecting their origin by a process of "Ashkenazation." As if the views and sensitivities of Israel-born citizens are determined by where their grandparents happened to be born. This is a one-dimensional approach that has allowed Netanyahu to remain in power. As part of this campaign of incitement, and to evade the criminal charges against him, a concerted and well-organized campaign was launched on social media and on the public television channels—including and especially Channel 14—to incite against the judiciary. Members of the judicial branch were branded leftists and traitors; the judiciary itself was portrayed as a corrupt entity, working against Netanyahu and seeking to end his tenure as prime minister. The theory that the criminal charges against him were a plot cooked up by the prosecution and opposition parties and that they were fabricated and baseless spread like wildfire thanks to the propaganda machine, conducted by the aforementioned television stations and the prime minister's older son through social media platforms and journalists close to Netanyahu.

The outcome is that the High Court of Justice is now under threat and is portrayed as hostile to Netanyahu and his government. Fake anecdotes about High Court justices who the propaganda machine suspected could rule against Netanyahu and his government were spread wholesale. Any state institution that did not act in accordance with Netanyahu's "instructions" or was not supportive of Netanyahu was subjected to a campaign of denigration, fake news, threats, surveillance, and lies. The atmosphere in Israel was polarized, filled with hatred and violence—verbal and often physical.

General elections were almost a matter of routine in 2019 and 2020. Netanyahu, to curry favor with right-wing voters, put forward an initiative to officially annex parts of the West Bank—the dream of many people in the national-religious, messianic, and right-wing camps. Anyone familiar with Netanyahu, however, knew that he had no intention whatsoever of implementing the plan, which was designed to do nothing more than attract voters from those camps. The annexation plan came after U.S. President Donald Trump unveiled, on January 28, 2020, the "Peace to Prosperity" plan, his peace plan, which was based on a proposal prepared by the Netanyahu government. The plan would designate certain parts of the West Bank as being under Palestinian control while safeguarding the security of Israel. The

Palestinian body, however, would not have the authority to enter into international agreements. The plan was rejected out of hand by the Palestinians, and there was no chance that they would accept it. The Israeli government never adopted it, though the plan was Netanyahu's. Another typical flip-flop by Netanyahu. However, during an election campaign, Netanyahu put forward his own plan for annexing parts of the West Bank, primarily the Jordan Valley area adjacent to Jordan. That plan was the start of the official annexation and would create an absolute situation of apartheid. It was also vehemently opposed by Jordan, Israel's neighbor to the east. The damage the plan would cause was inestimable but, from Netanyahu's perspective, it was a useful and cynical political ploy to woo voters from the right.

But then Netanyahu kept delaying the supposed date that the annexation would be announced, and the Israeli government did none of the practical preparation that implementation of a partial annexation would entail. These were the signs that Netanyahu had no intention of carrying out what he declared. But, in the random and meandering way of historical moves, the plan spurred President Trump and his closest advisor, Jared Kushner, to work on a peace deal with those Arab states that Israel had already been cooperating with on various issues for many decades. These agreements were conditioned, among other things, on the cancellation of the partial annexation. After negotiations kickstarted by the U.S. administration, Israel, the United Arab Emirates, and Bahrain signed the Abraham Accords. Following moderate American pressure and the signing of the Abraham Accords, Netanyahu backtracked on his plan to partially annex the West Bank. This is the twisting path that led to a historic peace agreement. A formal peace deal with additional Arab states—the Emirates, Bahrain, Morocco (and Sudan would later join). The agreement contributed much to Israel's integration in the region and its ability to contribute to the technological prosperity of our regional partners. Netanyahu tried to persuade the Israeli public that the Abraham Accords were just as important as the peace deal with Egypt—an absolute falsehood—and wanted to portray himself as the exclusive father of the achievement.[22] Netanyahu also used the Abraham Accords to bolster the baseless theory that he had been hawking to the Israeli public for years, according to which the so-called "Palestinian problem" is marginal and that Israel can forge agreements with Arab states without any genuine solution to the conflict that involves a Palestinian state in the West Bank (or a confederation with Israel). That theory, however, is an absolute mirage. As if it is possible to maintain peace agreements and advance them without courageous, difficult, and complex action on the Palestinian issue. Netanyahu adopted this cowardly and baseless theory as his own. He advocated for it vociferously and tried to persuade others—in Israel and overseas—of its veracity. Eventually, this theory would lead to its worst crisis since the War of Independence in 1948. Tragically, however, large parts of Israeli society bought into Netanyahu's fantasy. The Abraham Accords, in the eyes of some Israelis, meant that Netanyahu must be a master diplomat, a statesman of global standing. It was a totally false and baseless image, of course, but Netanyahu managed to persuade many Israelis that it is true. And so, Israel's march of folly continued.

In the meantime, various groups of Israelis—those who are not ultra-Orthodox, rightist settlers, or Netanyahu cultists (known as Bibi-ists[23])—started to demonstrate against the prime minister. These rallies began as far back as 2016, when a handful of people started protesting outside the home of the attorney general, who was deliberating at the time on whether to file an indictment against Netanyahu. The numbers gradually grew from dozens to thousands and then tens of thousands of people, with the

---

22. Netanyahu's contribution to the Abraham Accords cannot be denied but most of the initiative, vision and contribution was made by the United States, President Trump and his senior political advisor, Jared Kushner, as well as to the leaders of the UAE and Bahrain.

23. Bibi-ism is a phenomenon similar to what we have seen in parts of society in other countries, where people followed populist leaders for whom false promises and the spread of hatred were merely tools to seize and hold onto power.

epicenter of protests in Jerusalem, close to Netanyahu's official residence, and across the country. Slowly but surely, more voices were added to those calling for the government to be overthrown. These demonstrations, along with a worsening economic picture, a massive budget deficit, and the coronavirus pandemic adding to the economic and social pressure, created a rare opportunity in June 2021. Following yet another general election, a group of eight parties from different sides of the social and cultural spectrum came together to form a coalition that managed to win a majority in parliament and form the new government. For the first time in the history of the state, an Arab party—the United Arab List, headed by Dr. Mansour Abbas—joined the coalition and the government. The new prime minister was Naftali Bennett—a religious, rightist, and pro-settlement politician but one with the ability to listen to other views. He was joined in government by other parties from the right and the left. From the moment it was sworn in, the Bennett government was targeted with threats, violence, harassment, and lies. Members of the opposition, under Netanyahu, behaved raucously in the Knesset, hurling insults at and shoving members of the coalition. Many of the members of Netanyahu's party, a group of people lacking in practical and genuine talent, owe their political careers to Netanyahu. He handpicked them and, as far as he was concerned, the only tests were the extent of their loyalty to him and his ability to manipulate them as he saw fit. Under Netanyahu, they became a noisy and disruptive chorus in the Knesset. They had no interest in any issues of substance, instead trying to sabotage the new government at every turn. Even issues that were unquestionably in the interests of the State of Israel and its citizens were met with vehement opposition from Netanyahu and his party. For example, a plan that would have allowed Israeli citizens to enter the United States without a visa—something that would have been welcomed by everyone—was opposed by Netanyahu and Likud, simply because they wanted to deny the ruling coalition any accomplishments. The same happened with national plans to improve transportation, to invite tenders for the completion of the metro system in Tel Aviv, which suffered from terrible congestion; and the same happened with an international agreement with Lebanon over gas drilling rights in the Mediterranean Sea. Negotiations between Beirut and Jerusalem lasted over a decade under various Netanyahu governments but, because of Netanyahu's character and his inability to make tough decisions, they did not lead to an agreement. Finally, with the Americans mediating, an agreement was reached that satisfied both Israel and Lebanon and provided both countries with much-needed certainty in this area.

At this point, it is worth pointing out that the inclusion of an Arab party in the ruling coalition was a positive moment in terms of the integration of Arab society in the State of Israel. The vast majority of Israeli Arabs, who make up 20 percent of the population, want to be integrated into the life, culture, and economy of Israel—and they have the ability to make a massive contribution. Around 25 percent of the physicians in Israel, 40 percent of the pharmacists, and many engineers come from the Arab community. There is no reason not to allow them to integrate fully and equally into the State of Israel. This is what most of them want and what is a supreme national interest. However, the integration of an Arab party, under the leadership of Dr. Mansour Abbas—a devout Muslim, eloquent, intelligent, educated, and courageous—infuriated Netanyahu and his supporters. They began to refer to the government as one that "supports Arabs" and relies on the parliamentary support of "enemies of the state." They spread the fallacious claim that the government had promised to invest the massive sum of 54 billion shekels in Arab society—a lie that Netanyahu repeated in his speeches. In practice, less than 10 percent of that sum was invested, but these lies convinced many of Netanyahu's supporters. They were overcome with incitement, lies, and hatred. Netanyahu has great talent and skill in espousing lies, creating hatred and division, and the cynical use of the fear felt in some parts of Israeli society over Israeli Arabs, Arabs in general, and Iran. Netanyahu is exactly like populist leaders in South America and Europe in his use of intimidation, creating hatred, false promises, and the image of a strongman.[24] The prolonged campaign of violence, threats, harassment, intimidation, and lies against Knesset members from Prime Minister Bennett's party—a religious, right-wing party—gradually undermined the stability of the government and led some of them to quit the coalition. Some did so, and later, they served as ministers in the new government that Netanyahu had established. The systematic campaign waged by Netanyahu and his accomplices, which brought ruin to Israeli society, disgrace upon the institutions of government, the courts, and the state prosecution, and smashed the independent media, got results. In June 2022, just 12 months after it was sworn in, the government was forced to call fresh elections. Despite being in power for just over a year, the Bennett government recorded some significant achievements and rectified some of the iniquities of previous Netanyahu governments. In one year, it managed to bring normality to life in Israel; it got rid of Israel's massive budgetary deficit and even ended its tenure with a surplus and inflation at under 3 percent; GDP increased (at 5.5 percent, it was among the highest in the world!); it fostered closer ties to moderate Arab countries like Jordan, Egypt, the UAE, and Morocco—and with the U.S., Israel's most important ally. The toppling of the coalition put all of that in danger.

The election was held on November 1, 2022. Netanyahu's party won 32 seats in the Knesset—most of them filled with individuals whose entire careers were based on their total loyalty to Netanyahu—which allowed it to form a coalition.

While Netanyahu was busy tearing Israeli society apart and polarizing it like never before, spreading his incendiary and divisive messages through his mouthpieces on social media and in the press, he also launched a dramatic campaign to radically change the regime in Israel and crush democracy. The first

---

24. See above article by Prof. Shlomo Ben Ami, *"Tyranny past and today,"* *Haaretz,*27.12.2024.

anti-democratic piece of legislation passed by the Knesset was an amendment to the Basic Law: The Judiciary, which bans the court from interfering in decisions made by the cabinet and its individual ministers on the grounds that they are significantly unreasonable. This amendment was part of Netanyahu's effort to smash the Israeli judicial system and, along with it, the foundations of supervised rule. It would allow for the appointment of people to public positions and offices based solely on political and personal loyalty and personal considerations, irrespective of their capabilities, experience, and professional qualifications. Netanyahu and his current coalition have been doing just this for many years and, as a result, the functioning of Israeli government ministries (with very few exceptions) has deteriorated to the same level as that experienced in developing countries.

This plan to overhaul the Israeli judiciary was met by protests and demonstrations by the Israeli people, as well as threats by reservists in frontline units and the Air Force that they could refuse to turn up for reserve duty. The IDF's Military Intelligence division warned that the judicial overhaul, the public opposition to it, the division that was growing within Israeli society, the polarization, and the internal struggles were a golden opportunity for Iran and its proxies, Hamas and Hezbollah, to attack Israel. Military Intelligence, apparently aware that Netanyahu would deny ever having received verbal warnings, sent written warnings to the prime minister on no fewer than four occasions, including in March and July 2023. Netanyahu, however, completely ignored these warnings in an act of utter irresponsibility. Moreover, on two separate occasions—in the Knesset on June 25, 2023, and at a cabinet meeting four days later—he confidently declared that Hamas had been deterred from engaging in hostilities against Israel and that much of its military equipment had been destroyed in previous operations.[25]

---

25. See also the report published November 2024 by a committee established by civics. The Israeli government still declines any attempt to assign a formal Commission of Inquiry under the Commission of Inquiry Law,1969.

Netanyahu's response to these security warnings and his disregard for concern over a possible attack by Hamas or Hezbollah also influenced the functioning of the IDF. The Southern Command, which is responsible for the Gaza front, and the chief of staff were all influenced by Netanyahu's assertion that "Hamas is deterred" and would not dare launch an invasion of Israel. Therefore, even the warnings sounded by spotters stationed along the Gaza border, who warned a month before the barbaric attacks of October 7 that Hamas was engaged in unusual activity along the border, were ignored by their commanders, who told them to "stop bothering us."

The fallacious doctrine, inspired by Netanyahu, was the root cause of the unspeakable surprise that awaited Israel on that "Black Saturday" morning. And so, on October 7, 2023—a Saturday morning during the Jewish festival of Sukkot—residents of the kibbutzim and agricultural communities adjacent to the Gaza Strip woke up to an attack, planned many months in advance, by some 3,000 terrorists from Hamas' Nukhba Force. Ever since violently seizing power in Gaza in 2007, Hamas' rule of the coastal strip has been dictatorial and corrupt. It has trampled on the rights of minorities, women, and members of the LGBTQ community. The attack took the State of Israel, the Israeli government, and the IDF by total surprise. Netanyahu and his wife returned a day before from a vacation in northern Israel. The doctrine that Netanyahu had espoused for years was that Hamas was "an asset" for Israel and that it had been deterred from launching military action against Israel—a doctrine that was exposed as pure nonsense.

This theory suited Netanyahu. His only desire was to avoid negotiations—tough but essential negotiations—with the Palestinian Authority in the West Bank toward an agreement over the establishment of a Palestinian state. Such negotiations require determination, courage, leadership, and the ability to deal with extremists in Israel who demand more settlements in the West Bank—as well as tough talks with the Palestinians themselves.

Netanyahu has neither the desire, the ability, nor the character-istics required to deal with such vital and weighty missions. He is weak, afraid, and hesitant.[26] His only goal is to remain unchal-lenged in power. So, he chose what looked like the easy path: bolstering Hamas in the Gaza Strip (the transfer of Qatari money to Gaza, with the assistance of the Netanyahu government, allowed Hamas to build up its military strength and encouraged corruption among its leaders), weakening the Palestinians, and fabricating the nonsensical theory that Hamas had been deterred and that it is an "asset" for Israel.

And so, on October 7, when Israel was taken by surprise, there were only 550 or 600 soldiers (not all of them combat troops) along the 40-mile border with the Gaza Strip, and there was just one single battalion (Battalion 13 from the Golani Brigade) and only 12-14 tanks (not all in full-service condition). In contrast, at the same time, due to pressure from the Jewish settlers and their representatives in Netanyahu's government, without whom he would lose his grip on power, there were 30-32 infantry battalions in the West Bank. This situation is the direct result of the neglect by Netanyahu and his extremist government in favor of the West Bank settlers. This allowed highly trained Hamas commandos to take control and capture civilian Israeli communities and to try and take IDF bases. During their barbaric assault, Hamas terror-ists committed acts of murder; they butchered their victims, committed mass rape, tortured civilians, children, infants, men, women, the old, and female soldiers—and they burned entire communities to the ground, with their residents still inside.

Such was their barbarity that some of the Israeli victims had been so badly mutilated that they could not be positively identi-fied for many months, if at all. It was an attack lacking all human-ity. Unrestrained barbarity. The State of Israel was dealt a severe blow that day. The shock, the citizens' loss of faith in their govern-ment, the abandonment of southern communities, and the fact

---

26. See comments by many politicians who know him, including Ariel Sharon, Yair Lapid and U.S. President Donald Trump.

that the IDF was not prepared—not in terms of intelligence (even though there had been warnings and intelligence information suggesting that something was afoot) and not operationally—to deploy troops in case of such an attack. The United States, under President Joe Biden, recognized Israel's crisis of leadership and rushed to Israel's side. Washington understood how traumatic the event was and how it could have far-reaching ramifications, including the possibility of involvement from Iran (which supports Hamas and Hezbollah, its regional proxies) and from Hezbollah. Moreover, the United States recognized that the government of Israel—which, for the previous 12 months, had tried to carry out an unreasonable judicial overhaul by smashing the powers of the Supreme Court and undermining judicial oversight of undemocratic legislation and unreasonable decisions by the government—had moved Israel away from the values of democracy that were at the heart of the special relationship between Israel and the United States. The Biden Administration saw these proposals coming from a failed government, headed by a leader whose policies were leading to a disastrous situation. The conclusion was that Israel needed America's help to avoid slipping into a regional war. To this end, the United States sent two aircraft carriers to the Middle East (the USS Gerald R. Ford and later the Eisenhower), and the president himself visited Israel within a week. The war in Gaza is still raging, but one thing is certain: the events of October 7 have dramatically changed the State of Israel (which will be covered in detail in Chapter 10.

Thus begins one of the darkest and most devastating periods in the history of the State of Israel. It is mainly the result of Benjamin Netanyahu's failures and his omission of necessary decisions. More on that in the coming chapters.

But, before returning to these failings and the threats it faces, let's look at the extraordinary achievements of the State of Israel.

Chapter 2

The State of Israel

Despite difficult conditions and permanent security concerns, economic and scientific achievements

The journey to the establishment of the State of Israel began with the First Zionist Congress, which was held in Basel, Switzerland, in 1897, in a small hotel where a group of Eastern European Jews came together to promote the idea of a state for the Jewish people. It was a phenomenal, unprecedented, and historic accomplishment—a nation returning to its land after almost 2,000 (!) years. Likewise, the accomplishments of the State of Israel since its establishment in the fields of economics and science are nothing less than miraculous. The GDP of Israel in 1949 was $5,000. By 2022, that figure had risen to $53,400, making Israel the seventeenth-richest country in the world.[27]

1949-1967

By the end of the War of Independence, Israel had lost 1 percent of its population. It now became necessary to start running the country, with all that this entailed: education, academia, healthcare, security, the economy, industry, transportation, infrastructure, art, and culture. To all of these was added another extraordinary mission: by the end of the first three years of its existence, in 1952, the tiny and weak State of Israel—with a population

---

27. Israel' GDP for 2023 will be lower because of the attempted judicial coup that Netanyahu launched that year and, subsequently, the war in Gaza that followed the October 7 terror attack.

of 600,000 Jews and 150,000 Arabs—absorbed an additional 850,000 Jews who immigrated to the fledgling state. Half of them came from Arab countries and half were survivors of the European Holocaust. That would be like the United States absorbing 500 million people in three years. An impossible mission under normal circumstances and in a rich country—even more so in a country that had just been established in the aftermath of a War of Independence that claimed so many victims and created so much destruction—and which was on the verge of economic bankruptcy. However, Israel was blessed at that time with unique leaders, headed by David Ben-Gurion, who was one of the giant leaders of the 20th century. Under these difficult conditions, Israel introduced an economic policy of rationing, known as the "period of austerity." Israel introduced policies whereby the government was integrally involved in the running of the economy, which took the form of control over the country's main industrial activity, limits on imports, foreign currency, and bank credit, as well as supervision over raw materials. This policy of austerity allowed Israel to absorb hundreds of thousands of destitute immigrants and refugees. But it also led to the expansion of the government services needed to oversee the various teams and to the creation of a black market that operated in parallel to the official economy. In 1951, Israel experienced a severe balance-of-payments crisis. In February 1952, the Ministry of Rationing and Supply was dissolved, and Dov Yosef was fired from his position. The same year, the government introduced a series of new economic measures. The State of Israel engaged in negotiations with the West German government over reparations for Holocaust survivors. Some Israelis started getting reparations from the Germans, as well as financial aid from the United States. This led to more money in the economy, increased exports, and reduced the government's budget deficit. It was not until 1954 that Israel finally emerged from recession. From that moment on, for about 10 years, there was a period of impressive growth in GDP, which climbed by an extraordinary 10 percent annually.

But, in 1966, the Israeli economy was hit by a major recession. Unemployment had risen and was at around 10 percent of the workforce, and there was negative net migration. The economy was shrouded in a heavy atmosphere of crisis. But there was to be an unexpected change. The Six-Day War in 1967 and its rapid conclusion led to new impressive economic growth. In addition, there was a new wave of immigration **of** educated people from the West and Russia. The country's defense industries grew, in part because of the arms embargo that France imposed on Israel, and exports increased.

1973-1991

Once again, Israel experienced a harsh economic crisis and lost a decade. In 1973, the Yom Kippur War broke out. That caused a global energy crisis. The Israeli economy was again in dire straits because of the cost of defense. And so began what is known in Israel as the "lost decade," which was characterized by recession and economic stagnation. The late 1970s saw a dramatic political change in Israel. Likud was voted into power for the first time. A right-wing party that, on the one hand, advocated annexing the West Bank to Israel and building settlements and, on the other, was in favor of a free-market economy. However, when Likud took office, it relaxed restrictions on taking foreign currency out of Israel and other economic activities, which very soon led to rampant inflation between 1981 and 1985. During those years, the cost of living rose by up to 400 percent a year.

1992-2003

Starting in 1993, the Israeli economy recovered impressively. There were two main reasons for this. Firstly, hundreds of thousands of immigrants from the Soviet Union started arriving in 1991 after the collapse of the Soviet bloc. This wave of immigration was a cultural and economic blessing, contributing much to the fields of culture (including the wonderful Gesher Theater), as well as technology and engineering. Secondly, starting in

1993, the Oslo Accord peace process began. This courageous and impressive political initiative, which was accompanied by a peace accord with Jordan in 1994, turned Israel into a desirable place of operation for international corporations. The Arab boycott began to disintegrate, and companies which had once refused to invest in Israel or set up business there started operating in Israel. For example, Unilever invested in Israeli food company Strauss, and Nestlé invested in Osem. McDonald's even opened its first restaurants in Israel. Foreign investors also started to show an interest in the Israeli market. The country's technology and high-tech industries started to bloom. The fruits of the Israeli defense industry were seen in advanced technological capabilities in a variety of fields, including communications and computers. The growth of the high-tech industry was impressive, taking advantage of Israeli know-how gleaned from the defense industries and the IDF. Higher education in Israel, combined with the wave of immigration from the Soviet Union, the Oslo Accords, and the sense of optimism that led to a significant change in the region—along with Israel's basic industries in the fields of security, military, and telecommunications—gave the economy a massive boost. The State of Israel implemented new plans to support and assist start-ups in their earliest stages, where the element of risk is significant. Israeli venture capital funds began to emerge, in cooperation with investors from abroad, mainly from the United States. This boom had another benefit: Israeli companies quickly became the most floated on the U.S. stock exchange (after Canada). In 2001, however, there was another negative turn. A massive crash on NASDAQ caused many tech companies, including Israeli companies, to lose much of their value. The technology market worldwide entered years of stagnation. That was exacerbated by domestic woes in Israel. The prime minister at the time, Ehud Barak, returned from long meetings he held in the United States with the head of the Palestinian Fatah movement—meetings that were arranged and hosted by U.S. President Bill Clinton. These talks ended in deadlock and, as a result, the second

Palestinian intifada erupted. Incoming tourism all but ended. Foreign investments dried up, and the economy entered a massive crisis. Israel remained in economic crisis until 2006. Under the leadership of the new prime minister, Ariel Sharon, Israel engaged in various measures to deal with Palestinian terrorism. This military confrontation had a positive outcome within three or four years. The level of terror and sabotage dropped dramatically. Israelis' sense of internal security was greatly restored. In addition, the economic measures enacted by the Israeli government of Ariel Sharon, along with his finance minister, Benjamin Netanyahu, bore fruit. Among other things, the government reduced its deficit and cut stipends to the ultra-Orthodox sector and large families. These measures, along with economic support from the United States, backed by loan guarantees from overseas, helped Israel extricate itself from the crisis.

2005-2024

Since 2005, the Israeli economy and its security and technology sectors have advanced massively. The State of Israel has developed, using local technology, water purification systems and desalination plants. It solved the water shortage problem that Israel had been suffering from due to the Mediterranean climate and the lack of rain—an achievement of global importance! By the time of the global economic crisis of 2008-2009, which began with the collapse of the Lehman Brothers bank in the United States, the Israeli economy was strong and stable. Israel, therefore, was able to weather the global crisis with relative ease. Israel did not experience the worst effects of the crisis, unlike countries such as Portugal, Spain, Italy, and Greece. After 2010, the Israeli economy took off again. Export figures improved, and Israeli high-tech—the engine driving the economy forward—earned a global reputation. Israeli companies expanded and recruited excellent staff, and there was a marked increase in the number of acquisitions, mergers, and exits. Venture capital funds from across the world opened branches or offices in Israel to share in the prosperity and its handsome profitability. Israel slowly began to be known as the "start-up nation." The number of start-ups in Israel was among the highest in the world. In 2020, more than 120 Israeli companies were listed on NASDAQ. Israeli exports grew, and the debt-to-GDP ratio improved. In 2020, the ratio was 60.9 percent (compared to 68 percent in 2021 at the height of the coronavirus pandemic). By the end of 2022, Israel was experiencing an impressive economic recovery. Gross domestic product (GDP) had risen 6.3 percent, and per capita GDP was $53,400—an impressive achievement. However, following an election, a new government was installed in Israel. It was headed by Benjamin Netanyahu, who had a coalition of nationalist parties that supported West Bank settlements and ultra-Orthodox parties that demanded large sums of money, even though their voters refuse to study modern subjects and are therefore unable to contribute to the Israeli economy. Shortly after the election, the Netanyahu government launched a series of legislative initiatives designed to undermine the independence of the judicial system.

As a result of this unprecedented plan—which was designed to crush the independent judiciary, take control of appointments to the Supreme Court, and revoke the court's authority to intervene in decisions by the executive branch—a huge dispute arose in Israeli society. Israeli democracy, one of the main assets behind the state's prosperity and its ability to maintain a diverse culture and sustain the existence of top-quality institutes of higher education and research organizations, was in real danger of being destroyed. This was all for an irresponsible prime minister and a government made up of extremist, nationalist, and racist parties—some of which have zero interest in what happens in Israeli society, as long as they get their stipends from the state. As a result, there was a dramatic 68 percent drop in investments in Israeli high-tech. There were almost no Israeli IPOs on overseas stock exchanges. Even international credit rating companies like Moody's and S&P started to issue warnings about the direction the State of Israel was headed and expressed real concern over the high credit rating the country enjoyed.28 The Israeli economy entered a period of real crisis, alongside the threat to the democratic character of the state and internal struggles by various sections of Israeli society against the government and its leaders. These struggles had all the signs of potential civil war. And then Hamas launched its murderous and atrocious attack against residents of Israeli communities in the south and people attending the Nova music festival. The attack led to the outbreak of hostilities between the IDF and Hezbollah on the northern border and, a few days later, the IDF entering the Gaza Strip to fight Hamas. Some 1,250 people, most of them civilians, including women and babies, were murdered or killed. Approximately 150,000 Israelis became refugees in their own country, forced to leave their homes and fields in the south and the north. In addition, around 300,000 people were called up to the reserves to fight in Gaza. All of this additional expenditure on operations in Gaza and securing the northern border led to a dramatic downturn in commercial activity in the fourth quarter of 2023. Exports plummeted by 19.8 percent, as did GDP. In early 2024, credit rating company Moody's announced that it was downgrading Israel's ranking for the first time. Israel's finance minister, who represents the settlers' interests in Netanyahu's government, dismissed this decision. After all, the settlers still enjoyed generous funding at the expense of the Israeli economy in 2023 and 2024. This reality put the Israeli economy in jeopardy. Some people compared the impact of October 7 and the subsequent events to what happened to the Israeli economy after the 1973 Yom Kippur War—the so-called "lost decade," when security expenditure increased, GDP fell, and there was an increase in the debt-to-GDP ratio. The events of October 7 and their aftermath in Gaza and on the Lebanon border, coupled with the policies of an irresponsible government that continues

---

28. As of May 2024, both Moody's and S&P have lowered Israel's credit rating by one notch. On September 27, 2024, Moody's again downgraded the credit rating by two notches with a future negative trajectory.

to fund nonproductive sectors (the West Bank settlements and the ultra-Orthodox), could send the Israeli economy into a similar tailspin—probably even much worse than 1973—if the current government remains in power for any length of time. We will now move on to a review of some of the activities and successes in the Israeli economy, looking at industries that started as tiny ventures and grew to become global leaders in various fields. The brevity of this review does not reflect a paucity of such achievements. On the contrary.

Military and Defense Industries

Israel's industrial sector can trace its roots back to before the establishment of the state. There was already light industry manufacturing arms for the Haganah in Mandatory Palestine. When the state was established in 1948, these factories continued to develop and recorded impressive achievements. Today, companies like Israel Aerospace Industries, Rafael Advanced Defense Systems, and Elbit Systems manufacture advanced weapons systems, including fighter planes, unmanned aerial vehicles, missiles, and air defense systems. One of the most significant developments was the Iron Dome missile defense system, which has demonstrated superb tactical results and allowed Israel to live an almost normal existence even when hundreds or thousands of missiles were being fired at it.[29] Israel also developed and manufactured some of the most advanced tanks in the world, including the Merkava, which has several advanced models. These systems have built-in defenses against anti-tank missiles and are technologically impressive by any standard. All of them have become synonymous with quality across the world.

---

29. This technological power was demonstrated in April 2024 when, as part of an international coalition, with significant cooperation with the United States and under its direction, and in cooperation with other countries in the region, as well as the United Kingdom and France, Israel managed to prevent significant damage from 350 cruise and ballistic missiles fired by Iran at Israel.

Telecommunications

Many former members of the defense industry and operational activity acquired expertise in various technological and engineering fields, which allowed them to set up many telecommunications companies. The State of Israel became a telecommunications hub and, in the 1990s, was among the world leaders in the field.

Agriculture and Food

Israel now has a world-class food industry. Some Israeli companies are now owned by foreign concerns (Nestlé, Unilever, and the Chinese company Bright Food, which owns Israeli dairy producer Tnuva). In addition, Israeli companies and scientists have developed groundbreaking global technologies in the field of irrigation, citrus fruit and vegetable cultivation, and vaccines against various diseases, as well as innovations in the field of chemicals to improve crops of fruit and vegetables (such as Adama Agricultural Solutions, for example) and in various other agricultural fields. All of these international achievements gave Israeli industry a reputation for innovation and creativity. In the fields of food tech and artificial foods, Israel is also highly advanced. Hundreds of Israeli companies are involved in developing innovative foods, including meat substitutes. (The percentage of Israelis who are vegetarian is among the highest in the world!) In northern Israel, many business incubators have been set up to encourage innovation in food tech.

Water

Since its establishment, the State of Israel, which is located in an arid environment, has suffered from water shortages. It is a desert, after all. With the exception of the Kinneret—known as the Sea of Galilee, even though it is a lake—Israel does not have reserves of fresh water. The Kinneret, located in the north and fed by the Jordan River, is Israel's only source of fresh water, and its area is around 64 square miles—tiny compared to lakes in Europe. In addition, the amount of rainfall in Israel is low. As a result, for many years, Israel was forced to impose restrictions on the use of water in agriculture, industry, and for private use. In the 1990s, however, there were stunning technological developments that allowed Israel to purify wastewater and desalinate water from the Mediterranean—making them both potable. As a result, Israel now has around 87 water purification plants. The water shortage was solved, therefore, by groundbreaking Israeli technology and engineering! Another impressive achievement.

Biochemistry and Medicine

There were drug manufacturers operating in Israel even before the establishment of the state. For example, Teva Pharmaceuticals was founded in 1901. It would go on to become a global concern with innovative drugs and treatments—some of which were developed at the Weizmann Institute of Science in Rehovot.

Aerospace Industries

Israel has its own space agency. There is an advanced aerospace industry in Israel, which is among the eight most advanced nations in the world in the field, behind the likes of the United States, China, Russia, and India. Israel's aerospace industry has recorded impressive achievements in both military and civilian arenas.

Aeronautical Industries

Israel has developed a wide and advanced industry focused on planes and unmanned aerial vehicles, as well as cyber and radar systems for planes, missiles, and satellites for various purposes. It has also developed defense systems for planes and helicopters, surface-to-surface missiles, surface-to-air missiles, and air-to-air missiles. Israel's aeronautical industries have an unrivaled reputation, and their products are sold across the world.

Cyber Industries

Israel's various cyber technology companies—both defensive and offensive—are among the most advanced in the world and have an excellent reputation. From Check Point Software Technologies and Palo Alto Networks, which are traded on NASDAQ, to impressive private companies like Wiz Cyber30 Security and others, the country stands as a global leader in the cybersecurity industry. The fruits of Israel's achievements in cybersecurity were showcased in the response to the Iranian missile attack on Israel in April 2024.

Medicine

Israeli medicinal research and development has achieved breakthroughs of international importance. Israel's healthcare system, including its Health Maintenance Organizations and public hospitals, has garnered global recognition. The Sheba Medical Center at Tel Hashomer was ranked the ninth-best hospital in the world (!) in 2023. During the coronavirus pandemic, Israel's handling of the crisis was among the most impressive in the world, and it was no coincidence that global pharmaceutical company Pfizer chose Israel as the pilot country for its vaccine.

Technological Infrastructure and Higher Education

The foundations of Israel's technological infrastructure were laid at the state's establishment, first in the form of technological systems within the IDF and other security agencies. Subsequently, development progressed to private companies and semi-private companies with government involvement. The military has been fertile ground for creativity, imagination, and innovation among Israeli engineers, who found outlets for their extraordinary capabilities. In addition, Israel has established an advanced higher education system. The Technion—a public research university specializing in engineering, chemistry, physics, and medicine—began its activities in 1924. Since then, it has produced alumni who have gone on to do remarkable things in various scientific and engineering fields. For example,

---

30. Recently it was published that Google signed a definitive sale agreement to buy Wiz for $32 billion.

Mellanox Technologies, founded by Eyal Waldman and other Technion graduates, was sold to NVIDIA in 2019 for around $7 billion. By 2023, it was responsible for around 13 percent of NVIDIA's income. There is also the Weizmann Institute, founded in 1934 and named after Israel's first president. The institute is one of the world's leading multidisciplinary basic research institutions in the natural and exact sciences. Additional universities across Israel—in Jerusalem, Be'er Sheva, Haifa, Tel Aviv, and elsewhere—produce engineers, scientists, and researchers in many fields.

Israeli winners of the Nobel Prize and other prestigious awards

Thus far, the State of Israel has produced 13 Nobel laureates, six of them in the fields of science and economics: Prof. Israel Aumann in Game Theory; Prof. Ada Yonath in Biochemistry; Prof. Avram Hershko, Prof. Aaron Ciechanover, and Prof. Arieh Warshel in Chemistry; Prof. Dan Shechtman in Materials Science; and Prof. Joshua Angrist and the late Prof. Daniel Kahneman in Economics. In addition, in the fields of mathematics and computers, Israelis have been honored with the following awards: the Fields Medal (Prof. Elon Lindenstrauss); the Abel Prize (Prof. Hillel Furstenberg and Prof. Avi Wigderson); the Leonhard Euler Gold Medal (Prof. Doron Zeilberger and Aviezri Fraenkel); the Turing Award in Computers (Prof. Michael Rabin, Amir Pnueli, Adi Shamir, Yehuda Pearl, Prof. Shafi Goldwasser, and, in 2023, Avi Wigderson); and the Gödel Prize, which has been awarded no fewer than 20 times to Israeli scientists and researchers. These outstanding scientists represent the pinnacle of the world's research and scientific capabilities, and there are many others with phenomenal and impressive achievements.

Looking to the future

Israel's accomplishments in the fields of economics, science, research, development and technology are hugely impressive.

This is true when taking the tiny size of the country into account and even more so considering the complexity of Israel's reality, which entailed a constant struggle for security, and the many upheavals the state has experienced in the 75 years of its existence. However, if Israel wants to record such accomplishments in the future, it must ensure that the social, governmental and cultural infrastructure exist in order to provide first-rate education and exceptional researchers and developers. This can only happen in a vibrant and energetic democratic regime, if there is a free and independent media, if citizens have basic freedoms and there are equal rights in every area of life and public money is spent equally and impartially, in a responsible manner and for productive targets.

It became apparent between 2022 and 2024 that Israeli democracy has internal enemies. These enemies want to disrupt and enfeeble the democracy, to make the judiciary subordinate and obedient to the Government, and to take control of media outlets so that they fear criticizing the regime. This process will be covered in detail later in this book. They pose a severe threat—a genuinely existential threat—to the State of Israel as we used to know. To its economic, technological, scientific and education accomplishments of the State of Israel.[31] All made by Israeli politicians.

31. It was just recently published that two very prominent Israeli scientists from Jerusalem University and the Weizmann Institute are joining a prestigious faculty in Princeton, USA.

Chapter 3

A human tapestry from different countries

The Sephardi aliyah, Mizrahim and Ashkenazim—Complexity and diversity and the potential for social unrest

The State of Israel is a melting pot of Jews who immigrated to Israel at different times and from diverse lands. As a result, the population is made up of people united primarily by their shared Jewish identity—itself a broad and sometimes insufficiently precise definition. This shared identity is grounded in a tradition of reading and studying the Hebrew scriptures, recognizing Jewish traditions and festivals (such as Pesach, Hanukkah, Sukkot, Shavuot, Rosh Hashanah, and Yom Kippur), and a shared cultural heritage. However, it is essential to remember that these individuals arrived from various countries and cultural backgrounds.

For example, Jews who immigrated from Eastern Europe in the 19th century brought a vastly different culture from those who arrived from Germany in the early 20th century or from those already living in the region (primarily Sephardim and Jews from Yemen). Further waves of immigration brought Jews from devastated Europe after World War II and, following the establishment of the State of Israel and the War of Independence in 1948-1949, from numerous other countries, particularly Arab states.

In 1914, the Jewish population of the Land of Israel was approximately 85,000. Half were native to the Land of Israel, and half had come from Muslim countries, primarily Yemen. In the five years following the end of World War I in 1918, another 35,000 Jews immigrated to the region. Between 1924 and 1931, around

80,000 Jews migrated to Palestine, increasing the total Jewish population to roughly 180,000, although about 20,000 Jews left during this period.

A significantly larger wave of immigration occurred in response to the rise of the Nazi regime in Germany. Between 1932 and 1939, 250,000 Jews immigrated to Palestine, including 60,000 from Germany and a few thousand from Poland, Austria, and Czechoslovakia.[32] In addition, many Jews came. Many others also arrived from Poland and Romania, bringing the total Jewish population of Palestine to approximately 470,000 by 1939, on the eve of World War II.

After World War II, from 1945 to 1948, large numbers of Jews came to the Land of Israel from Europe, including Germany, Austria, Romania, Poland, and Italy. By the time Israel was fighting its War of Independence against Arab armies, the Jewish population had grown to 600,000. Around a quarter of these individuals were not Ashkenazi, a term referring to those who neither came from Muslim countries nor were born in Palestine.

Even then, distinct social divisions existed among the Jewish population. Native-born Israelis identified themselves as Sephardim, while immigrants from Muslim countries were categorized as Mizrahim, and immigrants from Europe were labeled as Ashkenazim. Following World War II, Jewish communities in Arab countries faced widespread violence, looting, and boycotts. These incidents, coupled with the murder of six million Jews during the Holocaust, significantly reduced the pool of potential immigrants from Europe. However, many thousands of Jews remained in Muslim countries and increasingly became targets of attacks and embargos.

---

32. Shmuel Noah and Chaim Adler, "Israel – An Emerging Society," Magness Press, page 14. Another version states that a total of 186,000 immigrants arrived during these years, of whom 36,000 were from Germany and about 76,000 from Poland.

Egyptian Jewry

At the time, approximately 66,000 Jews were living in Egypt. The Egyptian authorities confiscated Jewish properties in major cities, and Jewish homes were torched and looted. Hundreds of Jews were injured, and thousands were imprisoned. Prominent Jews who had held influential positions in Egyptian society and finance lost their assets and status. By 1956, the majority of Egyptian Jews had relocated to Israel.

Iraqi Jewry

The Jewish population of Iraq numbered about 138,000 and was one of the most ancient Jewish communities in existence. According to the *Book of Chronicles*, Jews had lived and thrived in Iraq since the destruction of the First Temple in 586 BCE. The region was home to famed yeshivas in Sura and Pumbedita. However, in the 1940s, antisemitism surged across Iraq.

In June 1941, during the Shavuot holiday, a pogrom erupted in Baghdad, later known as the *Farhud*. At least 179 Jews, including women, children, and the elderly, were murdered, and more than 2,100 were injured. Some estimates suggest the death toll may have reached 1,000.

On September 23, 1948, Shafiq Ades, a Syrian-born Iraqi-Jewish businessman, was publicly hanged in Basra after being accused of selling weapons to Israel and the Iraqi Communist Party. Denied proper legal defense during his three-day court martial, his execution shocked the Jewish community, leading many to no longer feel safe in Iraq.

The Israeli government, under David Ben Gurion, began planning a secret operation to bring Iraqi Jews to Israel. Between 1950 and 1952, the Iraqi government passed laws enabling the denaturalization of Jews and their subsequent emigration. Many Iraqi Jews were forced to sell their belongings for minimal sums and endured poverty and harsh conditions while awaiting their departure.

In May 1950, the Mossad initiated Operation Ezra and Nehemiah under the leadership of Mordechai Ben-Porat and Shlomo Hillel. The first flight carrying 86 Jews from Iraq to Israel took off that month. By January 1952, around 120,000 Jews had been airlifted to Israel through approximately 900 flights. During this period, attacks on Jewish centers in Iraq, including a bombing outside a Baghdad synagogue, intensified, further escalating the exodus.

Syrian Jewry

Syria's Jewish community numbered approximately 30,000. During the British Mandate over Palestine, the Haganah organized efforts to bring around 10,000 Syrian Jews to Israel. After the Six-Day War in 1967, additional waves of Syrian Jews migrated. The Mossad established a network to assist Syrian Jews in fleeing to Israel, often via Lebanon and then by sea. More than half of Syria's Jewish population eventually resettled in Israel.

Lebanese Jewry

At the time of Israel's establishment, Lebanon's Jewish population numbered about 10,000, primarily concentrated in Beirut. Over time, some Lebanese Jews immigrated to Israel, particularly after the Six-Day War. By then, around half of the Jewish population had left Lebanon.

Libyan Jewry

The Jewish community in Libya experienced two major waves of emigration to Israel. In November 1945, anti-Jewish riots broke out in Libya, then under Italian rule, forcing thousands of Jews to flee to Palestine. After Israel's War of Independence, approximately 30,000 Jews—90 percent of the Libyan Jewish population—migrated to Israel.

Tunisian Jewry

While Tunisia was under French colonial rule during World War II, it was home to around 100,000 Jews, many of whom were descendants of Jewish migrants from Livorno, Italy, in the 18th century. When Tunisia fell to the Nazis, members of the Jewish community were forced to wear yellow stars. Approximately 5,000 Jews were sent to labor camps, and many were killed in their homes, starved, or died in bombings. Historians estimate that about 600 Tunisian Jews perished.

After the War of Independence, Tunisia remained under French control, and the Jewish community largely stayed in the country. However, after Tunisia gained independence in 1956, Jews faced increasing persecution and incitement. As a result, most of Tunisia's Jewish community emigrated—half to Israel and the remainder to France.

Moroccan Jewry

Morocco was home to the largest Jewish community in North Africa, and there were three waves of immigration from there. Between 1948 and 1951, after the War of Independence, some 28,000 Jews made aliyah. Between 1952 and 1960, they were joined by another 96,000, and in the decade between 1961 and 1971, around 131,000 Moroccan Jews arrived. In total, approximately a quarter of a million Jews immigrated from Morocco, making it the largest community of North African immigrants in Israel. The absorption process for these immigrants was complex. There were many difficulties, especially in the years immediately after the War of Independence, when Israel was a very poor state and was, in fact, on the brink of bankruptcy. Between 1949 and 1951, there was a strict policy of austerity in Israel. The supply and price of food were controlled and monitored by the state, industry was weak, and the country was deep in debt because of the war. At the same time, Israel, with a population of around 600,000 Jews, absorbed approximately 850,000 Jewish immigrants (!) from various countries within a three-to-five-year period. In this period, an embryonic country—which had lost 6,000 people in its War of Independence, where the economy was on the brink of collapse and there was widespread poverty—was also dealing with the integration of immigrants from many different countries, who spoke different languages and came from utterly different cultures and educational, social and cultural backgrounds. The population of the new state skyrocketed by 150 percent over this period. A massive, almost impossible task. Nonetheless, despite the difficulties and with great effort, these immigrants were absorbed and integrated into Israeli society. This process, however, was accompanied and is still accompanied by many difficulties, anger, mistrust and hatred. The process of integration into Israeli society was different for each group of immigrants. While olim from Egypt, Iraq, Libya, Tunisia, Lebanon and Syria managed to integrate successfully into Israel's society, economy, industry and culture, as well as the worlds of law, accountancy, the military and the academy, and while there were many success stories among Moroccan immigrants, many of them also experienced problems integrating. There are many reasons why this community was less successful in integrating. As usual, there are many different interpretations and explanations. Some say that, while Iraq was under British control and Algeria was under French control for around 130 years, and Tunisia was a French colony for 76 years, Morocco was French for just 44 years. As a result, they claim, a large proportion of immigrants from Morocco did not experience or benefit from the influence of Western culture and education. In practice, this meant that the integration of Moroccan Jewry was more complex. In 1959, there was a series of street demonstrations and acts of vandalism in the Wadi Salib neighborhood of Haifa. In the aftermath of these riots, the state established the Etzioni Commission to examine the reasons for the violence. Various witnesses testified before the commission. Among its findings, the commission found that "a significant proportion of the neighborhood's residents are immigrants from North Africa, especially Morocco. We discovered that certain members of this community claim to feel a great deal of discrimination and deprivation, sometimes to the extent that they feel isolated from Israeli society, against which

they have many complaints" (Clause 11 of the Etzioni Report).
The report's conclusions indicated that there was a significant
wage gap between immigrants from North Africa and more
veteran Israelis, most of whom came from Eastern Europe and
were known as Ashkenazim. The government tried to address
the problems that arose specifically in Haifa. At that time, Mapai
was the dominant party in Israeli politics and its leader was Israel's founder, David Ben Gurion. The main opposition party was
Herut Party, headed by Menachem Begin, who took advantage
of the sense of discrimination felt especially by immigrants from
North Africa, and stoked up their antipathy toward the government and the ruling Mapai party. This protest still rumbles on
today. In the early 1970s, there was more public unrest, which
started in Jerusalem and which was spearheaded by immigrants
from North Africa.

They called themselves the Black Panthers, and they brought
the poverty and social gaps in Israeli society to the public's attention. The demonstrations began in 1971. After two months of
disturbances, the leaders of the movement met with Golda Meir,
Israel's prime minister at the time. A month later, the protests
resumed and escalated into violent confrontations with the police,
in which dozens of people were injured. In 1973, protest leaders
established a political party to compete in Knesset elections, but
they did not cross the threshold and did not win any seats. As a
result, there were divisions and disagreements within the movement, and the leaders all went their separate ways. However, the
tensions and the sense of discrimination among some members
of the North African communities, especially those who arrived
from Morocco, remained. In 1981, the Tami Party was founded—a
Hebrew acronym for the Movement for the Heritage of Israel—by
Morocco-born Aharon Abuhatzira, who was serving as Minister
of Religions on behalf of the National Religious Party at the time.
In the 1981 election, his party won three seats. It advocated for
Mizrahi Jews in general and Moroccan Jewry in particular. In the
1984 election, it won just one seat, but by that time there was

another party on the scene with aspirations to represent Mizrahi Jews. That party was Shas, on which we shall elaborate later. Before we tell the story of Shas, however, it is worth spending a moment on the condition of Mizrahi Jews—a broad definition covering anyone who immigrated to Israel from a Muslim country. The truth, however, is that it is an overgeneralization. Politicians make political capital from the ethnic issue and by using ethnic incitement, including Israel's current prime minister, Benjamin Netanyahu. Under the label of Mizrahi Jews, however, there are different groupings, and their integration into Israeli society has been very different. Jews from Iraq and Kurdistan, for example, have fully integrated into Israeli society. Iraqi Jews filled many high-placed roles in banking, insurance, finance, stock markets, high-tech, and academia, as well as law and accountancy. The story of Iraqi Jews in Israel is a remarkable success story.

This was due to the fundamental culture that they brought with them, combined with the fact that the British had ruled Iraq. Similar success stories are true of Jews from Syria, Lebanon, Iran, Libya, Algeria, and Tunisia, all of whom integrated highly successfully into Israeli society. More than half of the IDF chiefs and police commissioners in Israel between 1995 and 2023 have been Mizrahi Jews. Some of Israel's richest individuals are also Mizrahim, and many people who appear on lists of Israel's richest people are originally from Muslim countries. The same is true in many fields of Israeli life, including accountancy, medicine, engineering, high-tech, academia, commerce, and banking. At the same time, Moroccan Jewry—the largest group of North African immigrants—has experienced less success. There are countless explanations for this, but it is hard to pinpoint one. That said, these immigrants felt a great sense of discrimination. Various politicians utilized these feelings and eventually turned them into a reason for hatred. Internal strife of this kind is one of the major problems currently facing Israeli society. We will touch on that later, however.

Shas movement, the full name of which is officially known

as the Worldwide Sephardic Association of Torah Keepers. It is a Haredi-religious Sephardi party that was led for many years by the Sephardi Chief Rabbi of Israel, Ovadia Yosef, who was actually born in Iraq. From 1990, however, the party was run and controlled alongside Ovadia Yosef and, after the rabbi's passing, exclusively by Aryeh (Makhlouf) Deri. Born in Morocco, Deri studied in an Ashkenazi yeshiva, became involved in Shas and, gradually and, using various methods, took control of the party entirely.

Now, Deri is the sole leader of Shas. Even at the turn of the century, when he was convicted of bribery and was sentenced to three years behind bars, serving 22 months, he remained indirectly in charge of Shas' affairs. The party enjoyed the most electorally successful period of its existence, winning 17 of the 120 seats in the Knesset in 1999, having risen from just four Knesset members in 1984. In the 2022 election, the party won 11 seats. In its early days, Shas was in partnership with the Labor Party. At that time, Ovadia Yosef, Shas' spiritual leader, was at the height of his power. Considered a great Torah scholar, Ovadia Yosef was conciliatory and preferred a peaceful existence. In 1992 and 1993, Shas was part of the coalition headed by Labor and its chairman, Yitzhak Rabin. When the Oslo Accords were signed on September 13, 1993, Shas was part of the government. On that day, for other reasons connected to an indictment filed against one of its ministers, Shas left the coalition. Ten days later, however, when the Knesset was asked to ratify the agreement, Shas abstained from the vote, even though it was no longer in the coalition. From the 1996 election, however, a long-term alliance started to be forged between Shas and Likud, especially between Shas leader Aryeh Deri and Netanyahu. They have been together ever since. This political alliance strengthened Netanyahu and Deri, and they both garnered a lot of power, political influence and even a private future from it. Shas learned from the Ashkenazi political parties (see Chapter 4) and set up an independent school system, funded by the government. The children of many of Shas' voters attended these schools, most of them Mizrahim and from the more impoverished socio-economic strata. Inspired by the Ashkenazi model, these schools offered a lot of Torah study, as well as the Gamora and other Jewish texts, but—and this is the crux—offered very little, if any, of what is known as the core curriculum: history, civics, math, English, physics, biology, chemistry, and so on. The result has been damaging and severe. An entire sector of Israeli society, which includes people who vote for Shas, sends their children to an educational framework, funded by the government, which produces a generation that is ignorant of and ill-educated in the modern world of science, math, and world culture. Needless to say, the proportion of children graduating from this framework who go on to higher education is very low. As a result, a large section of the population—in the 2011 election, Shas won 11 seats—is unable to integrate into professions in the modern workplace. Therefore, they are reliant on state aid, which Shas, thanks to its powerful position within the government, is supposed to provide from the state's coffers. Moreover, due to a lack of a broad education, these people are totally unaware of general history or basic concepts like civilian rule, democracy, public management, a modern judiciary, the importance of the separation of powers, and the existence of a modern justice system. These people were never taught about these issues and so they are foreign to them. They are alienated and fail to understand their importance. These schools are a threat to the existence of the State of Israel and to Israeli democracy. In many respects, Shas is the Mizrahi side of Ashkenazi Haredi Judaism (more on whom in Chapter 4).

The budgets for Shas' schools are constantly growing. Like in the Ashkenazi ultra-Orthodox education system, they do not teach the core curriculum. The same phenomena that characterize the Haredi school system (see Chapter 4) also exist in Shas' network of schools, with equally devastating effects. In 2022 and 2023, under the Netanyahu government, Shas, along with the ultra-Orthodox parties and the right-wing messianic-Kahanist parties, managed to extort the prime minister into giving them new and improved financial packages, the result of which will be the destruction of the education system, higher education, integration, and economic advancement of the State of Israel. The budget for the Haredi and Shas school networks was raised by 40 percent (!), which means that investment per student in these schools is higher than for students in state-run and traditional schools—and, needless to say, far exceeds investment in schools serving Israel's Arab citizens. These education systems, where students do not study the core curriculum, do not provide the foundations needed to integrate into Israel's liberal democracy. Such concepts are utterly foreign to these parties and to the education systems they operate. Incidentally, it is not unheard of for Western governments to fund private education systems, but that is up to a ceiling of 50 percent, and the curriculum is always under the close supervision of state authorities (see the report by the Education Ministry's Budget Division). "Increasing funding to education without the requirement for work with and the obligation to meet the requirement of basic studies ('the core curriculum') will have a negative impact on students' participation in the employment market and their earning capacity, with an increasingly negative impact on the Israeli economy, given trends in population growth" (from the abovementioned report). And, of course, this is not only true of the ability to study modern, advanced professions. However, the report does not stress the lack of education toward understanding, internalizing and respecting the foundations of a democratic regime, the safeguarding of civil rights, the importance of a system of checks and balances, an independent judicial system, fundamental human rights, freedom of speech and expression, and so on. Increasing the funding for educational networks belonging to Shas and the ultra-Orthodox parties also encourages families, for purely economic reasons, to transfer their children from state-run schools to these private networks. In light of this, between 1992 and 2012, the number of students enrolled in these schools rose from 13 percent to 38 percent. A report by the Bank of Israel further shows that the spread of Shas schools to traditional communities in the early 1990s lowered the proportion of students who qualified for a 'bagrut' certificate (the matriculation exam which tests students' knowledge of the core disciplines at the end of high school) by 24 percent and reduced by 14 percent the employment rate of young people in the decade after they finished high school.

Given these channels for funding and supporting the education systems run by Shas and the ultra-Orthodox parties, coupled with the significant increase in the demographic numbers of these groups, and unless there is a dramatic change in these components, the result will be a very different Israel from the one we know in 2023. It will be a much poorer country, lacking in academic, scientific, and research capabilities, with a nationalist-religious infrastructure that rejects any liberal or democratic characteristics. As a result, there will also be a sharp decline in the strength of Israel's military and its ties with the most important countries in the world. This would be a disastrous process, the severity of which cannot be understated. It must be stressed that Benjamin Netanyahu, who has served as Israeli prime minister since 2009, with a short break between June 2021 and November 2022, is aiding and abetting this catastrophic process and has written blank checks to fund these educational systems—solely to maintain his grip on power. He has done so even though it is patently obvious that he is deeply aware of the destructive consequences of these processes on the economic, social, and military resilience and strength of the State of Israel.[33]

It is also worth noting that Shas changed itself over the years. It started as a social movement, in the framework of a respected rabbinical authority, Rabbi Ovadia Yosef. Born in Iraq, Ovadia Yosef was considered an expert in Jewish law and regulations and had a phenomenal memory. He was a respected authority in Halakha. He was in favor of integrating religion into education and expanding religious awareness while taking a pragmatic

---

33. See Netanyahu's comments when he was finance minister in 2004, under then-Prime Minister Ariel Sharon.

approach to political matters, especially in terms of relations with the international community and the Palestinians. In this respect, Ovadia Yosef was a suitable partner for the Israeli camp that aspired to a reasonable resolution of the conflict with the Palestinians. However, over the years, his influence over Shas waned. At that time, in the 1980s, a young, Morocco-born man was studying at the Porat Yosef Sephardi Yeshiva in Jerusalem before moving on to Yeshivat Chevron, which was an Ashkenazi-Haredi-Lithuanian yeshiva. Over the years, Aryeh Deri proved himself to be a charismatic and intelligent politician with impressive leadership qualities. As a result, he found himself becoming close to Ovadia Yosef and maneuvering his way within the party. By the early 1990s, when he was just 27 years old, he was running the party alongside the veteran rabbi, who remained the highest authority within Shas. At this time, Deri served as interior minister.

It would later transpire that he committed acts of corruption and accepted bribes, for which he would be indicted. Among the Mizrahi-religious community, which supported Shas, Deri's trial engendered intense feelings of hostility and hatred toward the Israeli judiciary. With the encouragement of Deri and his partners, the courts and the state prosecution were accused (almost entirely without foundation or basis) of discriminating against Deri due to his ethnic background and the political will to destroy both Shas and Deri's career. This campaign of incitement was joined by several public figures and various respected journalists (some of them, like Amnon Danker, who was editor of the *Maariv* newspaper at the time, were Ashkenazim). There were also mass protests outside the courts and the office of the state prosecutor, and tensions were inflamed by an energetic political and media campaign aimed at humiliating the courts and the prosecution. Deri himself tried everything in his power to sabotage the police investigation. Deri claimed that a large part of the money and assets that were discovered in his possession actually belonged to Esther Verderber, an American citizen who, along with her husband, had adopted Deri's wife. However, before Verderber could testify before Israeli investigators, she was mysteriously run over and killed; the driver, it turned out, was a former Israeli. There were unsubstantiated and unproven rumors that the "accident" was no accident. Under police questioning, Deri exercised his right to remain silent. After prolonged legal proceedings at the Jerusalem District Court, Deri was convicted of fraud, breach of trust, and aggravated bribery. He was sentenced to four years in prison. He appealed his conviction to the High Court, which upheld the lower court's decision but cut his sentence to three years. The verdict once again sparked violent disturbances, during which participants railed against the courts, shouted racist slogans about "the Ashkenazim" and chanted that "Deri is innocent." The atmosphere in Israel was volatile. Anger and sectarian incitement were again being vocally expressed. In practice, they reflected the feelings of people who were easily incited. Deri and his supporters expertly orchestrated the incitement. When he was released from prison, he was barred by law from returning to public life for a period of seven years. At that time, he was, of course, involved behind the scenes in Shas' activities while also conducting his private business affairs (for which he was later convicted of tax offenses). However, Shas was now led by Ovadia Yosef's chosen successor to Deri, Eli Yishai.

In terms of tensions between ethnic groups in Israel, these were relatively quiet years. The so-called "ethnic demon"—the Israeli term for the divide between Mizrahi and Ashkenazi Jews—which politicians like Deri and Netanyahu use for political purposes, was still in the bottle at that time. But not for long. Shas continued to expand its network of schools, and the same inferior education continued to be the basis of these schools. In 2012, Deri returned to Shas. He worked energetically to regain his previous position as party chairman and, even though Ovadia Yosef condemned him—in a leaked videotape from 2008—as "a thief" and "wicked," the nonagenarian rabbi's will weakened, and he was no longer able to withstand Deri's pressure. By October 2012, it was patently evident that Deri was once again Shas' strongman.

Ovadia Yosef died in October 2013, and Deri has been the sole ruler of Shas since then. It is worth noting at this point that Deri has remained Benjamin Netanyahu's political partner throughout all these years. The partnership began in 1996, when Shas joined the coalition that Netanyahu led, and continued in 1997, when Netanyahu and Deri joined forces to push through the appointment of a lawyer from the private sector as attorney general. The candidate in question was considered close to Netanyahu's party, and the suspicion was that the lawyer, once appointed attorney general, would recommend that Deri not be charged with corruption. The plot was quickly uncovered by the Israeli media, and the attorney general was forced to resign just three days after being appointed. This farcical plot to appoint a crony as attorney general was cooked up in secret between Netanyahu, then prime minister, and Shas leader Deri. This conspiracy—which was later the subject of a criminal investigation that the attorney general at the time decided to close without further action—was, in retrospect, part of the decades-long collaboration between Deri and Netanyahu.

Since 2009, Shas has been part of every governing coalition, and its Knesset members have filled various ministerial roles, most often in the interior, health, welfare, and religious services ministries, where they have access to generous funding, political power, and influence or the opportunity to employ scores of party members. This makes them reliant on the party for their income, as well as for generous funding for the schools in which future generations of Shas voters are being educated. An ignorant generation, that is, which cannot find employment in modern professions; a generation which will be incapable of acquiring higher education. And so, the State of Israel and its politicians are creating an enfeebled, impoverished, ignorant group of citizens who are dependent on Shas and its chairman.

Inciters of ethnic hatred

As already mentioned, ethnic background and tensions between Mizrahim and Ashkenazim were the reasons for the establishment of Shas. However, these tensions were, and remain, the broad basis for incitement and engendering hatred by certain politicians. As far back as the late 1960s and early 1970s, Menachem Begin, head of the Herut movement, which would later become Likud, reaped political dividends from the sense of discrimination felt by some of the Mizrahi population. During elections, Begin would campaign on the issue of the gap between Mizrahim and Ashkenazim, arguing that the ruling Mapai party was responsible for this discrimination and the economic gaps. In so doing, he deliberately created enmity toward Mapai in the 1970s. In his campaigns, Begin played up this sectarian message and used it to win over Mizrahi voters. In his speeches, Begin railed against the kibbutzim and their members, saying that while they enjoyed grassy lawns and swimming pools, the Mizrahim in development towns had no such luxuries. This kind of argument was very much in Begin's political wheelhouse. When Likud was elected to power, Begin continued in the same vein. To his credit, however, it should be said that Begin's rhetoric did not spill over into inciting hatred and, during his first term of office as prime minister at least, he did try to initiate a housing plan to help those sectors of society.

Tensions between Mizrahim and Ashkenazim continued to rumble on below and above the surface, however. From time to time, certain politicians—mainly from Shas and Begin himself—would cynically use them. When Netanyahu was elected prime minister in 1996, however, he adopted it as one of the key weapons in his political arsenal (even though he himself is from a highly educated Ashkenazi family and studied in venerated universities in the United States!). Discrimination and a sense of deprivation were turned into direct incitement and hatred between Mizrahim and Ashkenazim. Netanyahu worked energetically, systematically, and unrestrainedly—and exclusively for his own benefit—to incite the Mizrahi public against the Ashkenazim, whom he or his collaborators in the media started referring to as "the elite" or "the hegemony." The hatred that Netanyahu introduced into Israeli society over the ethnic divide is a massive social time-bomb, and the damage it will cause will be immense. Yet another example of how Netanyahu has succeeded in smashing Israel's internal social unity and sense of solidarity. Holding power and control were always the most important things for Netanyahu and, from his perspective, there has never been any limit on the use of incitement and internecine hatred in order to strengthen his grip on power. Anyone who deals with the power of a state knows that internal divides, tensions, and particularly internecine hatred between sectors of society are the fundamental elements in the resilience or weakness of a country and its civil society. Netanyahu has made a massively negative contribution in this respect. Moreover, as we shall see in Chapter 8, Netanyahu knowingly brought into the Likud party he chairs and the Knesset people whose abilities, experience, accomplishments, and education are, to put it mildly, inferior.

They do, however, possess two characteristics that make them ideal for Netanyahu: firstly, they are Mizrahim, either born in Morocco or second-generation immigrants, who have a strong sense of discrimination and deprivation; and secondly, they are crude, impertinent, and are willing to be used as mouthpieces for incitement and stoking hatred between Mizrahim and Ashkenazim. Hatred and incitement between Mizrahim and Ashkenazim have become a hallmark of Netanyahu's years in office and one of the political weapons he employs most often—either directly or through others in the press, in the mainstream media (Channels 12, 13, and 14 on television) and, of course, through the Likud Knesset members that he, in practice, handpicked.[34]

Subordination to Torah Law

One of the most critical issues for Shas, and something that founder Rabbi Ovadia Yosef advocated his entire life, was the implementation of Torah law in Israel. He said as much to

---

34. Even though there are primaries in Netanyahu's Likud, the chair has massive influence over the outcome of these primaries.

municipal rabbis and rabbinical court judges in a speech in Jerusalem on October 28, 1998.[35] In 2023, this goal was given clear and public expression in the coalition agreements that paved the way for the establishment of the current Netanyahu coalition. Clause 109 of the agreement between Shas and Likud states that "the government will act to pass legislation allowing the Rabbinical Courts to discuss, with the agreement of the parties involved, cases relating to including Monetary Law [civil matters] and shall determine that the Rabbinical Courts will have jurisdiction over civil matters which may be the subject of an agreement, or if the parties have agreed to this in writing and the event that one of the parties is a member of the religion of the court." This is indicative of Shas' goal of integrating Torah Law into the Israeli justice system. This could have dramatic ramifications for the democratic character of the State of Israel. A modern, advanced, liberal society in which there is equality between all citizens, including members of the LGBTQ community, Arabs, and women, cannot exist under Torah Law. These groups will necessarily have their rights trampled and denied under the harsh interpretation of Torah Law by Shas rabbis and their ilk. Netanyahu's willingness to include a clause of this kind in the coalition agreement that paved the way for the establishment of the current government is testimony to his limitless lust for power and his willingness to give his coalition partners whatever they want as long as they continue supporting him. This, of course, is a recipe for the destruction of Israeli society.

The sectarian divide is a source of great tension in Israeli society. Its roots are in the gaps between Jews who arrived in Israel after the 1948 War of Independence from Muslim countries and those who came from other countries (mainly Europe, known as Ashkenazim). This gap was widened over the years. Even though 30 percent of marriages in Israel today are between Mizrahim and Ashkenazim, and the offspring of these marriages are mixed, the

---

35. See Moshe Suissa, Haaretz, 11.4.2023.

tensions still exist in Israeli society. It is worth noting that the Mizrahim themselves are not one homogenous grouping. The Jews from Iraq, Syria, Egypt, Lebanon, Iran, Tunisia, and Algeria are different from Moroccan Jewry. Moroccan Jews are the largest group within the Mizrahi community, but it was amongst them that there was the greatest sense of discrimination. It's worth remembering that the leaders of all the protest movements— Wadi Salib in 1959; Ashdod port in 1971, when union leader Yehoshua Peretz led industrial action by workers; and the Black Panthers in 1973—were Jews who had immigrated from Morocco. Shas, too, is run by an immigrant from Morocco. During the life of Shas founder Ovadia Yosef, the party focused far less on the sense of discrimination. They gave impetus to allegations of discrimination and deprivation. Having said that, current statistics show that the conditions of Jews from Muslim countries have greatly improved and are now on par with Ashkenazi Israelis. According to a study by Prof. Momi Dahan, between 1992 and 2007, Mizrahim reduced income gaps by 1 percent per year, so over 15 years, they narrowed the difference by 15 percent. A Tel Aviv University study showed that among Israel's middle classes, the average income of Mizrahim and Ashkenazim was identical. The same is also true in other areas. Sixty percent of the heads of local councils and municipalities in Israel are from a Mizrahi background, as are union leaders. More than 50 Knesset members (around 43 percent) are Mizrahim, even though they make up just 35 percent of the population. There have been three Mizrahi IDF chiefs of staff: Dan Halutz, whose parents immigrated from Iran and Iraq; Moshe Levi, whose parents came from Iraq; and Gadi Eisenkot, the son of Jewish Moroccan immigrants. Among the list of Israel's richest individuals are many people who were born or whose parents were born in Muslim countries, and there are many successful Mizrahim in the fields of law and accountancy.

However, the sense of discrimination and deprivation—which now has no basis in reality—has left historical scars. As already mentioned, there were, over time, politicians who cynically used this for their own ends. But Netanyahu arrived on the scene and took it to a very different scale and level. He went even further than Begin and Deri in identifying the divisions between Mizrahim and Ashkenazim and systematically and consistently used them to engender anger, disdain, and even hatred between the two groups. He tried to create a link between "Ashkenazi" and "leftist," thereby portraying them as Arab supporters, as opposed to the Mizrahim. This portrayal is, of course, utterly baseless, but, in a world of images and within the sense of discrimination, it carried much power. The Mizrahi public perceives an integral connection between Jews and anyone who wants to connect or collaborate with Israeli Arabs—and even more so, the Palestinians—as sabotaging the Jewish camp and the interests of the State of Israel. And Netanyahu was "blessed" with an extraordinary ability to intensify this incitement, tendency, and these divisions, given his unrestrained nature and his irresponsible leadership. To him, all means are justified in order to remain in power, and he has managed to create wide gaps in Israeli society based on sectarian tensions. Israeli society is paying a heavy price for this. It is evident in daily life, in the media, and especially on social media.

There were even some people—people with academic degrees—who came up with a purported theory, allegedly based on research, according to which the country is divided into "First Israel" and "Second Israel" and argued that there is "a hegemony that is unaware it is a hegemony" (no less). At the heart of these theories is an attempt to differentiate between Mizrahi Jews and Ashkenazi Jews, with the latter portrayed as "the hegemony" or "First Israel." Clearly baseless claims, but they had the power to incite and expand hatred and enmity between groups within Jewish Israeli society, between Mizrahim and Ashkenazim. The harsh and threatening rhetoric employed by Mizrahim against Ashkenazim and leftists has intensified to levels never before seen in Israel. This could lead to extreme situations, including violence on the one hand, and could, on the other hand, also contribute to people's desire to leave Israel. If that were to happen, the emigrés would be the educated and capable population. This is a social timebomb which, even though every current statistic says has no factual basis,[36] is being cynically used by politicians from various parties (mainly Shas and Likud under Benjamin Netanyahu).

---

36. Including a high proportion of "mixed" marriages between Mizrahim and Ashkenazim.

Chapter 4

The Haredi-Ashkenazi community

The Haredi-Ashkenazi community is far from homogeneous. It is the community with the highest birthrate in Israel, currently standing at no fewer than 6.4 children on average per family. This is not only the highest birthrate in Israel—it's the highest in the Western world. Among other groups in Israeli society, the birthrate is much lower: 2.7 children among secular Israelis; 3.2 children in the Arab community; and 4.8 children in the national-religious camp.[37] These, of course, are growth rates which, on Israel's demographic charts, raise serious concerns about the demographic, economic, and social danger that could lead to the collapse of the State of Israel within 30 years. The story of the Haredi-Ashkenazi community, its character, and the existential danger that it poses to Israel will be examined in depth below. There is, however, a bright spot in this community, which, if Israel's leaders in the coming years—not Netanyahu and the members of his party but those who will come after them—are able to address effectively, with determination and wisdom, could ensure that this demographic timebomb does not explode and could even turn it into something of value.

The following is a comprehensive explanation.

First, we need to go back 75 years to 1948 and Israel's War of Independence. At that time, just 4 percent of the population of Israel was Haredi-Ashkenazi. Remember that number. Currently, between 11 and 12 percent of the population is Haredi, and they

---

37. Miskar Research and Polling Institute report, January 3, 2017.

make up 25 percent (!) of the population aged under 18. We will return to these figures and what they mean for Israel's society, economy, academy, and science. But let's stay in 1948 for now. The Declaration of Independence was signed by the 37 individuals who served on the People's Council, established by the Jewish community in Palestine, under David Ben Gurion, in preparation for independence. The members of the People's Council were selected according to party affiliation; Mapai, Ben Gurion's party, had two members; Mizrachi and Hapoel Hamizrachi (see Chapter 5) had five members; and Agudat Yisrael and Poalei Agudat Yisrael had one member. Among those signing the Declaration of Independence on behalf of Agudat Yisrael was Yitzhak Meir Levin. One of the leaders of Agudat Yisrael, Levin served as the first welfare minister during the first three governments of the State of Israel. He resigned from government in 1952 over his party's opposition to national service for women. He was also active in the effort to secure an exemption from military service for yeshiva students and was one of the initiators and founders of the Agudat Yisrael school network. None of these issues, which we will examine below, prevented Levin from supporting the establishment of the State of Israel and being an active partner. Another Agudat Yisrael representative on the People's Council was Meir David Loewenstein. He was born in Denmark, had six children—one of whom served in a frontline unit in the IDF and was killed in fighting in the Sinai Peninsula in 1956.

After the establishment of the State of Israel and the War of Independence, the Haredi-Ashkenazi community enjoyed two significant privileges: an ever-expanding exemption from military service and an independent education system.

The education system

In 1953, Israel passed the State Education Law, which unified the various education streams in Israel into two tracks: state education and state-religious education (which was affiliated with the Mizrahi National Religious Party). Both tracks were under the supervision of the Ministry of Education. But the Haredi-Ashkenazi community, which feared that its independence would be compromised, refused to integrate into these tracks and was given special status in the 1953 legislation.

At first, this education system was 60 percent funded by the state, but this gradually climbed to 100 percent. In 1992, Israel passed an amendment to the Budgetary Principles Law, which stipulated that the independent Haredi education system would receive identical funding to the state-run tracks. Since then, there has been more legislation and more political pressure by the Haredi-Ashkenazi community, which has become more politically powerful thanks to its stunning natural population growth, to increase state funding for its educational institutions.

Now, thanks to the coalition agreements that were signed as part of the Netanyahu-led government that was established in the aftermath of the 2022 election, we have reached the point where primary schools in the Haredi-Ashkenazi track receive more state funding than those in state-run schools (in NIS):[38]

Sector	Current situation	After the coalition agreements (12/22)
State-Arab	17,300	17,300
State-Jewish	18,100	18,100
State-religious	20,150	20,150
Haredi-Ashkenazi	15,500	18,900
Ma'ayan (Shas)	17,950	22,100

The outcome is an increase in state spending per student so that, as of 2023 and Netanyahu's sixth government as prime minister, funding for each student in primary schools in the

38. Source: The Marker, 19.12.2022

Haredi-Ashkenazi track is higher than for those in the state-run secular track. Here it is important to add another fact of paramount importance: Haredi-Ashkenazi schools do not teach their students math, physics, chemistry, biology, history, philosophy, civics, or English—and the Education Ministry's supervision of their curriculums, if it exists at all, is minimal. For comparison, look at the parallel education system that serves the Haredi-Ashkenazi community in New York. There, however, the community is a tiny minority in the massive United States, and its schools are not fully funded by the State of New York. As a result of the inferior quality of the content taught in Haredi-Ashkenazi schools, the proportion of students in that stream who qualified for a matriculation certificate was just 14 percent, compared to 83 percent in the state and state-religious tracks (and 91.3 percent in the Druze community). Thanks to the increase in state funding for yeshiva study between 2014 and 2021, there has been a sharp 46 percent rise in the number of yeshiva students (see the Israel Democracy Institute's report). This weakness has also manifested itself in the field of academic study. The Haredi population's representation in institutions of higher education stands at just 4.5 percent—one-third of their proportion in the general population—and, moreover, the professions chosen by ultra-Orthodox students generally allow them to integrate into the Haredi workplace, such as education and medical auxiliary professions, rather than medicine, business management, engineering, or sciences. The ultra-Orthodox generally also opt to study in colleges for which the entry qualifications are considerably laxer than universities, and only 8.5 percent of them study in a university, compared to 33.5 percent of non-Haredi Jews.[39]

As a result, graduates of the Haredi-Ashkenazi education system are ignorant and lacking in the basic knowledge needed for professions in the modern world. This has created a group of citizens—the proportion of which in the general population

39. Israel Democracy Institute, Annual Survey of Ultra-Orthodox Society in Israel, 2022.

is increasing consistently (statistics missing)—which is unable to contribute to the economy of the State of Israel. They are unable to participate in the worlds of advanced industry, high-tech, research, academia, science, technological development, and professions and services that require advanced professional know-how. Needless to say, the lack of knowledge in English prevents them from being exposed to different worldviews and broader perspectives. This ignorance leads to a very narrow worldview and an inability to understand what is happening in Israel in particular, events in the region or their implications for Israel—as well, of course, as broader phenomena in the world, some of which will have varying degrees of impact on Israel, some of which could be dramatic.

Another outcome is that there is a large and ever-growing section of society that lacks the ability to reach its own conclusions and come to profound understandings about events and their impact. This sector of society currently has significant influence over the composition of the Knesset and the Israeli government. As of 2023, in fact, if it were not for the Haredi-Ashkenazi Agudat Yisrael party, Netanyahu would not have been able to form a government. Due to his burning desire to be in power at any price (see Chapter 6 for more on Benjamin Netanyahu), this sector is able to extort extraordinary levels of financial benefits, budgets, and support for the Haredi-Ashkenazi community. Indeed, the coalition agreements that Netanyahu signed in 2022, ahead of the establishment of his sixth government, are stuffed with financial benefits and bonuses for the Haredi-Ashkenazi education system, as well as for housing.

For example: The 2022 coalition agreements with Netanyahu's government provided a massive addition of funding to the ultra-Orthodox education system and to salaries for teachers in those tracks. This was in addition to financial support for yeshiva students and other economic boons for the ultra-Orthodox sector, including kindergartens, municipal taxes, and public transportation. The following is a breakdown of annual spending per student in private and state-run schools before the additions of 2023 and 2024, under the Netanyahu government that was elected in November 2022.

Annual budget per student in private primary schools (in shekels)			
Secular	**Arab**	**Religious**	**Ultra-Orthodox**
11,285	7,900	9,700	15.490

Annual budget per student in state-run primary schools[40]			
Secular	**Arab**	**Religious**	**Ultra-Orthodox**
18,800	19,950	20,400	23,120

In practice, 96 percent of ultra-Orthodox students currently learn in the private education system. These schools, which are not state-run and are operated by nongovernmental organizations, are not adequately supervised, and teachers there are not civil servants. Just 4 percent of ultra-Orthodox students attend public, state-run schools in the state-religious sector.

An examination of the above tables shows that students in ultra-Orthodox education sectors always receive more state funding than other tracks—especially compared to state-run education.

Israel is the only country in the world that funds more than 50 percent of the costs of private educational institutions. In many countries, there is no state funding for private schools what-soever. The reason for this is obvious: countries want to teach content that they approve of, which will allow them to create a

40. Sources: Education Ministry report, 2023, and Lior Tal's article in "The Marker" (20.5.2023).

society with agreed-upon values, and to have an educational system that teaches students modern disciplines so that they can integrate into society and contribute to the economy and resilience of that country. Israel alone funds 100 percent of the cost of a private education stream. Moreover, the Haredi education system is not supervised and does not teach the core curriculum.

The schools serving ultra-Orthodox students in the two largest Haredi networks, considered "exempt" from both government policy and the law, were supposed to teach 55 percent of the core curriculum and, in exchange, would receive 55 percent of their funding from the state. It turns out, however, that these schools are not under supervision.[41] These schools systematically refuse to cooperate on international exams and government tests to assess the level of teaching on the core curriculum. The result is that the State of Israel, especially since 2009, when Benjamin Netanyahu took office, is funding the ultra-Orthodox education system without ensuring that they are teaching the core curriculum. Thus, Israel is using taxpayer money to fund an education system that produces citizens who lack the most basic knowledge in the core curriculum. This is most certainly a march of folly.[42]

Netanyahu and his current government have dramatically increased the budget for the ultra-Orthodox education system, solely to remain in power. A historic process is underway that, unless its course is changed dramatically, will ruin every social system in Israel, including its higher education, science, and research. An entire generation of engineers, technologists, and thinkers will simply disappear. Put simply, the largest sector in society—the Haredi-Ashkenazi community—will lack any skills

41. Supreme Court 07/4805, the Center for Jewish Pluralism vs. the Education Ministry, verdict from 27.7.2008.

42. See the April 15, 2024, report by the Reform Center for Religion and State, position paper on the boycott of national tests by Haredi institutions, High Court of Justice 586/24, Reform Center for Religion and State v. Ministry of Education, and High Court of Justice 10296/02, Union of Secondary Teachers v. Minister of Education, PDI 59(3),page 224.

in the core disciplines, including history, civics, geography, biology, and chemistry. This is nothing less than an existential danger to the State of Israel and will gradually but fundamentally alter the components of Israeli society.

In the coalition deal that was signed in December 2022, for example, between the ultra-Orthodox parties and Netanyahu's Likud, the following clauses appear:

Article 128: The independence, uniqueness, and relative budget of all types of Haredi education (including educational networks, exempt institutions, and educational institutions) within the general education system shall be preserved. This remains true even if there is an organizational, structural, or content change in the general education system. If there is a violation of such status, the government will act to correct the harm, whether by legislation or otherwise, according to the case and need.

Section 129: The status of exempt institutions shall be preserved, and the Education Minister shall sign an extension of the validity of the Compulsory Education Regulations (Provision of an Exemption Provision for Educational Institutions and its Budgeting), 5778-2017, which enshrines the Exemption Institutions Regulations.

Article 130: Following the conclusions of the State Comptroller's 2022 report on discrimination and the shortage of classrooms, kindergartens, and daycare centers in the Haredi sector, the government will prioritize the construction of classrooms, kindergartens, and daycare centers in the Haredi sector. It will act to reduce the gaps, including by adding 700 classrooms per year to the five-year plan to address the accumulated shortage in the provision of classrooms for the Haredi sector.

Article 137: The Education Minister will establish a team that will ensure equal distribution among all youth organizations starting in 2023, so the budget of the youth organizations will align with the budget of the youth movements. These organizations will be included in the foundations of the 2023 budget. The budget of the youth organizations will not decrease due to the increase in the number of youth organizations.

Article 148: The pedagogical independence of supervision and guidance will be maintained and strengthened according to the standard guidelines of the Education Ministry. The networks will receive independent status in the Education Ministry (similar to settlement education or any other solution). Accordingly, the networks will be NGOs, with all that this entails. (The Agudat Yisrael faction does not agree with the words "settlement education.") Government Decision 226 (Shasha Biton's Geffen Plan) regarding the program for managerial flexibility in the education system will be reexamined. If the plan is retained, it will be amended to accommodate the networks.

Article 154: In light of the recognition by the 37th government of Israel that all children must be treated equally and acknowledging the longstanding discrimination against the Haredi education system, the government will adopt and implement the principle of equality for all Israeli children. To achieve this, a professional team will be established on behalf of the prime minister, including representatives from the Finance Ministry, the Education Ministry, the Housing Minister, and the Chairman of the Finance Committee. The team will also meet with representatives of kindergartens, exemption institutions, educational institutions, independent education networks, Maayan Torah education schools, unique cultural institutions, seminaries, and institutions from the National Religious camp. This team will complete its work before the 2023 budget is finalized, and the government will consider this matter a top priority.

As of 2023, all Haredi institutions will enter the New Horizon program in full and in one phase, similar to general education, with the necessary adjustments. The remaining comparison issues, as appear in the Appendix, will be carried out for a maximum of up to three budgetary years, with 60 percent of the amount budgeted in the 2023 budget and the balance budgeted at 20 percent of the amount in the 2024 budget and in the 2025 budget, in accordance with the Finance Ministry's estimates as of the date of signing this agreement. If it turns out that the Finance Ministry's estimates as of the date of signing this agreement are higher than necessary for the purpose of making such a comparison, the implementation of the comparison will be accelerated accordingly. The United Torah Judaism faction announces that in order to achieve equality, it is necessary to act in accordance with what is detailed in the appendix to this agreement.

Supervision will be carried out in order to ensure that the budgetary comparison in the education system in all its components, including full educational activity and employment conditions, is actually carried out."

This tiresome text, which conceals itself in sanctimonious claims of "equality and recognizing ongoing discrimination," contains demands for massive financial subsidies and government support for the ultra-Orthodox community's independent education systems. And, indeed, in the state budget for 2023 and 2024 that was approved by the Knesset in May 2023, Netanyahu sold the future and security of Israel to the leaders of the ultra-Orthodox parties in exchange for another term as prime minister. In practice, an additional 13.7 billion shekels was allocated to the ultra-Orthodox education system, including pay raises for teachers in these institutions—even though they do not possess state-recognized teaching qualifications. These institutions do not teach the core curriculum, and most are not supervised by the Education Ministry. This is a highly destructive process for Haredi society and the State of Israel. However, Israel is paying and will continue to pay heavily in the future in terms of society, the deterioration of its economy, and the nation's security.

Without diving too deeply into the coalition agreements that set up the Netanyahu government in 2022, it is worth noting that the parties demanded that their educational institutions remain independent and that the Education Ministry not be authorized to inspect them. Who, then, will supervise them? The ultra-Orthodox themselves! Likewise, the government will not be entitled to withhold funding from them even if it emerges that they have failed to adhere to the various guidelines. Incidentally, these coalition agreements stipulate that salaries for teachers will come via independent educational networks. Since there will be no Education Ministry supervision of them, there is reasonable cause to believe that at least some of that money will not end up in teachers' pockets but elsewhere. An opportunity for corruption? We should not be surprised if, on the way to ignorance and isolation from the wider world and from a broader education, corruption also flourishes. Usually, as we know, the more insular a society is, and the more it is lacking in powerful mechanisms and institutions of supervision, the more corruption sprouts, flourishes, and spreads.

In addition, the coalition agreement (Chapter 9) means that any pay increase given to teachers in the ultra-Orthodox sector must also be given to ultra-Orthodox teachers and kindergarten teachers, even though they are not civil servants. This is another indirect way of increasing the income of ultra-Orthodox families. Moreover, the new agreement includes a demand for funding for students in the ultra-Orthodox sector and yeshivas **to** be linked to the number of yeshiva students. This means that there is no incentive for yeshiva students to go out and find paid work. Even today, the proportion of working men in ultra-Orthodox society is markedly low. While 83 percent of men in the general population work, among ultra-Orthodox and religious men, that figure is just 53 percent.

Here it is worth noting that experience shows that government funding for the ultra-Orthodox sectors has a direct effect on the proportion of people working. Thus, between 2003 and 2005, when Ariel Sharon was prime minister and Benjamin Netanyahu was his finance minister, public funding for the ultra-Orthodox sector was slashed. Up until that point, the government would give 150 shekels per month to a family with one child, and each extra child saw that figure rise to 850 shekels a month for the fifth child. As a result of these cuts, ultra-Orthodox families received 1,500 shekels less per month. This led to the employment rate among ultra-Orthodox men climbing from 35 percent to 40 percent—a jump of 15 percent over just two years!

Moreover, until 1977, when Menachem Begin—the leader of the Herut party, which later merged with the Liberal Party to create Likud—formed his first government, the employment rate among ultra-Orthodox men was 82 percent. That was similar to the employment rate among secular men.

Up until that point, ultra-Orthodox parties had stayed out of political life and refused to participate in government. This was due to their ideological opposition to recognizing the Zionist entity (that is how they refer to the State of Israel) and to receiving any favors or benefits from it. In 1977, for the very first time, they joined Begin's Likud, which had won the most seats and formed the government. Since then, the ultra-Orthodox have become engaged in power struggles, always siding with whichever party was most generous with them and their constituents financially and economically, supporting their schools, yeshivas, housing—and, later, discounts in municipal taxes and other handouts. This led to a dramatic drop in the number of ultra-Orthodox men in the workplace—from 83 percent to today's level of 53 percent. The many financial benefits that the ultra-Orthodox community currently gets are thwarting their return to the workforce. The outcome of these benefits to the Haredi-Ashkenazi community, funding educational systems that are not supervised and do not teach the core curriculum, and the high birthrate in this sector are indicative of the threat to the character of the state and its very existence.

Population increase

The Haredi-Ashkenazi population of Israel (as well as the Haredi-Mizrahi population; see chapter on Shas) increased at a dizzying pace. When the state was established in 1948, the Haredi population—Ashkenazi and Mizrahi together—made up 4 percent of the total population. Over the years, however, their proportion of the overall population increased significantly. While there was a significant decrease in the birthrate of Israeli Arabs (from six children on average to 2.97 children between 1949 and 2022), the birthrate among the Haredi population—both Ashkenazi and Mizrahi—remained high at around 6.4 children on average per family. In fact, it was only between 2003 and 2005, when the government cut its subsidies to large ultra-Orthodox families, that there was a significant downward trend in the birthrate of those communities (which fell to 5.7 children on average per family). Apart from that brief period, the ultra-Orthodox birthrate has remained steady. As a result, the ultra-Orthodox community, which made up 10 percent of the Israeli population in 2009, now makes up around 13 percent.

However, in the 3 to 18 age group, they currently make up 25 percent of the population. According to demographers, by 2065, the Haredim will make up 32 percent of the total Israeli population.[43] Assuming that this trend continues and there is no dramatic change, either in a reduction of the birthrate among the ultra-Orthodox community in Israel or, alternatively, if there is no dramatic change in the content of the material taught in the Ashkenazi and Mizrahi educational systems, the high proportion of ultra-Orthodox in the overall Israeli population means that the state cannot exist. The possibility that one-third of the residents of the state could be unable to participate in the advanced workforce places an unbearable economic burden on the rest of the population. Even today, the ultra-Orthodox population's contribution to Israel's tax revenue is a paltry 4 percent. In other

---

43. Central Bureau of Statistics projection, 2017.

words, the ultra-Orthodox make up approximately 13 percent of the population, but thanks to their yeshivas and their other indirect grants, they receive 300 percent more than secular citizens.

According to the Bank of Israel, while the average ultra-Orthodox household aged between 25 and 44 receives 2,800 shekels a month on average from the state (after taxes and other deductions), the non-Haredi household pays an average of 2,200 shekels (after taxes and other deductions).[44] Another report published in October 2024 claims that the average ultra-Orthodox household receives 18,000 NIS per month from the government and pays only 7,500 NIS, while non-ultra-Orthodox households (not including Arabs) receive 13,300 NIS per month while paying 14,000 NIS.[45] This also leads to massive public anger and intense tensions within Israeli society, including a sense of hatred for the ultra-Orthodox community for what is perceived as their exploitation of and parasitical relationship with the religious, traditional, and secular population. It is also worth noting that the high natural population growth of the ultra-Orthodox community, while being ideologically motivated, is also the result of economic considerations. As already mentioned, between 2003 and 2005, when Ariel Sharon was prime minister, support for larger families was cut.

This had a dramatic impact on the Haredi birthrate, which fell from 6.7 children on average to 5.7 children. The percentage of Haredi men participating in the workforce also increased during this period, from 35 percent to 40 percent. The cuts, however, were short-lived. Since 2009, with the exception of a short period between June 2021 and December 2022, Netanyahu has been prime minister. Throughout this entire period, Netanyahu's coalition partners received massive grants and financial support. After all, they are the people who gave him the thing for which he would be willing to sell everything and give everything: grabbing hold of power and remaining prime minister. This was particularly

44. See economists' warning, published May 28, 2024. "The Marker," economic newspaper.
45. See *"Shaldor" report, published August 2024 and based on data from 2019.*

evident when it comes to subsidized daycare for children aged between two and six.[46] This is in addition to grants for yeshiva students, discounts in municipal taxes, and payments from the National Insurance Institute for each additional child. This has encouraged the ultra-Orthodox community to continue with a high birthrate. Israel is rushing headlong into a demographic, economic, and social crisis; unless there is a dramatic change— either in terms of the subjects taught in the ultra-Orthodox education system, which would allow its graduates to continue tertiary studies in modern disciplines that would allow them to find work in advanced industries and high-tech, or otherwise in terms of a huge reduction of the high birthrate in that community—the Israeli economy will suffer and eventually collapse. The poverty rate will skyrocket. Even before Israel reaches breaking point, these demographic phenomena will encourage Israel's highest-achieving groups to reconsider whether they wish to remain or opt to leave the country. This, of course, is a recipe for catastrophe. As things currently stand, it does not appear that there is any Israeli leader willing to tackle these harsh realities. Certainly not as long as Benjamin Netanyahu remains prime minister. After all, his focus is fixed exclusively on remaining in power, and he puts personal interests above those of the state. He is willing to give the ultra-Orthodox anything they want.

Military service

Not only does the ultra-Orthodox education system produce citizens without training in civics, democracy, physics, mathematics, English, and other subjects required to train informed citizens who understand societal processes and governmental mechanisms in modern democratic countries and have the ability to integrate into the country's economy in advanced fields, but the same population refuses, for ideological and self-serving reasons, to serve in the IDF. This bizarre situation may sound absurd to an

---

46. See The Marker, Ms. Meirav Arlosoroff, 26.2.2023.

outsider, but it is the Israeli reality—and it both begins and ends with the position of the ultra-Orthodox population. The vast majority of them objected from the outset to the State of Israel and to Zionism. They refused to be part of the Zionist enterprise to establish the Jewish state. Large sections of them opposed the establishment of the State of Israel and rejected the Jewish population's desire for self-determination. As far as the Haredi population was concerned, maintaining their ancient way of life was enough, and they had no interest in self-determination within the framework of a Jewish state. Therefore, these people do not feel part of the State of Israel and do not feel obligated to contribute to its defense. Refusing military service aligns with the fundamental ideology of large parts of the ultra-Orthodox population. Indeed, even before the War of Independence, David Ben-Gurion agreed to exempt 400 Haredi Yeshiva students from IDF service. Given that the Jewish population of Israel at the time was around 600,000, if we translate that into 2023 figures, it would be the equivalent today of exempting around 5,000 yeshiva students. The problem, however, is that there are currently 135,000 yeshiva students (!)—more than 30 times the number in 1948!

How did we arrive at this extreme and unsustainable situation?

In March 1948, shortly before the outbreak of the War of Independence, David Ben-Gurion decided to exempt 400 exceptional Yeshiva students from serving in the IDF. The exemption was limited in numbers and was designed to maintain the connection between Judaism and the Torah, especially after the Holocaust, in which the Nazis slaughtered 6 million European Jews. This arrangement was extended, but the number of exemptions gradually rose. The situation reached such proportions that, in September 1963, when he was no longer prime minister, Ben-Gurion wrote a letter to his successor, Levi Eshkol. In it, he wrote:

"I now see how Haredi Jews are taking control, and I feel that I have a degree of responsibility. I released these men from their obligation to serve in the army. Although I made this decision

when the numbers were small, they continue to multiply and, in their unruliness, they are a danger to the honor of the country. Perhaps there is reason to revisit the question of men in yeshivas, if they actually do need to be exempt from their army obligation. But lawbreakers certainly do not deserve this questionable privilege."

Indeed, back in January 1951, Ben-Gurion wrote to the IDF chief of staff and the director of the Defense Ministry, saying, "In accordance with Clause 12 of the Security Service Law, I have released yeshiva students from military service. This exemption applies only to yeshiva students who are actively engaged in Torah study at a yeshiva and only as long as they are actively engaged in Torah study at a yeshiva." In 1958, with the approval of Ben-Gurion, Shimon Peres—who was director-general of the Defense Ministry at the time—reached a new agreement with the leaders of the Haredi yeshivas. That agreement formalized the process by which yeshiva students' military service could be deferred until reaching 25 years old, when they would undergo a short period of basic training, lasting three months. Thereafter, like every other citizen of Israel, they would be liable for mandatory reserve duty. In 1954, those 400 exemptions from military service grew to 1,240.

In January 1958, as prime minister and defense minister, Ben Gurion instructed Peres to annul the exemption from military service. He wrote this:

"The justification that existed when the state was established no longer exists. Every yeshiva student will be called up to the army. Only if there are special circumstances will they be allowed to extend their studies by half a year. They cannot defer their service more than four times. In other words, by the age of 20, and only if there are exceptional reasons to defer until that age."

This order, however, was not carried out since the government fell six months later. Therefore, the claim that Ben-Gurion was responsible for the current situation of ultra-Orthodox exemption from the draft is utterly spurious, like so many other claims. In 1968, one year after the Six-Day War, the number of yeshiva students climbed to 4,700—i.e., 12 times their number in 1948! As a result, IDF chief of staff Haim Bar-Lev demanded that the defense minister reexamine the issue of exemptions for yeshiva students.[47] As a result, a committee was established, and it eventually decided to leave the status quo unchanged so that 400 yeshiva students would be exempt from service every year. By 1972, annual exemptions (not cumulative) stood at 800 (see the aforementioned report, Page 65). In 1975, Peres, by then defense minister, revoked the restriction on new yeshivas joining the agreement. However, the limit of 800 exemptions per year remained. However, a dramatic change was on the horizon. The 1977 election result allowed Menachem Begin to form the first-ever Likud government.

That government, however, was set up with the support of the ultra-Orthodox parties, who, for the first time, sat in government. It opened the door for them to participate in the electoral process and the establishment of governments in Israel; in return, they began to demand increasing benefits, both in economic areas (support for kindergartens, schools, yeshivas, and discounts on municipal taxes and various other tariffs)—as well as exemption from military service. Israeli governments are always the result of agreements between parties, which then enter into a coalition together. The coalition agreement that Likud signed in 1977 with the ultra-Orthodox parties clarified how many yeshiva students were allowed to seek exemption from military service. After the 1981 election, in which Likud won a majority of seats in the Knesset, Begin again signed coalition agreements with the ultra-Orthodox parties—but, this time, the agreement was expanded to include yeshiva teachers, city rabbis, judges in rabbinical courts, teachers in private Haredi schools, and others. These changes had

---

47. See the historical appendix to the report of the Knesset Research and Information Center on "Implementation of the Deferral of Military Service for Yeshiva Students Law (The Tal Law)," published in June 2012.

ramifications beyond the military-security aspects and beyond the issue of how the burden is shared among Israeli citizens, between those who served full terms in the army and those who were exempted following the yeshiva students. This also led to a reduction in the proportion of ultra-Orthodox men participating in the workforce. Before 1977, around 87 percent of ultra-Orthodox men worked; by 1980, that figure had dropped to 63 percent, and by 2003, it was down to just 37 percent![48] This situation continued for years, and by 1998, the cumulative number of exemptions from military service issued to the ultra-Orthodox population was 25,000. And remember that in 1948-1949, there were just 400 of them. It was at this stage that Israel's High Court of Justice was asked to rule on the issue of the ultra-Orthodox draft and exemption for yeshiva students among the ultra-Orthodox population.

These cases made the High Court extremely unpopular and, indeed, hated among the ultra-Orthodox population. They started to perceive it as an obstacle to be overcome and removed. This hatred exploded publicly in 2023—more on which is in Chapter 9—but there were already signs of it in demonstrations and writing years before. In 1988, in response to a petition, the High Court ruled that the defense minister does not have the authority to determine the arrangement by which exemptions from military service are issued and that the arrangement must be enshrined in law. Following lengthy discussions, the Deferral of Military Service for Yeshiva Students Law was passed. It was also known as the Tal Law, after former Supreme Court Justice Tzvi Tal, from the national-religious camp, who headed the committee that formulated the law. Various petitions were filed against the law, and the Supreme Court tried to postpone its ruling for as long as possible in order to prevent a political crisis. In 2012, however, a ruling was handed down, and the court annulled the law, citing flaws in its instructions. In so doing, the court annulled the arrangement

---

48. See Dr. Asaf Malchi, the Israel Democracy Institute, Issue 81, 16.4.2018.

reached with the ultra-Orthodox public, who never forgave the justices for their ruling. Their enmity toward the High Court only grew over the years—and, as mentioned earlier, the ultra-Orthodox were never great fans of the Jewish state, to put it mildly, did not study the core curriculum, and were therefore strangers to social concepts, including the essence of democracy and the civil history of the world in terms of government and democracy.

In repealing the Tal Law, the Supreme Court ruled that the law lacked basic provisions, including, inter alia, a mechanism that would provide incentives for yeshiva students to serve in the army and the lack of supervision and implementation of national-civilian service. This sparked another round of political pressure and negotiations within the Israeli government—all of which were led by Benjamin Netanyahu. He turned capitulation to all of the ultra-Orthodox demands, for the sake of safeguarding his grip on power, into an instrument that he used limitlessly. The leaders of the ultra-Orthodox parties recognized Netanyahu's weakness and his uncontrollable lust for power, as well as his willingness to give them whatever they wanted if it meant their continued support. And they took full advantage of this. Their appetite and their demands grew from year to year, in every aspect of life—including the exemption from military service. In 2014, a new law was passed to replace the Tal Law, which had been struck down as unconstitutional. The 2014 law set limits and targets for the number of yeshiva students who would be drafted into the IDF every year and stipulated criminal punishments for violations. But it also said that there would be a three-year adjustment period, until June 2017, whereby the draft would not be implemented and yeshiva students would be allowed to defer their service. In Israeli politics, however, every agreement is just an opportunity for change, rejection, or amendment. The same was true this time. In 2015, Israelis went to the polls for the 20th time to elect a government. This time, under pressure from the ultra-Orthodox parties, an amendment was passed whereby the adjustment period was extended from three years to six, until

2020. In addition, the defense minister was given legal authority to defer the military service of anyone over the age of 21; this meant that the service of yeshiva students could be deferred to the age of 24, at which stage they would be eligible for a full exemption from service. By law, an unmarried ultra-Orthodox man aged 18 to 24 cannot work as long as his military service is being deferred. Once again, petitions were filed to the High Court against this amendment, citing various different reasons. In September 2017, the High Court of Justice annulled the amendment, finding similar flaws to those found in the Tal Law back in 2012. The justices ruled that the amendment must be repealed, saying that it was not equitable to other sectors of Israeli society and that it did not impose criminal penalties against anyone who refused to join the IDF.[49]

Throughout this entire period, a negligible number of ultra-Orthodox men were joining the IDF—around 2.5 percent. However, the political power of the ultra-Orthodox sector continued to grow, not only thanks to their high birthrate, which increased their proportion in the general public, but also because of Netanyahu, whose entire political existence depends on a coalition that includes the ultra-Orthodox parties. The Haredi politicians identified Netanyahu's weakness and his desire to stay in power at any price—and increased their demands accordingly. So, in the coalition agreement that was negotiated after the November 2022 election (and signed at the end of December that year), Clause 90, under the heading of "State and Religion," included a dramatic provision concerning military service. The clause stipulates that "by the time the state budget for 2023 is passed, an amendment to the Security Service Law will be passed, legalizing the standing of yeshiva students with the agreement of all members of the coalition." Indeed, once Netanyahu set up his government in April 2023, the ultra-Orthodox parties began to demand a law that would grant a blanket exemption from military

49. High Court of Justice 1877/14, the Movement for Quality Government in Israel vs. The Knesset, 12.9.2017.

service for any ultra-Orthodox man who is a yeshiva student up to the age of 21—after which they would receive a full exemption from military service. Once this legislation is passed, Israel will become a country in which there are two distinct groups: the first is a large section of society which serves in the IDF and which will, later in life, work and study, some in academia, will pay taxes and will participate in a dynamic and creative society; the other group, the Haredim, completely disavow themselves of military service and even any other kind of national service. Netanyahu's governments since 2009, and especially the most recent one, have also given the ultra-Orthodox everything they want in the area of military service. Currently, between 80,000 and 90,000 young Israelis join the IDF every year. Of them, around 12,000 to 13,000 are from the ultra-Orthodox population. They are not recruits. This is a significant proportion of Israeli society. This evasion of military service or, alternatively, national service, leads to bitterness, anger, and resentment amongst the public. This is especially true in 2024, in the aftermath of the events of October 7. Since then, IDF soldiers have constantly been fighting in the Gaza Strip and on the northern border against Hezbollah, while tens of thousands of ultra-Orthodox youths are not part of the war effort and are not taking the risks involved in defending their country. We are rapidly approaching the boiling point on this issue. At the current time, Netanyahu prefers to prioritize his continued reign as prime minister and does not dare to be a leader and change the situation. After all, he's afraid that the ultra-Orthodox parties on which his government relies will abandon him. But the explosion, like on so many other issues, is close.[50]

---

50. In March 2024, the High Court issued an interim order to the government, instructing it not to fund yeshivas in which there are draft-age students. In so doing, the court agreed to the request of the attorney general and echoed the feelings of the general public (apart from the ultra-Orthodox population). The discussion is ongoing. Later, the Supreme Court ruled that the ultra-Orthodox must serve. Netanyahu and his government, in the midst of war in Gaza and against Hezbollah, are discussing a new law to relieve the ultra-Orthodox from military service. At the same time, other sectors serve (and pay the ultimate price sometimes). Since October 7, over 800 soldiers have been killed in action.

Interim conclusion

So, what has been created here and what has intensified during Netanyahu's time in office, since 2009? The ultra-Orthodox population, parts of which deliberately and for ideological reasons refuse to play any active part in or contribute to Israeli society. Some of them are even ideologically opposed to Zionism. But their natural birthrate means that they have an average of 6.4 children per family. They make up 12-13 percent of the population and, according to demographic predictions, they will make up 32 percent of the population by 2065!

At the current time, their children study in independent educational institutions, which the State of Israel currently finances from the taxpayers' pocket! The State of Israel has no supervision of these educational tracks, and they do not teach modern subjects like math, physics, civics, history, English, chemistry, and computer science. Graduates of these schools are devoid of a broad education and unable to pursue further education in the fields of science or engineering. Therefore, their contribution to Israel's strength in the future, in technological areas, will be zero. On the other hand, they will need the State of Israel's financial assistance to support their families. Indeed, the State of Israel also does so, in the form of stipends to yeshiva students, discounts on municipal taxes, kindergartens, and payments from the National Insurance Institute for each extra child. Even today, the ultra-Orthodox sector contributes just 4 percent to Israel's tax revenues, while they make up three times that number as a proportion of the population. It is clear, too, that these people are not connected to and do not understand the principles of life in a modern state. Concepts such as democracy, equality, freedom of speech, freedom of expression, the right to ask questions, and an independent judiciary—all of these are totally alien to them. They do not recognize or understand them—or they reject them as unworthy values that should be subordinate to Torah Law. It is obvious, therefore, that if the current situation does not change, if the ultra-Orthodox birthrate remains high, and if ultra-Orthodox children are not taught key disciplines like English, history, and civics, the outcome will be that the State of Israel, within not many decades, will be a very different place from what we have known and what exists today. The State of Israel, unlike most other countries, including impoverished and developing countries, faces external threats to its existence. A large part of the State of Israel's resilience, as we saw in Chapter 2, comes from the quality of its human resources, which are equipped with high capabilities in the fields of technology, engineering, sciences, cyber, military industries, computer science, and medicine. It was thanks to these capabilities that, at the end of 2022, Israel's per capita GDP was around $51,500, as well as to significant military and economic capabilities.

However, if even 25 percent of the Israeli population are ultra-Orthodox and lack a broad academic education, which prevents them from studying or working in these fields, then Israel's relative advantage will be dramatically eroded. This will have devastating effects—not only on cultural life in Israel and, it seems, on the nature of the regime, but also on the economy. The Israeli economy will decline sharply, and, as a result, there will be devastating effects on transportation, infrastructure, and the healthcare system—all of which are areas in which Israel currently excels. And, of course, the defense and security establishment will also suffer. If 25 percent of the population is legally exempt from military service, lacks a modern education, and has an extremely limited ability to cope in the modern world, the State of Israel will become very different from how it is in 2025. The chances of survival are minimal, and the process of decline and collapse is ensured.[51]

Can Israel alter this catastrophic trajectory?

This is a genuinely existential question. Of course, time will tell. But this is not an overdramatized scenario. The ultra-Orthodox

---

51. See the dire warning published on May 28, 2024, in The Marker newspaper, by 130 senior Israeli economists.

population is already engendering an ever-increasing amount of hostility from the secular public and even the traditional sector. They see the insularity of the ultra-Orthodox and their refusal to serve in the army or any kind of national service. Many see them as parasites feeding off the educated, tax-paying public. The fury toward the ultra-Orthodox population will only increase. The tensions between Israeli society and the ultra-Orthodox are becoming more and more fraught and could erupt at any time. That could include violence or boycotts, including a refusal to pay taxes. On the other hand, within the ultra-Orthodox sectors, unlike their rabbinical and political leadership, there are some (and it's hard to gauge their numbers) who want to integrate with all the other citizens of the country in the fields of education and working in modern professions, including academia, sciences, technology, medicine, engineering, and even military service. Today, however, under the current political leadership and the supervision of the sector's "learned rabbis," these people in the ultra-Orthodox sector are not given the opportunity to study these disciplines.

This is not written in stone, however. If all the non-Haredi parties could come together in a coalition and decide to reduce the state's financial support for the ultra-Orthodox population, and if they could threaten to cut funding to the ultra-Orthodox schools unless they start teaching the core curriculum and allow state supervision, then it is just possible that, within five to ten years, there could be a significant change in this large sector of society. This is the only way that the State of Israel can escape from a trajectory that leads to self-destruction. Anyone who has encountered people from the Haredi-Ashkenazi community understands, on the one hand, that their world is not open to a broad education, including the core curriculum, and, on the other hand, recognizes the huge potential that these people have if they were given a fair chance to learn, to obtain knowledge, and to receive a broad education. This is a massive treasure that we are being denied because of a limiting education system that is funded in its entirety by the State of Israel and its taxpayers. Will the non-Haredi parties have the wisdom to unite and form a government that is not dependent on the mercy of the ultra-Orthodox parties? Will they have the wisdom to act as proposed herein? Time will tell, but there is no certainty that this will be the case. Based on how seats in the current parliament are distributed, this will also require cooperation from the Arab parties. Without a willingness to integrate the Arab parties, the chances of coming together and forming such a government are small. As of 2024, under Netanyahu's government, the march toward destruction is still in full swing.

This is the essence of Netanyahu—a weak man, lacking daring and decisiveness, whose skill is deferring decisions, treading water, and political dealings. As part of the coalition agreements with the ultra-Orthodox parties, the budget for yeshivas and teachers in the ultra-Orthodox Ashkenazi and Sephardic (Shas) education streams was dramatically increased. The salaries of ultra-Orthodox teachers in education rose by about 40 percent at an additional cost of six billion shekels to the budget. Currently, about 21 percent of Haredi men and 47 percent of Haredi women earn their living from teaching in Haredi schools. Therefore, increasing these budgets improves their income and makes them—not just the students—dependent on the leadership of the ultra-Orthodox sector and dependent on continued financial support, grants, benefits, and allowances from the State of Israel. Taxpayers, most of whom come from the secular, educated, or national-religious sectors, are getting increasingly disillusioned with this situation.

The tension in Israeli society is growing. Many people feel that they are bearing the burden of taxes, military service, and productive work—especially when a significant part of those taxes is used for the upkeep of schools, teachers, and yeshiva students from the religious and ultra-Orthodox sectors, whose share of the population is growing and whose contribution to the country's economy, higher education, industry, engineering, academic institutions, research, high-tech, theater, and art is minimal, if anything. This tension is increasing and could explode at any time. The explosion could take many forms, and it is difficult to precisely predict how. However, it could lead to a tax revolt, evasion of military service, perhaps even violence or a movement toward setting up federations within the State of Israel. It is a time bomb that is getting bigger and bigger. If Barbara Tuchman were to write *The March of Folly* today, she would have to include an entire chapter on what is happening in Israel. The Israeli government uses taxes collected from its productive and educated residents to fund the ultra-Orthodox, which is controlled by an extremist and self-interested leadership and which enjoys substantial funding for educational institutions and teachers who, at all stages of education, omit the core curriculum from their schools.

This increases the proportion of the Israeli population that lacks the tools for further education, academic studies, and the ability to cope in a modern society and economy. In so doing, they are dragging the economy and the GDP of Israel down. Like so many issues, Israel needs courageous and determined leaders who are willing to make tough decisions and engage in protracted struggles. At the current time, Israeli leader Netanyahu, whose only concern is safeguarding his personal grip on power, has refused to deal with these explosive problems and has acquiesced to every demand made by the ultra-Orthodox parties regarding funding for their education systems, exemption from military service, and non-enforcement of advanced curricula, including the core curriculum. In doing so, Netanyahu is destroying Israeli society from within.

If there is a change of leadership in the future, then it is possible that new leaders, with more courage and daring than Netanyahu, will step up and show a willingness to deal with the issue of the ultra-Orthodox population. If the necessary changes are made, the ultra-Orthodox community contains boundless human potential for significant advancement in the fields of science and engineering—provided that the disciplines taught in schools are fundamentally revamped. If not, Israel could find itself within two decades as a nation that is impoverished economically, culturally, scientifically, and technologically.

The cruel sands of time are running out.

Chapter 5

The Six-Day War, the occupation of the West Bank, the Palestinians and the growth of Jewish nationalism-messianism

On June 6, 1967, war broke out between Israel, Egypt, and Syria. Jordan joined the two other Arab countries after two days of fighting—due to the pressure, cajoling, and deception of Egyptian President Gamal Abdel Nasser. By the end of the fighting, Israel had secured a brilliant and surprising victory on all three fronts. While this book is not an analysis of the Six-Day War, we will address its consequences for Israeli society and the Palestinian issue. The occupation of the West Bank sent shockwaves through the Arab world. In Israel, the atmosphere was euphoric. Gradually, within the minds of the Israeli leadership, an idea began to take shape—that it would be possible to maintain control over the West Bank in the guise of an "enlightened occupation," in the words of then-defense minister and former IDF chief of staff Moshe Dayan. In other words, Israel sought to maintain military control of the territory while allowing residents of the West Bank to live their lives as normally as possible. To this end, Israel established the Civil Administration, which was subordinate to the military authorities and was responsible for the West Bank on behalf of the IDF (the head of the Civil Administration was usually an army general). There was also a lot of talk about how the occupation of the West Bank was temporary and that the territories were being held as a "deposit" for future negotiations with Jordan (and later, with the Palestinian residents of the West

Bank; see comments from then-Prime Minister Levy Eshkol). The outcome was a situation of waiting, stalemate, and indecision. This resulted in part from shock at the new reality and also from a lack of decisive leadership on the Israeli side. However, historic processes wait for no one. The phrases "there's nothing more permanent than something temporary" and "the occupation corrupts the occupiers" have become part of the Israeli lexicon. The State of Israel did not—and cannot—escape the truth of those sayings. Even within the first years of the occupation, some Israelis foresaw what was coming. They believed that continued Israeli control over the West Bank would have disastrous consequences for the State of Israel.[52] Author and historian Shabtai Teveth examined these ramifications in his book *The Cursed Blessing: The Story of Israel's Occupation of the West Bank.*[53]

Author Amos Oz:

"The ongoing occupation corrupts Israeli society.

The occupation is a crime and an injustice [and] there is no sensitivity to injustice in Israeli society. Sensitivity to injustice is a quality that has characterized the People of Israel for generations."

Prof. Yeshayahu Leibowitz in a letter dated September 8, 1967, to the editor the newspaper Davar, Mrs. Hannah Zemer:

"I am close to Amos Oz's opinion that the occupation of 'territories'—thereby enslaving a million and a half Arabs—will destroy the people and the country and will corrupt us as Jews and as people from a national, social and humanitarian-moral standpoint, and we will become an Israeli Rhodesia, condemned

---

52. Based on what he said after the Six-Day War and his past actions, it is safe to assume that, if David Ben Gurion had been prime minister after 1967, Israel would have returned the entire West Bank to Jordan, leaving Jerusalem in Israeli hands. At that time, King Hussein of Jordan was willing to make that deal, but, in the aftermath of Black September in 1970, that option was no longer viable. It was an historic mistake that cannot be rectified.

53. Weidenfeld & Nicolson. 1969.

to degeneration and destruction." Writing about the West
Bank settlements, Leibowitz added: *"A messianic cult, closed
and cruel, has emerged from some dark corner of Judaism,
threatening to destroy all that is dear and holy to us, to impose a
bloodthirsty, savage and wild cult upon us ... Nablus and Hebron
are just the means, just a stop on Levinger and Kahane's path
to imposing their brutish ideology on Tel Aviv, Jerusalem and
Dimona."*

Leibowitz was sounding a warning over destructive processes in
Israeli society. Ben Gurion, who stepped down as prime minister in 1963, voiced his opinion that Israel should withdraw from
the West Bank and only keep control of East Jerusalem (as well as
the Golan Heights, which were captured from the Syrians during
the war). In February 1949, toward the end of the War of Independence, when Ben Gurion—the determined, visionary, and
great leader—was serving as both prime minister and defense
minister, he was approached by Yigal Alon, the commander of the
IDF's forces in southern Israel. Alon suggested that, given how
the war was progressing and the IDF's success in repelling all the
Arab armies, Israel should quickly capture the West Bank and
forge ahead to the Jordan River border. In a historic decision that,
like all his decisions, highlighted his strong leadership qualities,
Ben Gurion rejected the proposal. He was concerned that adding
hundreds of thousands of Arab citizens to the fledgling State of
Israel would lead to a dramatic shift in the population balance
and make it difficult for Israel to maintain its democratic character—a principle that was central to his ideology. Indeed, it has
proven impossible over the years to maintain an occupation and
control over hundreds of thousands of Palestinians—a population that has now grown to between 2.2 and 2.5 million in the
West Bank—while simultaneously being a democratic country
committed to upholding equal rights, individual liberty, minority
rights, voting rights, and freedom of expression. An occupation of
this kind, especially when it includes the significant settlement of

civilians, as has occurred in practice, will inevitably and gradually undermine the democratic fabric of the State of Israel and lead to its collapse. A system like this necessitates two separate legal codes for two different populations: Israeli citizens within the pre-1967 borders and residents of the West Bank. This is a ticking time bomb that is slowly eroding Israel's democratic foundations and society in terms of its most fundamental democratic principles. This change in reality requires bold leadership on both the Israeli and Palestinian sides. If it becomes clear that there is no partner for negotiations on the Palestinian side, then the Israeli leadership must take unilateral steps—ideally with the support of the United States and other Western countries. But we will return to this later.

In practice, over the past 57 years, there has been a steady increase in the number of Jewish residents in the West Bank, while military rule continues over the Palestinian population, which must seek military permission for even basic matters, such as home construction. The Palestinian Authority, established in the aftermath of the Oslo Accords, has also weakened significantly in recent years—partly due to internal governmental corruption but also because of the deliberate policies of Netanyahu's governments between 2009 and 2024. The Palestinian Authority now lacks any real power in the West Bank. Large swathes of the West Bank have been appropriated through various legal mechanisms. Initially, Israel only appropriated public land that was not privately owned. However, there was a gradual expansion of this policy. Using various legal rulings and justifications, Israeli legal bodies—including the High Court of Justice and other state institutions—permitted and approved the appropriation of land privately owned by Palestinians (see the recent High Court ruling). Moreover, approximately 60 percent of the water in the West Bank is allocated for the Jewish population, which constitutes just 17 percent of the population.[54] At the same

---

54. See Avner Hopstein's investigation, "Zman," 19.10.2020

time, Israel began constructing infrastructure, roads, and public institutions for Jewish settlements. Massive budgets were allocated for roads and infrastructure in the West Bank—often at the expense of funding for projects within Israel itself. Numerous studies indicate that the State of Israel has invested three times more per capita in West Bank settlers than in residents of Israel proper. This process has been driven by the increasing influence of National Religious and messianic groups within Israeli society—and, of course, within the government and Knesset. The process of expanding settlements flourished. From a single small settlement, established in Hebron in 1968 by a single national-religious family—the Levinger family—the settlement movement quickly grew at a rapid pace. It is worth noting that in the years immediately following the Six-Day War, there was a strong nationalist fervor in Israel and a widespread desire to maintain control over the West Bank indefinitely. This sentiment was not limited to the religious population—it was also shared by many secular Israelis, including key leaders of the ruling party. Support for Jewish settlements in the West Bank and the concept of "Greater Israel" was widespread, ranging from Yitzhak Tabenkin—a leader of the Labor movement—and Yisrael Galili—a close advisor and ally of Prime Minister Golda Meir—to writers and intellectuals like Natan Alterman and Haim Guri, a renowned poet from the days of the Palmach and the War of Independence. In addition, there was a significant rise in religious-nationalist messianism within the National Religious camp.

The explosion of settlement activity reached a critical juncture in 1976, when Yitzhak Rabin—who had served as IDF chief during the Six-Day War—was prime minister, and Shimon Peres was his defense minister. The settlement in question was Sebastia, located on the outskirts of Nablus in the West Bank. The IDF intended to evacuate the illegal settlement, but violent clashes erupted between settlers and soldiers. The incident lasted approximately two weeks. In hindsight, those two weeks were pivotal in Israeli history. There were internal disagreements within the Israeli government. Peres—who, years later, would serve as foreign minister during the Oslo Accords negotiations—supported the settlers at the time. Some claim that this support was partially motivated by personal political considerations and was part of his campaign to undermine Prime Minister Rabin. Ultimately, the settlers succeeded in pressuring the government, which allowed them to remain. This was a missed historic opportunity to curtail the power of the settlement movement and, perhaps, halt its vision entirely. That opportunity vanished permanently in 1977, when the right-wing Likud party—committed to maintaining Israeli control over the West Bank—won the election. Likud was then led by Menachem Begin, who, before the establishment of the state, had been the leader of the underground Irgun movement.

At the time of Likud's victory in 1977, there were approximately 6,000 Jewish settlers in the West Bank and around 32,000 in East Jerusalem—beyond the "Green Line" (the border established in 1949 following the War of Independence). By 2012, it was reported that 330,000 Jews were living in West Bank settlements, while around 190,000 resided in Jewish neighborhoods of East Jerusalem. This marked a dramatic 15-fold increase over 35 years![55]

The question of what to do with the territories—hand them over to another power, possibly Jordan (which was a valid option until the Black September events of 1970), or to the local residents (but which ones?)—remained unanswered for years. Meanwhile, the occupation continued, bringing with it both damage and injustice, and the number of settlers continued to rise. During Yitzhak Rabin's second tenure as prime minister, there were contacts with the PLO, led by Yasser Arafat. These contacts, which began with many months of secret negotiations in various locations, including Europe, eventually led to the Oslo Accords. This was a historic breakthrough on the same level as the peace agreement between Israel and Egypt. It was on the back of the

---

55. It is worth noting that, despite the efforts of the Israeli government under Netanyahu, the Jewish population on the West Bank has hardly risen since 2012.

Oslo Accords that, in 1994, Israel signed a peace agreement with Jordan. However, the Oslo process was beset by many obstacles and numerous opponents—both among the Israeli population and the Palestinians. This is not the place to delve into the roots of these divisions or the details of the agreement.[56] What is important for understanding the developments within Israeli society— detailed herein—is that those Israelis who supported the settlement enterprise saw the withdrawal from the West Bank and the handover of territory to the PLO as nothing less than treason— not only against the state but also against the nationalist, religious, and messianic beliefs that were at the core of the settlers' ideology. The result was fierce opposition to any peace process with the PLO or the Palestinian people. The process—requiring withdrawal from parts of the West Bank and acceptance of Israel's existence—sparked violent opposition from extremists on both the Israeli and Palestinian sides. Since our goal is to better understand the Israeli reality at the time, we will focus exclusively on that side of the conflict.[57] Opposition to the agreement was accompanied by countless demonstrations, widespread verbal and physical abuse, and intense hostility directed at the government and its leader, Yitzhak Rabin. Finally, at a massive peace rally in Tel Aviv on November 4, 1995, an extreme religious rightwinger, a student at Bar-Ilan University, assassinated Rabin with three gunshots. With the benefit of hindsight, we can say that the most serious and meaningful attempt to reach a full agreement between Israel and the Palestinians was cut short before it could fully develop.

The process was historic, complex, and fraught with mutual risks. Both Israelis and Palestinians would have had to make

---

56. See Yair Hirschfeld, "Oslo: A Formula for Peace," Am Oved Publishing, and, for a different approach, Yuval Blumberg, "The Oslo Trap," Steimatzky Publishing.

57. There were extremists on the Palestinian side who opposed the process, especially the Hamas movement, the stated goal of which is the destruction of the State of Israel. Hamas committed many terror attacks in Israel during the Oslo process to torpedo the talks.

painful concessions for there to be any possibility of resolving the decades-long conflict and extricating Israel from its occupation and control over the Palestinian population in the West Bank. Had the process continued, it might have brought a worthy solution and prosperity. Since that murder, however, Israeli public opinion has gradually come to terms with the occupation; Israelis now not only see it as reality but also as a necessity in order to safeguard Israel's security and to avert any future security risks that would be created if Israel were to return the West Bank to a Palestinian state. As a result, Israel continues to control and occupy the West Bank, and there are ever-intensifying efforts by the Israeli government to bolster and develop the settlements while undermining Palestinians' ability to expand and prosper in their territories. These processes make Israeli society impervious to the suffering of Palestinians in the West Bank. They are treated only as an enemy. Military rule, by its very nature, results in violence, aggression, contempt for the law, harm to many individuals, and corruption. Israeli soldiers serving in the West Bank as part of their duties are compelled to act using excessive force and violence, entering civilian homes at night, making arrests, conducting violent raids on Palestinian villages and homes, and carrying out aggressive operations to track down suspected Palestinian terrorists or Hamas members.

This exposes them to violence and lawlessness. They bring all this back with them into Israeli society when they return to being civilians. If the atmosphere in Israel today is steeped in aggression, rudeness, and disrespect for others, at least some of this can be attributed to the military service of hundreds of thousands of Israelis in the West Bank. The various civil society organizations that attempt to document violent actions by IDF soldiers, including the "Breaking the Silence" group ("Ch'ovrim Schtika" in Hebrew), try to collect information and share it with the Israeli public, but they enjoy little traction. In practice, most of the Israeli public is unfamiliar with what is happening in the West Bank. The mainstream Israeli media deliberately ignores and denies what is happening there. The Israeli government has been trying for decades to suppress the issue. Netanyahu went even further. In his now-famous speech at Bar-Ilan University in 2009, he came out in favor of the two-state solution. Like many of Netanyahu's speeches, this one, too, was nothing more than lip service; he had no intention of delivering. In practice, however, during his 16 years in power, Netanyahu developed a baseless thesis that deliberately ignored the Palestinian issue. According to his thesis, Israel could "manage" the conflict with the Palestinians and should instead invest its efforts in reaching "peace agreements" with Arab states that do not border Israel rather than negotiating toward a two-state solution with the Palestinians. This theory was, of course, utterly detached from reality. After all, Israel has no century-long territorial or national dispute with these states, and peace accords with them—while welcome in themselves—do nothing whatsoever to resolve the conflict with the Palestinians or the occupation, which continues to have devastating consequences for Israel and the Palestinians. Israel cannot "manage" such a profound and complex conflict as if the sides were puppets. Rather, it must act responsibly and with leadership in order to find a complex solution to a complex conflict.

Alongside the Palestinian conflict, however, from an Israeli perspective it is worth examining the phenomena that emerged in Israel in the aftermath of the victorious Six-Day War. The huge military victory signaled the eruption of messianic religiosity in Israel. It is a massive and massively influential movement that has steered the State of Israel's course and is having a hugely destructive impact on its future.

The National-Religious messianic movement/the settlers

The national religious movement in Israel can trace its roots back to the religious-Zionist Mizrachi organization, founded in 1902. It was founded and led by Rabbi Yitzchak Yaacov Reines during the Zionist Congress and in cooperation with Theodor Herzl. It started operating in Israel even before World War I, but its activity intensified after 1918. In 1920, it relocated its world headquarters to the Land of Israel. Two years later, activists from Mizrachi founded the Hapoel HaMizrachi movement. In 1957, those two parties would merge to become the National Religious Party, known in Israel as the Mafdal, an acronym of the Hebrew name. The party advocated a combination of socialist values, such as social equality and justice, along with a deeply held faith in and adherence to the Jewish religion. As such, it was a movement that recognized the importance of work, learning, education, protecting the weak, social solidarity, and preserving the value of the Jewish religion and traditions. It was a loyal partner of the Mapai party, headed by David Ben-Gurion. There were never any elements of messianism, nationalism, or racism in the movement. Ideologies of the latter were not only alien to the leaders of the movement but contradicted its principles. It was, therefore, an active partner in building the newborn state and establishing religious kibbutzim, as well as Hapoel HaMizrachi's Union of Moshavim.

During the Six-Day War in 1967, Hussein, King of Jordan, ordered his troops to bomb Jerusalem with artillery shells. In doing so, he launched a campaign of violence and war against Israel after having been incited and deceived by Egypt's President Nasser with regard to his country's "successes" in the war. The Israeli government tried to dissuade King Hussein of Jordan from continuing hostilities and, in various secret meetings, tried, unsuccessfully, to explain to him that Nasser of Egypt was deceiving him. A cabinet meeting was called to discuss whether Israel should retaliate against Jordan's hostility and enter a war with Jordan. Internal Affairs Minister Haim-Moshe Shapira, the leader of the National Religious Party, also expressed his view. He opposed war with Jordan because he feared that Israel would be forced to rule over millions of Palestinian residents of the West Bank and would be subjected to sanctions and international pressure.[58]

---

58. In the aftermath of the Deir Yassin massacre in April 1948, during the Jerusalem war campaign, in which Israeli soldiers killed dozens of Arab civilians,

Understanding how we went from a peaceable, responsible, sane party, which advocated a combination of socialist values, social justice, and observing the Jewish religion and its traditions, to the situation that exists today—which will be described in detail below—is to understand the most tragic and disastrous process that took place in the State of Israel, to Israeli society, and to this stream of Judaism. The change that this national-religious camp underwent in terms of its position on Israeli control of the West Bank is the basis of the destructive process that Israel is currently experiencing. It is doubtful that Israel will extricate itself from this position. It is true that the Six-Day War was a stunning military success. The existential threat that Israel was facing was removed. Israel suddenly and rapidly captured large areas of territory, on the Golan Heights, in the Sinai (from Egypt), and in the West Bank (from Jordan). But this wonderful blessing also brought with it the seeds of calamity—a blessing that was also a disastrous curse.

The Rabbi Abraham Isaac Kook-messianic religious stream[59]

Alongside the measured and responsible religious Zionism of Hapoel HaMizrachi and the National Religious Party, there always existed a stream of Zionism headed by Rabbi Abraham Isaac Kook. HaRav Kook, as he was known, was one of the leaders of religious Zionism; he was a great rabbinical scholar whose writings also dealt with philosophy and morality. In 1921, he established the Chief Rabbinate of Palestine and was named Ashkenazi Chief Rabbi in the Land of Israel, which he saw as a

---

same Mr. Haim-Moshe Shapira condemned the incident, saying, "This is unacceptable behavior from a Jewish point of view. Jews cannot do that."

59."For excellent analysis of this specific trend in Israel and its origin, Oriel Tal, Myth & Reason in Contemporary Jewry,"1987,page 136-168 and bibliography therein; Prof. A. Sagi & D. Schwartz, "From Reality to Language: Religious Zionism and the Yom Kippur War," and the other "From Realism to Messianic," and Prof. Jacob Israel Yashar, "the Zionist messianic religious," Ishar bulletin, November 23,2023.

step toward reestablishing the Sanhedrin.[60] He also founded the Mercaz HaRav Yeshiva in Jerusalem, where his son, Rabbi Tzvi Yehuda Kook, would later become the head rabbi. Rabbi Abraham Isaac Kook's scholarship and activities were extensive, but one aspect is particularly relevant to this book. He viewed Zionism as the start of redemption ("Atchalta De'Geulah," in Aramaic) and a harbinger of the coming of the Messiah, for which Jews in the 2,000-year exile had been yearning when they said, at every Passover seder, "Next year in rebuilt Jerusalem." When he died, he left behind many students, some of them well-known, including Rabbi Tzvi Yehuda Kook, who later took over as head of the Mercaz HaRav Yeshiva. By 1950, Rabbi Tzvi Yehuda Kook had become the spiritual leader of the religious Zionist camp. Ideologically, he followed in his father's footsteps, supporting the approach whereby Zionism and the State of Israel were the realization of the Jewish prophets' vision of the People of Israel's rebirth and return to their homeland. He also believed that secular Zionism was "the Messiah's donkey"—that it was doing the dirty work for religious Zionism and that its energy and capabilities would gradually lead to a state in which there would be a religious utopia, the Sanhedrin would be reestablished, the Kingdom of David would be revived, and King David's laws would prevail. Therefore, concepts like democracy, individual rights, freedom of expression, equality, equal rights, a free press, the freedom to make proposals, separation of powers, regime change through elections, the rights of minorities, the LGBTQ community, and women are entirely foreign to this ideology.

The stunning military victory—which shocked the international community, including Jewish communities worldwide—gave Rabbi Tzvi Yehuda Kook, as well as his many followers and students, a massive boost. It empowered his belief that the triumph and the occupation of the West Bank—Judea and Samaria—were a clear expression of God's will for the redemption

---

60. The legislative and judicial assembly in the ancient land of Israel.

of the People of Israel and their return to the Land of Israel. In this spirit, his followers began to turn their vision and their fervent belief that all of Judea and Samaria should be controlled by Jews, who should be able to return to the very places their forefathers lived two millennia ago, into practical measures. In 1968, they rebuilt Kfar Etzion, which had existed as a national-religious kibbutz until 1948, when, before the establishment of the State of Israel, it fell into the hands of the Arab Legion of the Jordanian Army. The re-founding of Kfar Etzion was welcomed by all parts of Israeli society at that time, since the massacre perpetrated by the Jordanian Army and Arab gangs was particularly brutal.[61] The kibbutz was located close to Jerusalem, and the Israeli public felt that it was a symbolic act of historic justice. That, however, was just the first step in the rise of the settlements. Moshe Levinger and Eliezer Waldman, two rabbis from Kfar Etzion, went on to establish a new Jewish settlement in Hebron called Kiryat Arba, which was one of the names of the ancient city in the Bible.[62]

Hebron is profoundly connected to the Jewish people's history in the Land of Israel; according to Jewish lore, it is the location of the Cave of the Patriarchs, the burial place of the founding fathers of Judaism and their wives: Abraham and Sarah, Isaac and Rebekah, and Jacob and Leah. During the first years of King David's reign, Hebron was his capital city. The Kiryat Arba settlers then established settlements in Elon Moreh, Kedumim, Itamar, and Ofra, and in February 1974, an organization called "Gush Emunim." Rabbi Tzvi Yehuda Kook was among those who participated in the establishment of Elon Moreh on June 5, 1974. Later, Gush Emunim would establish the settlement at Sebastia. On seven occasions, Gush Emunim activists tried to build a settlement there, and they were ejected by the IDF each time. On the eighth such attempt, in December 1975, on the eve of the

---

61. Around 125 Israeli soldiers, men and women, were killed and some slaughtered – some of them after they had surrendered.

62. "Sarah died in Kiryat Arba, that is, Hebron, in the land of Canaan." Genesis 23:02.

Hanukkah holiday and shortly after the General Assembly passed a resolution equating Zionism with racism, settlers arrived at the Palestinian village of Sebastia in Samaria. This time, there were many more of them. Over the next nine days, Gush Emunim and settler leaders were engaged in angry arguments with the Israeli government, which Rabin and Peres headed. At that time, there was a lot of tension and mutual distrust between Rabin and Peres—and the settlers took full advantage of it. Peres supported the settlers' position. Moreover, Rabin would later claim, in an interview with journalist Avi Bettelheim, that Peres and his people acted as the settlers' "Trojan horses." Peres himself, in a speech to the Knesset on December 3, 1975, declared that "the wording is not about the need for a settlement, or even about the map and dimensions of the settlement, but about arrangements for leaving it." And when Dr. Meir Pa'il, the representative of the left-wing Moked party, warned at the same meeting that Israeli settlements in Judea and Samaria would lead to the formation of a binational state and the imposition of an apartheid regime, Peres mocked him, saying: "I understand that Knesset member Pa'il is predicting that Israel will become a binational state. I want to ask all the members sitting in this parliament whether anyone really believes that, even if such a disaster were to happen, Israel would turn to apartheid?"[63]

Today, of course, Peres' words sound ridiculous, since the establishment of a binational state and apartheid is already on our doorstep. In any case, after nine stormy days and the intervention of various public figures, Peres reached a compromise with Gush Emunim, according to which the settlement in Sebastia would be evacuated to a nearby location. Rabin subsequently acquiesced to this compromise. It was a huge victory for Gush Emunim. A large crowd sang "Am Yisrael Chai" and "Samaria is ours," and members of the Gush Emunim delegation to the negotiations

---

63. Peres' shortsightedness at that time is incredible. The question of whether Israel is an apartheid state in the West Bank, is not a theoretical one and is something that the global discourse has addressed.

were wildly applauded. This was a historic moment in the settlement process, whereby Gush Emunim proved that, with militant faith, determination, and organization, the Israeli government could be defeated and forced to accept the settlers' demands. Less than two years later, in May 1977, there was an election, and, for the first time in the history of the State of Israel, the right-wing bloc headed by the Likud Party and Mr. Menachem Begin was voted into power.

From that moment on, the ideology of Gush Emunim and HaRav Kook took over. Suffice it to say that, while in 1976, there were 6,200 Jewish settlers in the West Bank (not including East Jerusalem), there are now 475,000 of them (around 6% of the entire population of Israel). The settlers are spread across the West Bank, from relatively large settlements—most of them in the Jerusalem area—to dozens of smaller settlements, which are home to between 10 and 500 families. In total, there are 126 settlements, and around one-third of the settler population lives in two cities (Modi'in Illit and Beitar Illit, with ultra-Orthodox residents).[64] Moreover, since 1977, the Israeli government—and even more so during the sixth Netanyahu government from 2022—has supported communities and the further settlement of Judea and Samaria in various ways, mainly budgetary. The State of Israel foots the bill for public utilities, infrastructure, roads, electricity, schools, clinics, and jobs in the civil service for settlers living in Judea and Samaria. In fact, Israel funds settlers three times more per capita than Israelis living within the Green Line! The result is that substantial financial resources are funneled into settlements in Judea and Samaria—the West Bank—instead of going to residents of the State of Israel. In fact, the settler community, in general, is supported by the State of Israel and taxpayer money, which substantially deprives the rest of the residents of Israel, including struggling towns in the south and north of the country. The IDF has also found the West Bank to be a drain on

---

64. See "Haaretz," April 7, 2023: Dr. Shaul Arieli, Prof. Sivan Hirsch-Hoefler and Prof. Gilad Hirschberger.

resources since troops are deployed there not only for counter-terrorism operations but also to defend the settlers. The training that is so vital to maintaining the quality of the army is also severely impaired, given that around 60% of the IDF's infantry soldiers are stationed in the West Bank.

These are enormous social, economic, and security costs that the country's residents bear. It is clear, therefore, that the ideology of Gush Emunim and HaRav Kook has won. The spirit of the Mizrachi Movement, Hapoel HaMizrachi, the National Religious Party from before the Six-Day War, and people like Haim-Moshe Shapira and others, who advocated Torah combined with moderation, tolerance, and recognition of the various aspects of democracy as essential components of the State of Israel, became an insignificant minority. This large and important group of people was taken over by the spirit of HaRav Kook. The outcome has been fateful for Israel and has fundamentally changed the face of the country, including its government regime, which may result in Israel becoming a binational state, with all the harsh and destructive ramifications of this political manifestation. As part of their campaign to take control, Gush Emunim—particularly followers and disciples of HaRav Kook—advocated Israeli control over the whole of Judea and Samaria; they also sought to impose Torah law on the State of Israel.

Therefore, even though they still used the vocabulary of a liberal democracy, such values were already alien to them. Among themselves, they scoffed at these values. Their goal was the re-establishment of the Kingdom of David: Sanhedrin, Torah laws, the exclusion of Reform and Conservative Jews, changes to the status of women (including modesty laws regulating clothing) and to women's ability to progress professionally, increasing the role of rabbinical courts, imposing Torah law everywhere in Israel, the systematic discrimination of Arabs, a disregard for non-Jews, rejection of any foreign culture that is un-Jewish in their view, and an isolationist policy when it comes to international relations. This is a very different Israel from the one we knew and the one that its founders envisaged, aspired to, and described in the Israeli Declaration of Independence.

In 1993, Israel launched efforts to reach an agreement with the Palestinians, headed by the PLO's leaders, Yasser Arafat and Mahmoud Abbas. This process, known as the Oslo Accords, was a significant breakthrough on the way to a historic attempt to bring about a fundamental change in relations between the two peoples. It entailed the withdrawal by Israel from territory in the West Bank and the establishment of the Palestinian Authority, which would be given weapons and granted governmental powers. There was also an economic agreement between Israel and the Palestinian Authority, known as the Paris Protocol. However, Gush Emunim and followers of HaRav Kook saw this as a national disaster, betrayal, and were concerned that it would crush the foundations of their faith. They launched a series of protest actions, including violent and raucous demonstrations at which Rabin—IDF chief-of-staff during the Six-Day War and a great fighter in Israel's wars—was depicted wearing a Gestapo uniform! These demonstrations were supported and encouraged by rabbis from the national-religious group, including students of HaRav Kook, such as Rabbi Eliezer Waldman—a graduate of Mercaz Harav Yeshiva and one of the founders of Nir Yeshiva in Kiryat Arba—and Rabbi Dov Lior, who is also rabbi to Bezalel Smotrich, currently Finance Minister under Netanyahu's government. These rabbis decreed that not one inch of Israeli land should be ceded and that anyone who hands off Jewish land to foreigners—the Palestinians—is a traitor! So inspired, a messianic religious Jew named Baruch Goldstein, a resident of Hebron, entered the Cave of the Patriarchs in February 1994, where he murdered 29 Palestinian worshippers.

This atrocity sparked the fire of violence and was followed by waves of Palestinian attacks against Jews, especially headed by the Hamas group. Some 18 months later, on November 4, 1995, a young law student from Bar-Ilan University (a member of the national-religious stream) shot and assassinated Rabin.

Ironically, it happened after a massive peace rally in support of the Oslo Accords and Rabin. The camp of HaRav Kook became hugely powerful within Israeli society. As noted, not only did the moderate thinkers in this community, Mizrachi and the National Religious Party, disappear and fall silent, but followers and disciples of HaRav began to occupy key positions. Recognizing that taking hold of the reins of power in Israel would require them to spread their ideology among the general public, as well as ensuring that their supporters were in positions of power, they began a years-long process of integrating their supporters into various established media channels, including radio, television, and newspapers. They also started to be active in the military. Many pre-military colleges, where students are trained both in Torah and religious studies as well as military service, have been established. Some of them are even funded by the State of Israel! They were able to reach an agreement with the authorities whereby students attending these colleges would serve in the IDF for half of their three-year enlistment period and would spend the rest studying in a yeshiva.

This strategy paid off. Currently, about 25 percent of IDF officers are from the national-religious camp—around double their proportion in the general population (12 to 15 percent). Moreover, several yeshivas have been established in Judea and Samaria, also funded by Israel, with various rabbis teaching the students— primarily in the spirit of HaRav Kook. In recent years, books have been published about the direction that teachers in these educational establishments were leading their students.[65] Occasionally, photographs from these lessons are also published. The impression we get from them is dangerous and is a genuine threat to the democratic character of the State of Israel. Anyone who believes that Israel cannot continue to exist if it ceases to be a democratic state in the full sense of the word (and not just semantically or technically, holding elections every four or five years

---

65. See articles by Prof. Rachel Elior and Prof. Israel Jacob Yuval, including from October 8, 2023, in *Yashar.*

and nothing more) must see this as an alarming warning sign before the impending disaster. The foundations of HaRav Kook's ideology lie in finding signs of redemption in the Bible and the words of the Jewish sages, with each crisis explained as part of the redemption process and "God's plan," as they describe it. If you tell them that they are like other messianic movements in the history of the Jews in exile (such as the 17th-century self-proclaimed messiah Jacob Frank, who later converted to Christianity, or Shabtai Zvi from the 16th century, who later converted to Islam), they will deny it and find countless arguments explaining why they are not a messianic movement and why their faith is logical and grounded both in reality and in the Bible. Meanwhile, their power in the State of Israel continues to increase, permeating the IDF at the junior and senior officer level, the mainstream media (TV channels), including the printed press (*Makor Rishon*), and the field of education.[66]

The various yeshivas, therefore, including the pre-military academies, are thriving and producing new generations who have been educated by rabbis who adhere to the ideology of HaRav Kook. They believe in redemption and the time of the Messiah. They prohibit handing over any part of the Land of Israel in Judea and Samaria, they aspire to limit the rights of the Palestinian population of the West Bank, they believe in Jewish supremacy over the Palestinians, they want to impose Orthodox Jewish law and trample on the rights of other streams of Judaism in Israel, including Reform Jews. Later, their greatest dream will be the establishment of a Torah state, inspired by the law of King David, with the Sanhedrin and the Holy Temple. It should be noted that several other sectors of Israeli society, even if they do not support the national-religious movement, nevertheless support all or some of its views. They are blind, therefore, to the dangers it poses. Jewish history in the Second Temple of the Jewish State, and later in the reign of Roman Emperor Hadrian and then the Jewish leader Bar

---

66. See Yair Nehorai's "The Third Revolution," self-published and Micha Regev's "The Intoxication of Redemption," Yedioth Ahronoth Publishing.

Kochva, supported by the religious scholar Rabbi Akiva, and in the Diaspora, is full of messianic incidents. They all ended in disaster. This time, the existence of the State of Israel may be in similar hands. These segments of the population, headed by settlers from the messianic-nationalist-religious establishment, also prevent any possibility of peace with the Palestinian Authority. At this rate, because of the proliferation of settlements and various Israeli policies in the West Bank, coupled with the declining influence of the Palestinian Authority and moderate elements within Palestinian society, Israel is slowly but surely marching toward a situation in which the two-state solution and sharing the land will become an unfeasible idea. They will be replaced by destructive "solutions," such as a binational state, apartheid, and perpetual military conflicts. This will lead to intense international pressure on Israel, will adversely affect Israel's standing in the world, especially in the United States, and will usher in a period of economic and scientific research boycotts against Israel. Israel's brightest scientists will leave as part of a brain drain, and, lacking significant American support, Israel will not be able to exist in a situation of constant struggle and war. This is nothing short of an existential danger.[67] Another parade of Folly.

The national-religious movement, which was created by Mizrachi and the old Mafdal, has changed completely. From a religious movement, it has become a nationalist, racist, and messianic movement. They now want to turn Israel from a democratic country into a Jewish one. The High Court and its rulings are an anathema to them. They want to gradually introduce laws from the time of King David. Women's rights will be curtailed. Many of them believe that the woman's place is in the home and that

---

67. It is worth mentioning the recent Opinion by the International Court of Justice (July 19, 2024) discussing the occupation and its legitimacy under international laws. It is essential to read the specifics of events and actions taken by Israel authorities and settlers to understand the meaning of the occupation in practice, e.g. the two-tier legal system for settlers and Palestinians, the confiscation or requisitioning of land (sec.120 et.al), transfer of civilian population (sec.115-119), demolitions for lack of building permits (sec.214-222).

women are not equal to men. A woman's role is to serve in the home, to produce children, to raise them, and to ensure domestic tranquility. They believe that the Palestinians are inferior and that they should be grateful to the Jewish majority for the right to live in a Jewish state, with all its benefits.[68] Amongst themselves, they want the Sanhedrin to replace the Supreme Court. The concept of "equality," which is the basis of modern life in a democratic framework and is one of the basic values of a civilized society, is a jaded concept that they view with contempt.[69] The reason for this is that "equality" would require them to grant equal rights to Reform and Conservative Jews, not just the Orthodox, something they vehemently oppose.

The same applies to members of the LGBTQ community, Arabs, women, and other minorities. Therefore, they oppose the very concept, mock it, and refuse to enshrine it in Israel's laws. It has come to the point that their rabbis preach discrimination, Jewish supremacy, condemnation of the LGBTQ community, segregation between men and women in the public sphere, and, most recently, 14 Knesset members from the parties that make up Netanyahu's coalition—including Likud, Otzma Yehudit, the Ashkenazi and Sephardic ultra-Orthodox parties—backed a petition for leniency for someone who horrendously burned down a Palestinian house in the West Bank, murdering a father, mother, and small child in the process. And no one in the government spoke out against this petition. We are now seeing, therefore, how settlements, occupation, and ruling over the Palestinians for 55 years have totally distorted the ideology and attitudes of the national-religious camp. They gradually became more messianic, more radical, less accepting of different opinions, lacking openness, and adhering to their extremist beliefs. This, of course, is a recipe for destruction and disaster. One may find similar patterns

---

68. See Oriel Tal, supra. note 63 pages 156-168 and article published in The Jerusalem Quarterly, no.35, (1985), p.36-45.

69. See, for example, MK Simcha Rothman's remarks in Haaretz, February 24, 2023.

of behavior between the leaders of the Jewish revolt against the Roman Empire during the Second Temple period and these modern-day religious, nationalist, and messianic groups. In both cases, there were extremist groups, motivated by nationalist and religious impulses, full of hatred, hostility, and xenophobia. They refuse to give any serious consideration to facts, logic, and an understanding of the international arena in their decisions and policies. They overcome every shocking event with their belief that God will help solve the problem. Anyone familiar with Jewish history, therefore, must be filled with anxiety when confronted with the current results of this nationalist-religious-messianic version of Judaism. Now they have representatives not only in the Knesset but, thanks to Netanyahu, in the Israeli government as well. What, then, is their position regarding how to rule Judea and Samaria? The answer can be found in an article from 2017 by Israel's current finance minister, MK Bezalel Smotrich, published in the national-religious newspaper *Srugim*. In his article, Smotrich laid out his position on this subject. An analysis of the article shows that its author does not see the bigger picture, ignores the rights and interests of other parties, and that his understanding of the dynamics of the processes at play, the involvement of the international community, headed by the United States, as well as American Jewry, is less than minimal. He either ignores them or belittles them with his arrogance and total ignorance. Or perhaps it's a combination of all of these. It is a messianic and racist article, which completely ignores the international community, the power of the United States vis-à-vis Israel, the dependence of Israel on the United States, and the fact that Israel is a small country in need of support and relations with the international community. Here is part of the article:

"*My belief is that Israel must bolster the settlements in Judea and Samaria. We must move full steam ahead to increase the Jewish population of these areas. The Arabs of Judea and Samaria will, in my opinion, accept this move and will come to terms with the fact that Judea and Samaria are part of the State of Israel. And then, slowly but surely, we will be satisfied.”*

In the interim, the author says that *"the IDF will act forcefully against instances of violent resistance and will eradicate them. Until the Arabs accept that Judea and Samaria are part of the State of Israel."* And what about the rights of these Arab residents? The author says that he envisages several stages. In the first stage, Arab residents will have the right to vote in municipal elections and on local civil matters. He proposes dividing Judea and Samaria into six regions, which, according to him, reflect the clans and tribes of the residents of Judea and Samaria. In his view, this is a democratic system, and, although not "perfect," it would be a "partial democracy" (as he puts it). He predicts, however, that over the years, when the region is calmer and the Palestinians come to terms with the situation, some will even be entitled to vote in elections for the Israeli parliament; he adds, however, that most of them will have the "right" to vote for the Jordanian parliament. Jordan has not and will not agree to such a "solution"! Moreover, his proposal includes incentives for Palestinians to leave Judea and Samaria—a kind of "soft" deportation. The article talks about incentivizing this mass migration with money and grants, but there are possibly other intentions that he refrains from putting into writing for obvious reasons.

Such views are fundamentally based on a worldview and a faith that are religious and nationalistic and, above all, messianic—and which view societal and global processes as something directed by God.

It is an ideology that completely ignores a wide range of perspectives and possibilities; it builds a path for itself—in which everything goes the way of the believer. Messianism. We will not list the shortcomings of this ideology, as embodied in the article—and they are immeasurable—but it is worth noting these two: First, it is an accurate reflection of the position of the national-religious camp, whose leader currently serves as the finance minister. Moreover, as part of the coalition agreements signed following the November 2022 elections, the same minister has also been given control of the Civil Administration in Judea and Samaria, along with massive budgets. He has become the de facto ruler of Judea and Samaria and has the power to increase the momentum of settlement construction and expansion. Appointments of this kind and this kind of authority are not far from the de facto annexation of Judea and Samaria. Secondly, the idea that expanding the settlements will bring about a "change of consciousness" among the Palestinians in the West Bank, and that they will consequently see "a resolute State of Israel in control of the West Bank," as he puts it, and then accept their status as inferior residents under Israeli control, while ignoring the processes that this would involve, is unrealistic.

It is a proposal that completely ignores what will happen within Israeli society with regard to those citizens who oppose the process, as well as its effect upon Israel's relationship with the United States and European countries. It will also slowly but surely erode the fundamental and emotional link between American Jews and the kind of Israel that this proposal would create. This is just a very partial and short list of the important processes and ramifications that the author chooses to ignore. Ignoring the influence that the occupation has had on the character of the State of Israel, concerns that Israel may stop being a democratic country, that there will be waves of violence and brutal conflicts (as already exist now in the West Bank), that the rule of law will no longer be respected—all of these and many other concerns are simply absent from the proposal. It also ignores prominent historical examples of other countries' occupations and how they ended. Relatively recent examples, such as the French occupation of Algeria between 1830 and 1962, South Africa, the British and their colonial holdings, like India, and so on. Anyone who knows history knows that it is a recipe for disaster.

As stated, Smotrich, the author of the article, currently represents the majority position within the national-religious, messianic camp. He is now finance minister in Netanyahu's government. He is also the leader of one of the parties that make up the National Religious Camp. At the head of the other party is Itamar Ben-Gvir. In his youth, Ben-Gvir was a member of Meir Kahane's party—which was banned in the United States as a terrorist organization and is fueled by racist hatred of Arabs. During the period when the Oslo Accords were being negotiated, he was an admirer of Baruch Goldstein—the perpetrator of the Hebron massacre in 1994—and had a photograph of him in his home. He was one of the instigators of the violent demonstrations against Rabin and the Oslo Accords. He continued over the years to sow hatred, division, and violence between Arabs and Jews in Judea and Samaria. He now lives in Hebron and serves today as national security minister under Netanyahu! Obviously, Ben-Gvir and his party wholeheartedly agree with the opinions expressed by Smotrich in that article on the Palestinian issue. Ben-Gvir did not serve in the IDF, but that does not prevent him from being aggressive, hating Arabs, and advocating the ideology whereby Jewish rights trump those of others.[70]

The result is that the national-religious camp has slowly transformed over the course of 57 years into an extremist, nationalist, and messianic movement. The occupation and all that it entails brought out the messianism and the faith in a divine power that promised redemption to the People of Israel—as well as Greater Israel, including Judea and Samaria with its 2.5 million Palestinian residents. Many members of that camp, which once used to respect others and recognize the importance of rational considerations and the international community, have become increasingly religious, extremist, and messianic. This messianism involves confrontation with the foundations of democratic governance, violating the rights of minorities, the LGBTQ community,

---

70. In a television interview after he was named national security minister, Ben-Gvir said: "My right to life is more important than the right to movement for Arabs. Sorry Mohammad, but that's the reality. That's the truth. My right to life is superior to their right to movement."

women, and Arabs. At a later stage, this process will also entail increasing extremism; Israel will turn its back on international relations, reject Israel's need for a democratic regime—which is also a fundamental metric and factor in the precious relationship with the United States—as well as give up on the vitally important relationship between Israel and world Jewry, especially American Jewry. It is a process that could have disastrous ramifications.

In some respects, today's messianic National Religious movement, which was created and originated by Harav Kook and later formed in the image of rabbis like Dov Lior and others, is not just the source of the messianic approach, which seeks to engage in a massive confrontation with the Muslim world over the holy places in Jerusalem. It believes in Jewish supremacy; it is racist and xenophobic. It views the Palestinians as inferior human beings and wants to keep the whole of Judea and Samaria under Israeli control. It also wishes to impose Torah Law, as in the days of the Second Temple, with the Sanhedrin and fewer rights for foreigners, women, and members of the LGBTQ community. In terms of Jewish history, they bear a chilling resemblance to the radical groups who, some 2,000 years ago, led the Jewish revolt against the Roman Empire (66 BCE to 70 CE) and later the Bar Kochba revolt (132 to 135 CE). Those revolts ended in utter failure, the deaths of hundreds of thousands of people, the destruction of the Second Temple, and the exile of the Jews from the Land of Israel. Then, too, it was the zealots and messianic believers, whose faith that God would help them stand up to a vast empire, led them to act with complete disregard for reality, facts, and *Realpolitik*—holding an extremist belief that, by virtue of divine intervention, they would be able to defeat the greatest and most powerful nation in the world at that time. In practice, Israel could now find itself being dragged into a situation whereby it may end as a binational or an apartheid state. If either of these comes to pass, it would mean the destruction of the Jewish-democratic state and, subsequently, the undermining of Israel's standing in the Western world, a potential embargo like the one imposed on South Africa, as well as severe and dramatic harm to Israel's economic, academic, scientific, diplomatic, and military power. On the other hand, it is worth remembering that France ruled over Algeria for 132 years. Over the years, more than one million French civilians moved to Algeria. And yet, in 1962, when France withdrew from the North African country, one million French nationals left within two months (!) and returned to France—even though they considered Algeria as their colony for decades. In the meantime, Israel is being dragged into a prolonged and expensive campaign, which entails a religious, nationalist, and messianic group controlling Israeli policy in the West Bank—with all the destructive ramifications this will have. Clearly, the occupation is the main existential threat facing the State of Israel. In terms of historical irony, the great victory in the Six-Day War brought with it the seeds of this national disaster, in the form of national-religious messianism, which is threatening the very existence of the state.

The power that this group wields in Israeli society is now evident. As for the impact it will have, only time will tell. In Chapter 9, we will examine the most recent signs of its increased power, given that Netanyahu—motivated solely by purely personal considerations and a desire to preserve his political power, thereby remaining prime minister and sabotaging the criminal trial he is currently embroiled in—gave these extremist, messianic, and Kahanist racist forces tremendous power within his government. During the writing of this book, Israel was taken by surprise on October 7, 2023, when Hamas launched a barbaric and murderous attack, filled with hatred and atrocities, during which terrorists murdered, burned, tortured, beheaded, dismembered, mutilated, raped, and marauded over the entire day—which also happened to be the Sukkot holiday. They attacked peaceful civilians in the Israeli communities bordering the Gaza Strip and a number of communities in the Negev—in small towns like Ofakim, Netivot, and Sderot. The fact that Israel was taken by surprise is a major failing on the part of the IDF, whose senior officers ignored stark warnings from their subordinates, leading to the military being unprepared for a surprise attack—despite the fact that there were dozens of intelligence alerts from various sources (spotters, many intel reports, and even video clips circulated by Hamas). But the political leadership, the government of Israel, headed by Mr. Netanyahu, also shares massive responsibility for the disaster and the surprise. This is also intrinsically linked to the occupation of the West Bank. A few words are needed to explain how all these dots are connected. The Gaza Strip, located in southern Israel, was under Egyptian control from 1948 to 1967,[71] when it was occupied by Israel during the Six-Day War.

It remained under Israeli control until 1979. It is populated mainly by local residents and, since 1948, by Palestinian refugees, who now make up 75 percent of the population there. In 1979, as part of the Camp David talks between Israel and Egypt, which were mediated by the United States, it was clear that Gaza would return to Egyptian control. Israel had no intention of ruling the Strip. But Egyptian President Anwar Sadat also did not want control over Gaza, which he viewed as nothing but a headache that had no benefits whatsoever. And then Sadat encountered a rare opportunity. Ariel Sharon, who was serving as housing minister at the time, opposed handing over territory to Egypt. In an attempt to nix the process, Sharon decided on the immediate establishment of a number of settlements in Gaza. This was happening at exactly the same time that peace talks were taking place at Camp David. Sadat was clever enough to take advantage of the situation, threatening with his usual sense of dramatics to leave the talks. During the intense negotiations that took place to placate Sadat, U.S. President Jimmy Carter pressured Begin to accept Israeli control over the Gaza Strip. Begin caved in to the massive American pressure, and Israel found itself continuing to rule over Gaza.

---

71. Gaza is mentioned 22 times in the Bible. During the period of the biblical judges, it was occupied by Philistines, who came from Greece.

Later on, a number of Jewish agricultural settlements were established in the southern Gaza Strip, along the Mediterranean coast. They were home to around 8,000 Israelis. They were also targeted by deadly terror attacks perpetrated by Gazans, while Palestinian groups regularly attacked IDF soldiers. In 2005, when Sharon was serving as prime minister, the government made a decision of real leadership to withdraw Israeli forces from Gaza, dismantle the Jewish settlements there, and evacuate residents. This difficult decision meant that Gaza was no longer under Israeli control. However, the withdrawal was unilateral and was not coordinated with the Palestinian Authority. This was the root of a major error. Since it was a unilateral withdrawal and was not coordinated with the PA, Ramallah tried to assume control of Gaza. It encountered fierce opposition from Hamas, a Palestinian extremist Islamic movement that shares much of its ideology with the Muslim Brotherhood. In the 1970s, when it was led by Sheikh Ahmed Yassin, it was an Islamic social and religious organization.

Among its goals is the annihilation of the State of Israel and the imposition of Islam across the region; it views the whole of the territory of Israel as Waqf land.[72] It advocates a stream of radical Islam that has no place for foreigners, Christians, and Jews, in which women have a very subordinate position in society and which attacks the LGBTQ community. Hamas vied with the Palestinian Authority, which was created by the PLO, for dominance in Gaza. In 2006, there were elections in the Strip—the credibility of which must be viewed with a great deal of suspicion—and the people of Gaza elected Hamas. The Palestinian Authority, however, refused to cede power. There were violent clashes, including brutal murders, which ended with Hamas in power. At that time, Israel was easily able to deal with Hamas' military capabilities. In 2009, however, Netanyahu came to power again in Israel. As someone who was preoccupied exclusively with gaining and maintaining power, he made the conscious decision not

---

72. Waqf is a permanent, irrevocable land to Allah, never to be gifted, sold or inherited.

to engage in any kind of dialogue with the Palestinian Authority, preferring instead to strengthen Hamas. In so doing, he believed that he escaped the need to engage in tough negotiations with the Palestinians to enter into the hard talks on the future of the West Bank, which would put him against the Israeli right-wing parties and the settlers, who were an important source of political power for him. Instead, he opted to strengthen Hamas, with which it was, in any case, impossible to negotiate since it is dedicated to the destruction of Israel. In so doing, Netanyahu secured his grip on power by avoiding confrontation with the settlers and their supporters, who were part of his coalition.

This cowardly and nefarious "plan" was the foundation of Israeli policy from 2009. As a result, Netanyahu initiated and facilitated the transfer of cash from Qatar to Hamas—sums that fluctuated between $10 million and $30 million a month![73] Officially, this money was for the humanitarian needs of the people of Gaza, such as education and healthcare, but at least half of it was used to bolster Hamas' military strength (military equipment and training and a massive network of tunnels under Gaza). And, of course, much went to the corrupt leaders of Hamas. As a result, instead of dealing with the issue of the occupation and the West Bank, which Israel simply ignored, Netanyahu played for time and tried to strengthen Hamas, which, from time to time and for its own reasons, launched military operations against Israel, including rocket attacks and occasional attempts to infiltrate Israel from the ground and the sea. Israel responded with military operations that often included minor ground incursions into Gaza. Hamas, however, never gave up on its desire to attack Israel and its citizens, to instill fear and terror into them, and to try to eradicate the Jewish state. With his rhetorical capabilities and his façade of self-confidence (even though he is a cowardly

---

73. In February 2020, acting on Netanyahu's orders, Southern Command General Herzl Halevy (who was IDF Chief of Staff on October 7) traveled to Qatar together with Mossad chief Yossi Cohen, in order to persuade Qatar to continue transferring millions of dollars every month to Hamas.

and hesitant person), Netanyahu managed to cast his spell over Israeli public opinion and convince Israelis that Hamas had been "deterred" from using military force against Israel and that the monthly cash transfers from Qatar, along with around 20,000 permits for Palestinian workers to enter Israel to work, meant that it was not in Hamas' interest to carry out acts of terrorism or to start a war.[74] That, of course, was an illusion.

Hamas prepared for a long period for its murderous attack. In 2023, while Israeli society was facing a major domestic crisis over the legislation that Netanyahu was trying to introduce in order to strengthen his grip on power, limit the authority of the High Court, increase the power of politicians to appoint officials who would agree with their policies and unreasonable governmental decisions, and decide who is appointed a judge. In addition, differences of opinion were emerging in the United States following the government's efforts to undermine Israel's democratic regime. Moreover, there were reports about a possible agreement between Israel and Saudi Arabia, something that would contradict the goals of Hamas and its military and financial patron, Iran. Against this backdrop, the terrorist leadership of Hamas decided to launch a surprise attack. Alongside Israel's intelligence failure, there was also a failure in preparedness for such an offensive. Around 30 infantry battalions had been deployed to the West Bank, where there is a large population of settlers who need military protection, combined with political pressure from the settler and right-wing parties, which prop up the Netanyahu coalition. Meanwhile, along the 40-mile border between Israel and Gaza, the IDF had barely two battalions! A few days before the Black Saturday of October 7, a commando unit and a battalion of infantry soldiers were redeployed from Gaza to the West

---

74. Even as late as June 2023, Netanyahu gave a speech declaring that Hamas "has been deterred for next several years from taking military measures against Israel." In 2021, cabinet minister Tzachi Hanegbi even said that Hamas would not take military action against Israel for at least "the next 15 years." See also recent summary report by the Israeli Security Agency ("Shin Bet") from March 2025.

Bank to provide additional security for a settler outpost during the Sukkot holiday. As a result, security for the southern communities adjacent to the Gaza border was neglected in favor of the West Bank settlers. This was a practical manifestation of how the occupation not only created chaos in Israel's domestic culture, intensified nationalist and messianic trends, generated violence in the West Bank, and empowered the nationalist, religious, and messianic sectors in Israel, but also impeded the basic defense establishment from protecting and defending regions other than the West Bank. What happened in the aftermath of October 7 also highlighted what decades of occupation of the West Bank have done to Israel's image and international support for Israel—up to and including people calling into question its right to exist. All this can be attributed not only to the typical antisemitism that does exist, particularly in Europe, but also to decades of occupation and apartheid policies that emerged in the West Bank. Israel's image and international support for Israel are also the cornerstones of Israel's strength and power.

The West Bank occupation has systematically and continuously eroded them, and the harm it has done is only growing. Israel desperately needs the support of the West, especially the United States. The occupation and all of its manifestations erode this support. And it is worth mentioning here: Hamas started as an Islamic social movement but turned into a monstrous and extremist terrorist organization. During the sixteen years that it controlled Gaza, instead of investing the money it was given to develop the Strip and improve education, healthcare, industry, science, and education, it spent much of those funds on corruption and upgrading its military capabilities in order to plan violent military attacks on Israel, harm it, and ultimately eliminate it. Indeed, this terrorist and extremist regime brought disaster and economic hardship to the people of Gaza. The GDP there was a meager $1,600 per person. Indeed, not all the Palestinian people support Hamas. Within the Palestinian public, there is a significant group that wants to live a normal life that provides them with education, healthcare, and infrastructure—especially in the West Bank. This group will grow as more positive processes are nurtured in the West Bank. Israel, under a different government, of course, must secure its future and its existence by responsibly, seriously, and systematically pursuing an agreement with the Palestinians in the West Bank. It is true that the PA is not an easy partner for peace talks—not at all. It, too, is not innocent of corruption, and the system of government there leaves a lot to be improved. There is also a considerable chance that a Palestinian state, if established, would not be democratic in the conventional sense and may not even be a state to take any pride in. It is also understood—and the 2023 Gaza war has only highlighted this—that as part of any agreement in the West Bank, Israel must have the right to impose the security measures necessary to ensure that events leading up to October 7 do not occur in the West Bank and that radical Islamic forces, such as Hamas and others in the West Bank (Islamic Jihad and so on), do not take hold of power in whatever Palestinian entity is established, thereby controlling the West Bank. All of this is essential to ensure Israel's security.

In any case, however, it is in Israel's supreme interest to liberate itself from the occupation of the West Bank—at the very least, from considerable parts of the territory. In doing so, Israel will ensure that it remains a democratic state. A country cannot be democratic in the full sense while occupying neighboring territories. Israel cannot exist as a prosperous state for long and maintain its values, its cultural, economic, scientific, and industrial power, without a democratic regime—with all that this entails. However, it is clear that this will necessitate a totally different Israeli leadership from the one currently ruling the country. And it will require massively courageous leadership since such processes will require courageous decisions, determination, daring, and willingness to engage in struggles, including against those extremist forces within Israel. These forces will not hesitate to use physical force and violence, as well as acts of terror, shooting, and sabotage. The assassination of Prime Minister

Yitzhak Rabin is just one example. Time will tell if courageous leaders can be found on the Palestinian and Israeli sides to ensure the peaceful coexistence of the two states, as the United Nations resolution passed in 1947 stipulated almost 80 years ago. From an Israeli perspective, it is impossible to overstate the importance of this issue. Liberating Israel from the reality of occupation, with all of its ills, requires a combination of complex conditions and processes, including on the Palestinian side. It requires a strong, new, courageous, and non-corrupt Palestinian leadership willing to accept Israel's existence within the borders of a demilitarized Palestinian state.

A demilitarized Palestinian state must be a precondition from Israel's perspective. This will be a difficult process for Palestinian society, which will also entail violent internal struggles. In 2006, the battle against Hamas in Gaza led to severe violence, which ended with hundreds of Fatah members being killed by Hamas members, including some who were thrown to their deaths from rooftops. The events surrounding the Oslo Accords, which ended with the assassination of Prime Minister Yitzhak Rabin by an extreme and fanatical right-winger, provide us with a taste of the process of liberating Israel from the occupation. Indeed, many countries, at different stages of their history, have experienced civil war. The American Civil War came some 80 years after independence; the French Revolution, including the murderous violence that followed; the Paris Commune in 1871; and the English Civil War, between 1642 and 1651. The United States would not be what it is today if it were not for that bloody and devastating civil war. There is a very real fear that Israel will have to face itself in a difficult internal situation to liberate itself from the dangers of occupation and the reality of apartheid, with all the damage that would cause. But Israel cannot afford itself such a civil war. Israel can, of course, still escape the dangers of occupation, apartheid, global boycott, religious-messianic-nationalist fanaticism with its disastrous consequences, and so on by simply withdrawing unilaterally from most areas of the West

Bank. Of course, doing so as part of an agreement would be preferable, but it is highly doubtful that one can be reached under the current circumstances and given the settlement expansion. Even unilateral withdrawal, however, requires daring leadership, determination, and a person of stature, along with the full cooperation of the United States and the West.[75] At the moment, there is no such leader in Israel. Netanyahu is weak, cowardly, and hesitant; his only power is his rhetoric. However, history teaches us that sometimes such a leader appears out of nowhere, and in retrospect, everyone applauds that leader. There are plenty of examples, e.g., Ben-Gurion, Egypt's Sadat, Abraham Lincoln, and Mahatma Gandhi, all of whom gradually and surprisingly became great leaders—people of courage and vision.

---

75. Israel currently has an historic opportunity to join forces with the Arab states, headed by Saudi Arabia, and the support of the USA, in a comprehensive deal that includes the start of long-term moves to establish a demilitarized Palestinian state in the West Bank, which would be heavily supervised, and an agreement on Palestinian forces, together with foreign support, in the Gaza Strip, and a full diplomatic agreement with Saudi Arabia. The current Israeli government is neither interested nor able, in the absence of bold leadership, to take advantage of such a historic opportunity. President Trump's former "Peace for Prosperity" plan, which was rejected or not accepted by both parties, may now be a rough basis for such discussions.

Chapter 6

Deterioration of Israeli democracy

Benjamin Netanyahu is Israel's longest-serving prime minister, having accumulated more years in power than even the
country's founding father, David Ben-Gurion. Apart from the
longevity of service, however, there is no room for comparison
between Netanyahu and Ben-Gurion, who was a leader of international standing. During his tenure in office, Netanyahu acted
as a populist politician who was more interested in preserving a
grip on power than leading changes and vision. He caused severe
damage to Israeli society, the Israeli economy, Israel's standing
in the world, and its relationship with world Jewry. He is considered by many to be the worst prime minister Israel has ever had.
Many experts consider that his contribution to the destruction
of entire systems within Israel and to Israeli democracy itself has
been immense. Many scholars, experts, and journalists opined
that in order to take control and maintain his grip on power, he
has deliberately and systematically destroyed the relationship
between various parts of Israeli society—including between the
religious and secular communities, Mizrahim and Ashkenazim,
rightists and others. He worked vigorously, with much success, to
engender hatred, incitement, and division over jealousy and took
advantage of preexisting disagreements between these groups.
He cynically used these cracks, disagreements, and gaps within
Israeli society, which he identified, expanded, and intensified
without any inhibitions. And he was systematic and talented.
Already in the 1996 election, shortly after the assassination of

Yitzhak Rabin (when Netanyahu was head of the opposition[76] and was greatly responsible for some of the incitement against Rabin), Netanyahu ran against Shimon Peres, who was a far more skilled and experienced politician than him. During that campaign, he produced a totally fallacious slogan, claiming that "Peres will divide Jerusalem." It was a slogan that was nothing more than groundless incitement. In the 1999 election, when he lost to Ehud Barak, he was caught on camera whispering into the ear of a revered rabbi in the ultra-Orthodox community that "the leftists have forgotten what it means to be Jewish."[77] As far back as 1992, Yitzhak Shamir, prime minister at the time, described Netanyahu as "the angel of sabotage." In this way, he also demolished Israel's governmental system, scoffed at the idea of having qualified civil servants, and appointed unworthy and unqualified people to positions in the Knesset or other government jobs. He also appointed people close and loyal to him, whose only "quality" was being a "Yes Man."

He encouraged and engendered public disdain for the institutions of the state, including the judiciary, the police's criminal investigations department, the state prosecutor, and the High Court of Justice. Each of these is a subject unto itself, as is the historic indictment filed against the weakest and, considered by many—including scholars—the most dangerous prime minister Israel has ever had. The harm he has caused to Israel is historical in scope. History is a series of events that, for the most part, stem from multifaceted, complex processes. Sometimes, however, for better or for worse, individuals can have a decisive impact on events. Over the past two centuries, for example, there have been people like Napoleon, Abraham Lincoln, Mahatma Gandhi, Winston Churchill, Lee Kuan Yew, the founder of modern

---

76. His infamous appearance, for example, at a demonstration in Jerusalem's Zion Square, when protesters held placards of Rabin dressed in a Nazi uniform. Rabin himself, in an interview just days before his assassination, spoke about Netanyahu's involvement in the incitement against him.

77. At a meeting with Rabbi Yitzhak Kadouri.

Singapore, and Sheikh Zayed bin Sultan Al Nahyan, who founded the United Arab Emirates—all on the positive side. On the negative side are people like Benito Mussolini and many, many others.[78] Given the extent of the damage and disaster he has brought to Israel, Netanyahu can rightly be grouped with those individuals who had a significantly negative impact on their country.

Throughout his career, in many instances, he behaved as if personal and political interests were always in preference to the good of the state. He changes his position based on his personal and political interests. He has no direction. For example, at the start of his first term of office, he accepted the Oslo Accords, continued to negotiate with the Palestinian Authority, even calling PLO chairman Yasser Arafat "my friend," signed the agreement on the implementation of the Oslo Accords (at the Wye Plantation, USA, in September 1998), and withdrew from 13 percent of the West Bank, which was transferred to the control of the Palestinian Authority. During his second term in 2009, he gave his famous "Bar-Ilan speech," in which he agreed to the "two-state solution" and backed a demilitarized Palestinian state. Thereafter, however, for reasons of political expediency and safeguarding the coalition he formed, he changed his position; he distanced himself from the Palestinian Authority, ignored it, and systematically tried to undermine it.

He did not do one single thing to kickstart the process of recognizing a Palestinian state. At the same time, he used the 2009 election campaign to promise that he would "eliminate Hamas" in the Gaza Strip. In practice, however, he did exactly the opposite. He stopped meeting with the head of the Palestinian Authority in 2010, started to weaken it by expanding Jewish West Bank settlements and turning a blind eye to acts of violence by groups of settlers. At the same time, he started to nurture and strengthen Hamas. He tried to sell the idea that Hamas was "an asset." He opened communications with Qatar and made sure that the

78. One interesting book on the subject is Ian Kershaw's "Personality and Power: Builders and Destroyers of Modern Europe" (Penguin Press, 2022).

Qataris sent Hamas $15 million a month. That sum would only increase over time.[79]

Under Netanyahu's government, Israel ignored the fact that Hamas was using this money to increase its military strength and to construct a massive network of underground tunnels in Gaza, which it would later use against Israel. Netanyahu refrained for more than a decade from taking preventative military action against Hamas to thwart its military buildup.[80] On several occasions, he even stopped military commanders from carrying out plans to assassinate senior Hamas members. In so doing, Netanyahu led Israel to its greatest disaster: the October 7 massacre. His insistence that Hamas had been "deterred from attacking Israel" led to the country's intelligence agencies failing to warn of irregular Hamas activity since they did not want to disrupt the "Hamas coma" that the prime minister had adopted. Further examples of the mistakes Netanyahu made can be found in his handling of the Iranian nuclear program.[81] Under its current regime, Iran is a genuine threat to Israel and to other countries in the Middle East. Its nuclear program is also a serious threat. In 2015, the world powers were negotiating an agreement whereby Iran's nuclear facilities would come under international supervision. The deal would ensure that Iran would not progress with its nuclear program for at least the next decade. Netanyahu launched an aggressive campaign against the deal. He joined forces with the

---

79. Per several news sources, it reaches 30 million USD per month for a significant period,, and most of it is in cash.

80. In his book, *Bibi: My Story (page 487)* he describes the 2014 military conflict with Hamas. While then-minister Naftali Bennet urged launching a full-scale war to eradicate Hamas, Netanyahu was inclined otherwise as he feared there would be tens of thousands of civilian casualties in Gaza and Israel would need to manage two million Gazans, which he did not want.

81. Incidentally, while not serving as prime minister, on September 12, 2002, Netanyahu appeared before the U.S. House Government Reform Committee, during a hearing entitled Conflict With Iraq, an Israeli Perspective, where he spoke about concerns over nuclear and chemical weapons. He claimed, with absolute confidence, that military action would cause enormous shocks in the region, including Iran, and would lead to the fall of the Ayatollah's regime. Of course, this prediction turned out to be nonsense.

Republican Party in the United States and campaigned against President Barack Obama. He wrangled an invitation to address Congress, during which he gave a bombastic speech against the deal about to be signed and, with untold arrogance and chutzpah, came out against a sitting American president. In so doing, he harmed Israel's relations with the Democratic Party and created a rift. Until that moment, every Israeli prime minister treated both parties the same—for obvious reasons. But Netanyahu preferred to bolster his image as a "strong leader" in the eyes of his supporters instead of putting the good of the country first. A few years later, when Donald Trump was president, Netanyahu foolishly and fervently tried to persuade him to withdraw from that agreement. Netanyahu was "successful" in this respect, but because the American withdrawal from the deal was not replaced with a viable alternative, and there was no contingency planning (something that Netanyahu is guilty of in so many areas), the result is that Iran is now closer to having a nuclear bomb than ever before, and the threat to Israel has increased tenfold.

Once again, Netanyahu—who has created for himself an image of "Mr. Security"—made a dramatic and historic mistake. In many respects, Netanyahu reflects and implements the guidelines drawn up in *The Prince*, the 16th-century political treatise written by the Italian diplomat, philosopher, and political theorist Niccolò Machiavelli—and as practiced by other figures from the 20th and 21st centuries.[82]

Netanyahu has revealed himself to be a weak individual. Although his rhetoric is strong, he prefers inaction, lacks initiative and vision, is hesitant, and is averse to making significant

---

82. According to Machiavelli, a ruler is not obliged to keep his promises; he must act cunningly and duplicitously; he must create rifts between different groups among the people to ensure that they do not unite against him; he must always divert responsibility for failures away from himself and find others responsible for failures; he must always take credit for any successes; and he must always justify breaking his promises on the grounds of law and order. See also Mussolini, in Prof. Ruth Ben-Ghiat's book, "Strongmen: Mussolini to the Present."

decisions.[83] He never takes responsibility for his failures. It is no coincidence that he has surrounded himself—in the Knesset and in his bureau—with low-quality people. People with no record of impressive public activity, who lack any practical leadership or managerial skills, and almost all of whom are loyal to him since they owe their political careers and their positions to him. Most of the ministers he appointed are mediocre at best; they lack the skills for the positions they are in and, under normal circumstances, they would come nowhere near serving as ministers in the Israeli government. In 2021, the ultra-Orthodox community celebrated, as it does every year, the Hillula of Rabbi Shimon bar Yochai (a festival) on Mount Meron in the Galilee. Every year, many more ultra-Orthodox people come to the site than it can safely hold. This time, fears of a mass disaster became reality, and 45 people were killed in a nighttime stampede. It happened on Netanyahu's watch, but it was only after he was (briefly) voted out of office that the government set up a commission of inquiry; Netanyahu himself refused to do so, fearing it would point the finger of blame at him. In March 2024, the committee published its findings, which included much criticism of Netanyahu. It detailed how he tried to evade responsibility, refused to deal with the root of the problem, fudged and avoided making the necessary decisions, and dealt with his ultra-Orthodox coalition partners, without whom he would not be in power. The committee determined that Netanyahu was responsible for the disaster and even noted, in somewhat restrained language, that he did not tell the truth during his testimony.

"We found an evil culture in our own home. Within public bodies, governmental authorities, and public officials, both elected and appointed. We found a culture primarily concerned with appearances;

---

83. In 2020, Israel and the USA were on a mission to kill Gen. Suleimani from Iran. The planning spanned months and then, just before the crucial moment, Netanyahu backed down and told President Trump that Israel would not participate. President Trump, as he spoke of the incident, was very disappointed of course.

a culture of ignoring repeated warnings, of complacency, and of inflexibility on significant matters relating to public safety and the preservation of human life. A culture of disrespect for governance and the rule of law, and a pattern of procrastination and avoidance of decision-making. Conduct that was adversely influenced by political interests and external considerations. A culture of narrow-mindedness and evasion and abdication of responsibility. This culture led to the terrible disaster on Mount Meron. The writing was on the wall. This catastrophe could have been prevented, and it should have been prevented.[84]

Netanyahu's utter failings, his pathological aversion to decision-making, his fear of dealing with any substantive issues, and his avoidance of taking responsibility for failures have been demonstrated in countless incidents, the worst of which occurred on October 7. Hamas terrorists broke through the border between Gaza and Israel in an attack that took Israelis totally by surprise. They were unimpeded, as the IDF was caught utterly unprepared—both in terms of intelligence and military deployment and preparedness in case of a surprise attack. For years, Netanyahu claimed that Hamas had been "deterred" and would not dare any decisive military action against Israel. He was responsible for the monthly transfer of vast amounts of money from Qatar—money that Hamas used to build up its military strength, train its fighters, and build a network of underground tunnels. And so, for the first time in the history of Israel, under the Netanyahu government, there was a barbaric, murderous, and horrendous attack on Israeli civilians. For many hours from that Saturday morning, Israeli residents of communities close to the Gaza border and thousands of young people attending the Nova Music Festival were left defenseless in the face of marauding terrorists, who slaughtered them and mutilated their bodies. Subsequently, approximately 150,000 people were forced from their homes in southern Israel and along the northern border with Lebanon, becoming internal refugees—the first time in the history of the State of Israel since

---

84. The Report by the State Commission of Inquiry into the Mount Meron Disaster, 2024, Page 274 of the Hebrew transcript.

the War of Independence. Netanyahu brought Israel to the lowest point in its history—militarily, in international standing, socially, and economically. Fifteen years of rule by this man culminated in indescribable chaos and destruction. Netanyahu led his country to the same kind of destruction and devastation as other populist leaders from the 19th and 20th centuries, such as fomenting division and hatred toward small groups of "domestic enemies."[85]

Netanyahu's main harm and destruction that he has brought to Israel is not limited to the fact that he is someone who has no problem serially making untrue statements and comments,[86] or to the fact that he is a braggart who cannot deliver on his promises, or even that he is hesitant and lacking basic skills needed for management, let alone leadership[87]. His main weakness is his lust for power and willingness to sell off all the state's assets and institutions to achieve his personal goals. To this end, he incited parts of the population against others. He incited against leftists ("The left has forgotten what it means to be Jewish," Netanyahu said during the 1999 election) and against Arab citizens ("The Arabs are coming out to vote in droves," he said on Election Day in 2015). Slowly but surely, leftists became synonymous with traitors in the eyes of some Israelis. In contrast, incitement against journalists who did not toe the Netanyahu line turned them into enemies of the state. They came under verbal attack, slander, lies, insults, threats, and eventually physical violence to intimidate anyone who did not follow Netanyahu's line. Later on, when criminal investigations were launched against him—eventually leading to indictments for bribery, fraud, and breach of trust—Netanyahu

---

85. See, for example, Napoleon III until his eventual defeat at the hands of the Prussian army, under command of Otto von Bismarck, as well as Mussolini and others. Denis Mack Smith's book "*Mussolini*," especially the chapter on "Mussolini as leader," is especially recommended. There are many similarities between the Italian despot's conduct and that of Netanyahu.

86. See the appendix A to this book.

87. This book was sent to publishing prior to June 13,2025 the day when Israel launched its strikes on Iran's nuclear facilities .Netanyahu in this instance was certainly resolute.

even began to use those journalists beholden to him and the social media platforms they operate to incite the public against police investigators and the person who was serving as police commissioner at the time (who was, incidentally, a right-winger who happened to respect the rule of law above all else). And when the police investigation ended with a recommendation for a formal indictment to be filed against Netanyahu, he launched a comprehensive and systematic campaign of incitement, allegations, invective, and harassment against the officials from the state prosecution dealing with these criminal allegations.

Later, when it came time to decide whether to indict the prime minister, Netanyahu turned the beams of incitement and threats against the state prosecutor and his officials, as well as against the attorney general at the time, whom the Netanyahu government had appointed. Even today, Netanyahu is engaged in his campaign of incitement, division, hatred, and polarization between sectors of Israeli society—between left and right, between Ashkenazim and Mizrahim, as well as against the institutions of the state. He has incited against the Shin Bet (some of his ministers see the Israeli security agency as traitors and leftists, and Netanyahu never calls them out for such comments, even though it is clear that none of them would say a word unless they had the tacit or explicit approval of Netanyahu), against the High Court of Justice, and especially against its former president, Justice Esther Hayut. Incitement, creating and fanning hatred, and inventing imagined enemies whenever he needed to are Netanyahu's main political arsenal.

He makes systematic and effective use of them. And the harm and destruction to Israeli society and the State of Israel are of strategic proportions. As part of his willingness to concede to coalition parties' demands just to remain in power and his willingness to do unthinkable things to the same end, Netanyahu signed coalition agreements after the 2022 election with various ultra-Orthodox parties and with religious, racist, messianic parties from the far right, headed by Bezalel Smotrich and Itamar

Ben-Gvir. These agreements promised Netanyahu's partners huge budgets—at the expense of the rest of the Israeli population and the state-run education system, the healthcare system, and universities, as well as research and development facilities. Moreover, for his own personal political interests, which come before the good of the state if there is any contradiction between them,[88] he appointed Smotrich to the key position of finance minister. Not only is Smotrich devoid of any understanding or experience in the field of economics, but his interest is mainly to entrench and expand the occupation and bolster the West Bank settlements while doing whatever he can to harm Israel's Arab sector. He also appointed Ben-Gvir, the head of the Otzma Yehudit party, as national security minister, with responsibility for the police and the Border Police. Ben-Gvir is a nationalist racist and a former member of Meir Kahane's outlawed Kach Party, who never served in the IDF. He currently resides in the West Bank settlement of Kiryat Arba. For Ben-Gvir, Dr. Baruch Goldstein—the ultranationalist settler who murdered 29 Muslim worshippers in Hebron in 1994—was a hero; for years, Goldstein's portrait was proudly displayed in Ben-Gvir's home.[89]

Netanyahu's willingness to destroy Israeli society from within, to demolish all the institutions of state and their standing (including the High Court, the state prosecution, the police, the Shin Bet, and the IDF), and his culture of appointing people as ministers and to other senior positions based solely on their loyalty to the leader, without even bothering to examine whether they are suited to or have the skills for the position, have had a massively destructive impact in the long term on Israel and are a negative influence on Israeli society. For example, for state comptroller, he appointed a candidate who, in practice, during his tenure, had barely written any reports critical of Netanyahu. In

88. Prime Minister Yitzhak Shamir once said of Netanyahu that his personal interest takes precedence over the interest of the State of Israel.

89. In the run-up to the most recent election, Netanyahu said that it would be inconceivable to appoint Ben-Gvir to a ministerial position in his cabinet.

2024, he changed the method of appointing the person responsible for the Civil Service, whose job it is to ensure that appointments to the civil service are made solely on a professional and substantive basis and not by connections and acquaintances. According to a cabinet resolution, Netanyahu, as prime minister, is now exclusively responsible for appointing the next civil service commissioner. In August 2024, Netanyahu made sure that one of his ministers, who is responsible for appointments to the board of directors of government-controlled companies, named Prof. Alon Pikarsky, head of surgery at Jerusalem's Hadassah Medical Center and personal physician to Netanyahu and his family, to the board of directors of the state-owned Rafael, a renowned arms manufacturer. Why on earth would a surgeon serve as a director for a weapons manufacturer?[90]

Finally, Netanyahu has almost never admitted to making a mistake and has always avoided taking any kind of responsibility for failures attributed to him. At the same time, he fully appropriates others' achievements and successes (often without being in any way connected to them).[91] The culture of evading responsibility is destructive, and it is slowly but surely seeping through to every level of the Israeli establishment—with predictable results. In 2011, during the Carmel Forest fires, for example, 45 people were killed due to negligence and neglect by the fire-fighting service, which turned out to be woefully lacking in training and equipment. The same was true of the abovementioned Mount Meron tragedy, when 41 people were trampled to death due to illegal overcrowding of a religious site. The commission of inquiry that was established found that Netanyahu was outrageously ineffective, negligent, and unwilling to take any decision

90. A petition to the Supreme Court to nullify the appointment was dismissed.

91. Most recently, on June 9, 2024, when, in a heroic operation, Israeli security forces rescued four hostages from the Gaza Strip, Netanyahu rushed that very same day – which happened to be Shabbat – to more than one hospital for photo ops with hostages and to take the credit for the success. See also, Netanyahu took some credit after the successful attack on Suleimani as President Trump later complained, supra. note 86.

that might upset his ultra-Orthodox coalition partners, notwithstanding the risk to life and limb, and, most critically, that he evaded all responsibility. His testimony to that commission is a shocking catalogue of refusal to admit that mistakes were made or to admit any culpability, an inability to make decisions, and incredibly inadequate management. All of these are characteristics of Netanyahu's time in office.[92]

As one commentator described him after discussion of Netanyahu's omission to take the required decisions in order to release the last 101 Israeli hostages captured by Hamas since October 7, which destroys the basic solidarity sentiment that was a T-bone of Jewish life for thousands of years and of Israeli society since its foundation: "Netanyahu is not only responsible for the greatest disaster which occurred to the Jewish people since the Holocaust, not just the greatest inciter and corruptor of Israeli society in the history of Israel, he is also a leader who is so detached from the spirit of Jewish history and basic tradition and the cultural strings that survived for thousands of years."[93]

However, the start of Netanyahu's career was much more promising.

He is, after all, an eloquent speaker, of English and Hebrew, with a broad base of knowledge, intelligence, and a gift for persuading people. He was raised in a home in which the arts and education were revered. His father was a history professor who specialized in Spanish Jewry during the Inquisition. The family spent several years in the 1950s and 1960s in the United States, where Netanyahu was enrolled in local high schools. It was there that he picked up his English, which he used to such advantageous effect back in Israel, and he says he was active in the

---

92. In many respects, the October 7 disaster and the military failures before and during that day, including the lack of organized military forces for immediate military intervention for more than 10 hours, and the subsequent month-long paralysis of the government when it came to treating the Israeli victims, all stem from the same behavior and culture that has taken root in the country.

93. Prof. Dimitri Shomsky, "Haaretz" newspaper. October 23, 2024.

school's debating society. He returned to Israel and, alongside his older brother Yonatan (Yoni), served in the elite Sayeret Matkal, a commando unit. He returned to the United States when his military service ended, studied at prestigious universities, and worked as an economic consultant for the Boston Consulting Group. He returned to Israel to fight in the Yom Kippur War in October 1973. After serving briefly, he soon returned to the United States—unlike his comrades-in-arms, who continued serving for many more months. While he was still in the United States, his brother was killed in an operation called "Entebbe" in Uganda—a daring IDF mission to rescue 104 Israeli and Jewish hostages who had been captured by Palestinian terrorists working in collaboration with German militants. The audacious rescue mission was meticulously planned, and almost all the hostages were freed unharmed.

Apart from Yoni Netanyahu, who was hit by Ugandan fire during the operation, one Israeli soldier, Surin Hershko, was severely wounded. Netanyahu used the death of his brother to turn himself into a well-known and well-connected public figure.[94] He was, as mentioned, living in the United States at the time. He changed his name to Benjamin Nitai and worked as a financial advisor. If it were not for Operation Entebbe and Yoni's death, it is possible that Netanyahu would have stayed in the United States. History, however, takes a long and winding path. In a well-planned and executed campaign, Netanyahu raised money for a foundation to memorialize his brother, to publish books about him, including a collection of the late hero's letters. By memorializing his brother, Netanyahu became a well-known figure in certain circles in the United States, while in Israel he became familiar to the public and especially the political community. Even then, there were obvious signs of his character. On the one hand, his incessant and indefatigable march toward positions of power, while manufacturing different versions of the truth; facts, fact-checking, and

---

94. Yoni Netanyahu was considered a paradigm of virtue: moral, a courageous fighter and a uniquely positive person.

sticking to the truth are irrelevant to him. Even in his most recent autobiography—"Bibi: My Story"—his description of Operation Entebbe, especially his brother's role in planning the operation and his involvement in the actual execution, is very different from how people who took part in the operation described things—especially the deputy commander of Sayeret Matkal and Yoni's deputy, Col. (Res.) Muki Betser.[95]

Over the years, this phenomenon of ignoring the truth and facts, of creating "alternative facts," became Netanyahu's modus operandi—so much so, in fact, that foreign leaders (French President Nicolas Sarkozy, for example, along with President Obama and even Donald Trump's Secretary of State Rex Tillerson, among others) have been quoted as saying that they do not believe him.[96] History, however, is dictated by what can seem to be random events. If it were not for Operation Entebbe, Netanyahu may have remained in the United States. However, following the heroic death of his brother in that operation, Netanyahu returned to Israel. He slowly but surely entrenched himself in public life.

Between 1993 and 1995, Netanyahu was chair of the Likud Party, the largest opposition party at that time. While the Oslo Accords were being negotiated, there were mass violent protests against the process itself and specifically against Prime Minister Yitzhak Rabin. Netanyahu was one of the leaders of those demonstrations and opposition to the Oslo Accords. Here, too, he was duplicitous, however, as he participated in the incitement while occasionally making more conciliatory noises—apparently so that, many years later, he would be able to point to those comments and say that he did not contribute to the incitement and polarization against the government and its leader. Behind closed doors,

---

95. See Muki Betser, "Secret Soldier" (London: Simon & Schuster); and "Bibi: The Story of My Life." This book itself includes dozens of other examples of Netanyahu's "alternative truths" and factual accounts that are sometimes untrue and sometimes are only part of the truth, a distortion of the truth or a "substitute" for the truth. See the appendix for more.

96. Even Netanyahu's own finance minister, Bezalel Smotrich, called him "a liar and son of a liar."

Netanyahu fanned the flames of opposition and the incitement against Rabin and his government; he was a little more restrained in public.[97] When demonstrators held aloft images of Rabin in a Nazi uniform, however, he spoke out against this. In the days before his assassination, Rabin was asked why he did not talk to the leader of the opposition—that is, Netanyahu—to lower the flames and the insanity of those protests. Rabin explained that there was no point in doing so because Netanyahu says one thing and then does the exact opposite. Many people contributed to the incitement against Rabin, and many were responsible for that horrific assassination, the devastating consequences of which Israel is still experiencing. But Netanyahu played a role in it. In the election that was held six months after the assassination, Netanyahu was elected prime minister for the first time (1996 to 1999), having defeated Peres partly due to a campaign of incitement and defamation based exclusively on the slogan that "Peres will divide Jerusalem."

During this three-year tenure, Netanyahu's character traits were already becoming evident. On the one hand, he was a sophisticated person. His oratorical and rhetorical skills were unmatched, and he was a hugely impressive interlocutor. He was well-read and made an excellent first impression. At the same time, there were already indications that he was prone to losing his head under pressure and that he tended to panic and make ill-considered decisions in tense situations. This was especially evident during the attempted assassination of then-Hamas leader Khaled Mishaal in Jordan in 1997. The plan to poison him failed, however, and, following threats from King Hussein of Jordan, Israel handed over the antidote to the toxin, and Netanyahu later freed 70 Palestinian terrorists, among them Hamas's spiritual leader, Sheikh Ahmed Yassin. The same tendency to panic was evident in 1996 when riots erupted in Jerusalem over Israeli excavations at the Western Wall Tunnel during his first term of

---

97. This was described by the Late PM Rabin in an interview couple of weeks before he was assassinated.

office.[98] There was also a tendency toward political deals that utterly ignored the principles of democracy, such as the independence of the attorney general, in an embarrassing affair in 1996 known as the "Bar-On–Hebron affair," when Netanyahu and Shas leader Aryeh Deri conspired to appoint a private attorney to the position of attorney general, knowing full well that this attorney, Roni Bar-On, would not pursue the criminal investigation that was being conducted at the time into Deri's affairs. But one has to acknowledge that up until that point, Netanyahu had not posed a concrete threat to Israeli democracy. In the 1999 election, he lost to former IDF Chief of Staff Ehud Barak, and there was an orderly handover of power, after which Netanyahu retired from public life, focusing instead on his business interests (through which, incidentally, he made a fortune, mainly by giving lectures and serving as a consultant with several companies). He would later return to political life. Between 2003 and 2005, he was finance minister under Ariel Sharon. It was during this period that he showed an ability to take in economic information quickly, and he took several courageous decisions that improved the Israeli economy.

In light of Ariel Sharon's understanding that the ultra-Orthodox community was growing at a rapid rate (see Chapter 4) and was a heavy burden on Israeli society and the economy, one of the necessary actions was to reduce these subsidies to a level that they would not be seen as an incentive to bring more children. Netanyahu, in his capacity as Sharon's finance minister, decided to drastically reduce the allowances for large families. This led to three important results, the last of which is truly disastrous. Firstly, the reduction in allowances led to more ultra-Orthodox Israelis joining the workforce. Prior to that, just 42 percent of ultra-Orthodox men worked, but within two years, that figure climbed to around 50 percent. That is a phenomenal increase. Secondly, the average family size in the ultra-Orthodox

---

98. See Amy Ayalon, chief of Shien Bet at the time, describing that Netanyahu was "paralyzed" during the events.

community fell from 6.7 children to 5.7 children within two years. Again, this is a dramatic decrease, proving that there is a connection between allowances for large families and the birthrate, even in this specific sector. That is an astounding statistic. Thirdly and finally, Netanyahu's popularity among the ultra-Orthodox population and leaders of the Haredi parties plummeted. In the 2006 election, his Likud party only garnered 12 seats, its lowest total since 1977. Netanyahu learned the lesson the hard way: if he wanted to retake and hang on to power in Israel, he would have to placate the leaders of the ultra-Orthodox parties, give in to their demands, and stop cutting their allowances. Instead, he would have to increase these stipends across the board. As already established, the process by which the proportion of ultra-Orthodox in Israeli society is growing is an existential threat to Israeli society and even to the State of Israel itself. This will remain true until the ultra-Orthodox educational institutions radically change their core curriculum and teach modern disciplines like mathematics, physics, history, civics, chemistry, and English. Netanyahu, however, since he was single-mindedly focused on taking and retaining power, was willing to give the ultra-Orthodox whatever they wanted as long as they agreed to join his future coalition. And that's precisely what happened.

The State of Israel became enslaved to the ultra-Orthodox population under the leadership of Netanyahu. Between 2009 and 2015, Netanyahu continued to win more elections to serve as prime minister. The ultra-Orthodox sector was his loyal partner throughout this period, as was the national-religious settler camp. Issues fundamental to Israel's future—including the occupation of the West Bank—remained unaddressed under Netanyahu. Another conclusion reached by Netanyahu was that to win power in an election and remain in power, he had to control public opinion. He did so via the media. He was highly active in this area, even while still in opposition. In 2007, after negotiations with Jewish-American billionaire Sheldon Adelson—the owner of hotels and casinos in Las Vegas and Macao—and his wife, Dr. Miriam Adelson, a new newspaper called *Israel Hayom* was launched in Israel. The Adelsons bankrolled the newspaper, which, from day one, was clearly and uncritically supportive of Netanyahu. Almost every article appearing in the newspaper was encouraging toward and supportive of Netanyahu and his positions. His every appearance, speech, and interview were covered in full, while his rivals were painted negatively.[99] Unlike other newspapers in Israel, *Israel Hayom* was handed out for free. The fact that it was free meant that the newspaper grew in popularity, and by 2012, it was the most-read newspaper in Israel. Not only did it serve to advance Netanyahu and his positions among the Israeli people, but it also started to work against the economic interests of its rivals, especially *Yedioth Ahronoth*, which was the most widely distributed newspaper until that point. *Yedioth* is owned by the Mozes family, and its publisher at the time was Mr. Arnon Mozes.Netanyahu continued to try and take control of the media sphere. To this end, he worked decisively to embed journalists who supported him on Israeli television networks (Keshet and Reshet, the two main television networks, were both owned at the time by businessmen with an interest in maintaining "peaceful coexistence" with the prime minister).

Over time, many of the people working in news on Israeli television networks were supporters of Netanyahu and his policies, either out of ideology or because they opportunistically decided to back the prime minister. Netanyahu even tried to change the structure of the state-run television channel (*Channel 11*). He wanted to dismantle it and reassemble it with employees who were on his side—and he assumed that his supporters would select these journalists. Although he did manage to dismantle the channel, which was forced to operate in a new format, Netanyahu failed to plant his supporters on the inside. He later "admitted" that he had failed to do so because, as he put it, he was preoccupied at the time with Operation Protective Edge

---

99. Later in years to follow this tendency was significantly changed.

(*Tzuk Eitan*) in Gaza. Netanyahu's obsession with controlling the media to control public opinion, thereby ensuring continued public support for him at the election booth or during his tenure, was, and still is, a cornerstone of his approach. Between 2015 and 2016, several incidents suddenly surfaced in the media, all of which, without exception, were related to Netanyahu's obsession with controlling the Israeli media. All of them revealed potential criminal acts, such as fraud and breach of trust. Even suspicions of bribery came to light.

In the next chapter, we will review these affairs and how they led to dramatic changes in Israeli democracy and spawned efforts to crush it.

Chapter 7

Netanyahu's Trials and the "Submarines-navy vessels-Shares" Affair

In 2015, the pressure on Netanyahu was increasing. *Israel Hayom*, the freebie newspaper established by the late Jewish-American billionaire Sheldon Adelson and his expat Israeli wife, Dr. Miriam, became the most widely read newspaper in the country, overtaking *Yedioth Ahronoth*. The owner and publisher of *Yedioth Ahronoth*, Arnon Mozes, was concerned about the financial status of his publication. A lawmaker with ties to Mozes began to put forward legislation that would forbid the distribution of free newspapers. Netanyahu, under pressure, worked hard to nix the legislation. Once the bill had been approved in its first vote, despite his best efforts, he sought to dissolve parliament. In the meantime, the Israeli media (especially in *Haaretz*'s financial newspaper, *The Marker*) started to publish investigative reports into Netanyahu's conduct.

At first, the articles focused on deals he tried to strike with Mozes, whereby the *Yedioth* owner would hire journalists who would write positively about Netanyahu and his wife, in exchange for Netanyahu persuading Adelson to reduce the number of copies of *Israel Hayom* that were distributed on Friday—the day with the highest number of newspaper purchases. Later, there were reports that Netanyahu had proposed passing laws that would support and benefit *Yedioth*. Such activities, if proven in court, constitute a profoundly serious crime. In addition, reports emerged about Netanyahu and his wife receiving hundreds of thousands of shekels worth of lavish gifts from Arnon Milchan, an Israeli billionaire. Milchan, a successful and famous Hollywood movie producer (*Pretty Woman* and *Fight Club* are just two of his blockbusters), was keen on fostering a relationship with Netanyahu. On occasion, he turned to Netanyahu for assistance. For example, allegedly the prime minister helped Milchan extend his expired U.S. visa and tried (unsuccessfully) to help him amend and extend the effect of Israeli tax law to grant citizens returning from more than ten years overseas an exemption from Israeli taxes and from having to report worldwide earnings to the Israeli authorities.[100] In exchange for this relationship and occasional help—or so the claim went—Milchan showered Netanyahu and his wife with lavish gifts.

They apparently felt comfortable enough to take hundreds of bottles of expensive champagne and Cuban cigars from Milchan's home, and the Hollywood mogul also bought expensive jewelry for Sara Netanyahu. According to the Israeli prosecution, these gifts were valued at up to $200,000. When these reports started to emerge, Netanyahu vehemently denied them and launched a well-orchestrated campaign, spearheaded by political activists, to refute the claims. In the meantime, a new government took office. But 2016 brought fresh allegations. It became clear that Netanyahu had been working energetically to take control of the Israeli media since he recognized how important it was for influencing and manipulating public opinion, navigating narratives, and ensuring that he did not have to rely solely on *Israel Hayom*. Netanyahu began embedding journalists into different media outlets—people whose careers he wanted to advance and who either worked and received instructions, directly or indirectly, from the prime minister's bureau or from people working with Netanyahu, or who were inclined to favor Netanyahu. Indeed, Netanyahu had his own special team that dealt with media matters, including social media platforms. According to reports,

---

100. The latter ended unsuccessfully.

he also tried to take control of the content of an online news site called *Walla*, owned at the time by Israeli tycoon Shaul Elovitch—who also had a controlling interest in Israel's largest telecommunications company, Bezeq. Netanyahu and Elovitch would go on to develop a close relationship. At the time, Netanyahu served not only as prime minister but also in four other ministerial posts, including communications minister. In these roles, according to reports, Netanyahu granted regulatory benefits to Bezeq at Elovitch's request in exchange for turning *Walla* into a mouthpiece for Netanyahu and his wife. According to the indictment that would later be filed, the benefits that Netanyahu granted Elovitch totaled around $250 million. An investigation was launched into the affair. At the time, Israel's attorney general was Dr. Avichai Mendelblit, a member of the national-religious sector who had served as Military Advocate General and risen to the rank of major general. When he left military service, Netanyahu appointed him as Cabinet Secretary.

This is an administrative position designed to coordinate ministerial activity and serve as an aide to the prime minister. It requires working closely with the prime minister. We will return later to Mendelblit's tenure in this position. In 2016, the position of Attorney General became vacant. Up until that point, most Israeli AGs had been individuals with considerable legal experience who were unconnected to the political echelon. It is a particularly critical position because the attorney general in Israel fulfills two roles: he is not only the legal advisor to the government but is also responsible for the state prosecution and the submission of criminal indictments. The attorney general wields great power, and the position has been filled by some of the best legal minds in Israel, including Justice Meir Shamgar, under whom the author of this book interned at the Supreme Court. For his own reasons, however, Netanyahu wanted Mendelblit as attorney general. So, the five-person committee, including the Supreme Court chief justice, which decides on the appointment of the attorney general, was convened. After examining the various candidates, the committee voted to appoint Mendelblit. It was not a unanimous vote, however, with committee chairman Dr. Asher Grunis, at the time the Supreme Court chief justice, opposing. Dr. Grunis argued that Mendelblit's years of service as cabinet secretary meant that he was too close to Netanyahu, which could color his positions and opinions. Grunis, however, was in the minority. Prof. Gabriela Shalev and two Knesset members—Anat Berko and Moshe Nissim—also served on the committee that chose Mendelblit. Prof. Shalev, a professor of contract law at the Hebrew University, had also served for two years as Israel's ambassador to the United Nations.

Nissim, a former justice minister, had been a Likud party activist his entire political life, making a living from it, in part, by working with or for government bodies or similar entities. Dr. Berko, who spent 25 years in the IDF and reached the rank of lieutenant colonel, was a Knesset member representing Likud—the party headed by Netanyahu. The committee selected Dr. Mendelblit from a list of six candidates. It would later emerge in the media that another candidate for the vacant position of attorney general, a former District Court judge, told a friend that before the decision was made, she was approached by someone close to Netanyahu's bureau and asked, in no uncertain terms, whether she would drop an ongoing case against Mrs. Sara Netanyahu if she were to be selected as attorney general.

Soon after his appointment, an investigation into Netanyahu's potential involvement in the aforementioned cases began following major reports in several newspapers and the start of small public demonstrations every Saturday evening in a square near Mendelblit's home. Dr. Mendelblit was ineffective. He slowed the investigations down and eventually reduced some of the charges against Netanyahu. In one specific case, he even prevented an investigation from being launched at all against Netanyahu (see the section below on the *Submarines and Navy Vessels Affair*). At a tough and turbulent time for the Israeli legal system, with the prime minister under suspicion and criminal investigations underway, the attorney general must have a high degree of integrity, civic courage, and the ability to withstand threats and pressure. On this, one may argue, Mendelblit failed. He was hesitant, and Netanyahu took full advantage. Mendelblit's laxity was evident in the investigations against Netanyahu. In the case of Netanyahu's connection with Arnon Mozes and the proposal that Israeli law be amended to benefit *Yedioth Ahronoth* in exchange for the newspaper appointing reporters who would write favorably about Netanyahu and his wife, conversations between the two men were recorded. It turned out that Netanyahu and his advisor at the time made five recordings of conversations with the newspaper publisher.

These recordings ended up in Mendelblit's hands because of a separate investigation into the same prime ministerial advisor. Had this information not been leaked to a reporter who published the details, it is safe to assume that the whole affair would have faded away and not come to the public's attention—let alone led to an investigation or an indictment. Even when he was forced to release the tapes, Mendelblit did not act with any urgency to open an investigation and procrastinated. Meanwhile, the investigations into Arnon Milchan and the tycoon owner of Bezeq continued. As part of the probe into Milchan, the need also arose to investigate Sara Netanyahu, since the prime minister's wife allegedly received hundreds of cases of champagne from the Hollywood producer. . In regular investigations, police usually interview suspects simultaneously to ensure that they do not coordinate their stories. In an unusual move, Mendelblit intervened directly in how the investigation should be conducted, barred police from interviewing the Netanyahus at the same time, and insisted that they be questioned on different days. Later, he sought to delay the investigations and postpone decisions, including whether to indict Netanyahu and his wife. Eventually, pressure began to mount within the state prosecution for three indictments to be filed against Netanyahu (and his wife, over the Milchan and Elovitch affairs). Mendelblit, however, still tried to prevent this from happening. He took the extraordinary step of summoning all the living former attorneys general, including Prof. Aharon Barak and Meir Shamgar. At the meeting he convened, they all came out in favor of professional conduct and backed the prosecution's approach. Left without a choice, Mendelblit moved toward indicting Netanyahu. Here, too, however, he failed to listen to the prosecution's recommendations and was lenient with the prime minister. He exonerated Sara Netanyahu from all the charges, leaving the prime minister as the sole defendant. In the Milchan and Mozes cases, too, he reduced the severity of the charges against Netanyahu and dropped the recommended charge of bribery. In doing so, he went against the recommendations of most of the team of state prosecutors working on the case. An analysis of the indictment that was eventually submitted— which Mendelblit signed off on—shows that he even managed to use phrasing that favored Netanyahu. Netanyahu took full advantage of this and launched a campaign of division and incitement. At first, he targeted the Israel Police and its commissioner, Roni Alsheikh. Alsheikh, a nationalist and religious yeshiva graduate who lived for many years in Hebron, was also deputy director of the Shin Bet. Although he was a staunch right-winger, he was also a person of integrity and values, and he gave his full backing to police investigators, even though he knew that Netanyahu would not extend his three-year term as police chief by the traditional extra year. This is exactly what happened, and the police recommended filing three indictments against Netanyahu and his wife on a variety of serious corruption charges.

After inciting against the police and its investigators, Netanyahu then launched a campaign of slander and incitement against the State Prosecutor's Office and individual prosecutors after they accepted the police's recommendation. As a result, the lead attorney on the case was forced to use bodyguards, and both she and her family required protection. She and her husband were subjected to slanderous accusations, and even the permits she obtained for building work at her private residence were rigorously scrutinized. The other members of the prosecution team were also targeted. These attacks were conducted in the media—on television, radio, and social media networks—by journalists working on behalf of Netanyahu. The protests became violent, vicious, and brazen, filled with threats and curses against the State Prosecutor's Office, individual prosecutors, and police investigators. The state prosecutor, who gave his full backing to the investigating team, was ostracized. Netanyahu labeled anyone who worked against him a "traitor," a "leftist," or someone who "hates Netanyahu." The process of incitement—the agitation against law enforcement authorities, the police, and the State Prosecutor's Office—gained momentum to the point that these bodies lost the public's trust.

Surveys have shown that more than 50 percent of the public does not believe that the police and the State Prosecutor's Office have acted with integrity and honesty. The campaign of incitement and agitation later reached the court system as well, especially the Supreme Court. Netanyahu's campaign sought to portray the Supreme Court and its justices as a branch of the liberal and "leftist" establishment, insinuating that their credibility and integrity could not be trusted. In so doing, he undermined the status of the Israeli Supreme Court, which until then had enjoyed a reasonable level of prestige. It was no coincidence that when indictments were eventually filed against Netanyahu for the three aforementioned offenses (the *Milchan gifts affair*, the *Bezeq affair*, and the *Yedioth affair*), the opening of his trial was accompanied by thousands of agitated demonstrators gathered outside the Jerusalem District Court and in the adjacent streets, shouting slogans against the State Prosecutor's Office and the courts. Meanwhile, Knesset members gave strident speeches claiming that the prosecution and the police had manipulatively manufactured the indictments against Netanyahu. On the first day of the trial, Netanyahu appeared at the entrance to the courthouse, flanked by a dozen or so government ministers, where he delivered a speech inciting against the prosecution and the police to the media and the Israeli people. He stood behind a lectern bearing the official emblem of the State of Israel. Because of the coronavirus pandemic, they were all wearing facemasks.[101] This behavior, which is that of a ruler who has lost all restraint, continued Netanyahu's campaign of incitement and his efforts to crush the public's trust in every branch of law enforcement: the police, the prosecutor's office, and the courts. It should come as no surprise, therefore, that progress in the trial was glacial. Over four years since it began, the end of the trial is nowhere in sight—and it is doubtful whether it will continue at all. Then, after an indictment was filed and criminal proceedings had commenced, it appeared that Israel was heading toward its fourth general election within a two-year period. In the run-up to the election, civil rights groups filed several petitions with the Supreme Court, arguing that, according to the laws of the State of Israel, an individual against whom three indictments for serious offenses—including bribery—have been filed cannot be appointed prime minister.

This might sound like a reasonable argument. Nonetheless, a panel of 11 Supreme Court justices unanimously ruled that there was no impediment to Netanyahu serving as prime minister while on trial for three criminal charges. The court ruled that the rules which apply to every civil servant, no matter how junior, and also to ministers under Israeli law and court rulings, miraculously do not apply to the Israeli prime minister. There can be almost no doubt that the public atmosphere of terror, threats, and incitement against the Supreme Court, created by Netanyahu and his supporters in the months preceding this hearing, directly or subconsciously influenced every justice on that Supreme Court panel. It is impossible, of course, to prove this, but given the circumstances, there is no way to explain this unanimous ruling without even a single judge offering a minority opinion. This was a critical turning point in the history of Israel's fragile

---

101. See picture on page 120.

democracy—a moment of truth and a historic juncture for the Supreme Court. It had to stand courageously and prevent the destruction of the system of honesty and public decency. But the High Court was overwhelmed and did not pass the test—the greatest test in its history.

By this stage, the battle over the fundamental elements of Israel's system of government and the status of the Supreme Court had been determined. The fact that the Supreme Court could be browbeaten by a campaign of intimidation, agitation, and threats became evident to all. History is full of decisive and fateful confrontations. This one ended in an 11-to-zero ruling in Netanyahu's favor.

The Submarines and Navy Vessels Affair

From within this maelstrom of investigations, reports suddenly started appearing in the media that Netanyahu's cousin—an American businessman named Nathan Milikowsky—had given Netanyahu hundreds of thousands of dollars between 2008 and 2010 to pay taxes on a dividend that Netanyahu had received from a private company based in the United States in which he owned shares. The case came to light by pure chance. By that time, Netanyahu was already serving as prime minister and had approached the Exemptions Committee for permission to receive additional loans from Milikowsky. A Pandora's box was suddenly opened, and its contents were gradually revealed. While all this was unfolding, suspicions grew that, in 2010, Prime Minister Netanyahu was involved in the decision-making process for the procurement of submarines and had pushed for Israel to purchase advanced submarines[102] from the German conglomerate ThyssenKrupp. Once stories began appearing in the press, there was a public campaign demanding that a criminal investigation be launched into those involved in the deal. The investigation revealed that at least three submarines—each worth around

---

102. This was expected to be the 6th submarine in the service of the Israeli Navy.

$600 million—had been purchased from ThyssenKrupp while Netanyahu was prime minister. It also emerged that the Defense Ministry had requested to procure four missile boats to defend Israel's offshore gas drilling platforms from terrorist attacks or state aggression. Another of Netanyahu's cousins, an attorney, interfered in the process and invoked Netanyahu's name in an effort to annul the tender. As a result,[103] the tender was canceled and the contract for the boats (with different specifications) was instead awarded to ThyssenKrupp. Each missile boat cost 100 million dollars. Once again, Attorney General Mendelblit was asked to rule on the issue. Here, too, he stymied the investigation—first by refusing for weeks to allow the police to launch a criminal probe and then by referring to it as an "examination," a concept that does not exist in Israeli penal law. Moreover, immediately after initiating the so-called "examination," he publicly declared that Netanyahu had nothing to do with the case and was not under suspicion at all. In so doing, he effectively exonerated Netanyahu from a case that was just starting to come to light— without even the most preliminary investigation having been completed. This was fundamentally odd behavior, and eyebrows were raised.

There were, however, deeper and more concrete reasons to explain Mendelblit's conduct.[104] Whenever he had an opportunity to thwart or limit the scope of the investigation, he took it. In doing so, he caused grave harm to the rule of law, which is a critical pillar of any democratic society. Some claim, without concrete evidence, that while serving as attorney general, Mendelblit may

---

103. One should also take into account that the German government provided a grant of 115 million Euros.

104. This puzzling announcement by Mendelblit at such an early stage of the investigations might also have sabotaged the work of the police investigation, because the moment the head of the public prosecution publicly announced that the main suspect here, Prime Minister Netanyahu, "is not a suspect at all," it sends a message to others involved in this very serious affair that they should not cooperate with those investigating Netanyahu – including perhaps even turning state's witness and testifying against him – since the head of the public prosecution has already expressed his opinion that Netanyahu is not a suspect at all.

have unwittingly or inadvertently been involved in the submarine sales to Egypt—possibly without full awareness of other vested interests at play. Courageous and diligent journalists, assisted by citizens rallying to save Israeli democracy, managed to expose the bigger picture—despite the absence of a substantive police investigation. Their revelations brought to light some horrifying facts and raised concerns that Netanyahu might have committed grave criminal offenses, perhaps even compromising national security. How so? It became evident that in August 2007, while serving as chairman of the opposition, and Knesset member, Netanyahu "purchased" shares in NMSD, a U.S.-registered private company owned by the Milikowsky family. NMSD held shares in another American company—Seadrift Coke.[105] Thus, Netanyahu indirectly owned approximately 1.0 percent of the shares in Seadrift, headquartered in Texas, which the Milikowsky family had acquired through NMSD in 2005 for a relatively low price. According to Netanyahu, he purchased that 1.0 percent share in the company, indirectly through NMSD, for $600,000. However, he has never presented a contract for the purchase of those shares, nor has he shown proof that payment was made and transferred. Of course, Netanyahu was not required—and therefore did not present—any of the standard documents that typically accompany a legitimate share purchase. These include an orderly purchase agreement, customary due diligence procedures, expert valuations, negotiations, site visits to company facilities, or any prior assessment of the shares' value before the acquisition. This is particularly unusual given that the shares were in a private company, meaning they were not freely traded and could be difficult to sell, if at all. The lack of transparency surrounding the transaction raised significant concerns, but Netanyahu never provided a satisfactory explanation.

In itself, this conduct is unusual. But this is just the start of the story. It subsequently transpired that, six months later, a

---

105. Seadrift Coke manufacturer of petroleum needle coke.

company called GrafTech, which was traded on the New York Stock Exchange, purchased 18.9 percent of the shares in Seadrift for $115 million—valuing Seadrift at approximately $715 million. Netanyahu purchased his shares in Seadrift[106] from his cousin, Mr. Milikowsky, at a valuation of about $55-$65 million. That represents a discount of about 90 percent (minus liabilities in NMSD, the family company). The result, of course, is more than bizarre and raises serious and pressing questions. This kind of "gift" prompts questions about why Netanyahu was allowed to purchase the shares at such a massive discount (assuming that he actually paid the sum of $600,000[107]). Later, the picture worsened. When acquiring a private company that is not traded on the stock exchange, the question of an "exit" is critically central at the time of acquisition. The buyer wants to know how (and when) they can sell the asset; otherwise, they could be "stuck" with the shares, unable to realize their value through resale. At this stage, the story takes an even more egregious turn. In 2008, a major financial crisis in the United States affected economies worldwide, including Seadrift, which experienced difficulties as revenue and profitability declined. Seadrift applied to GrafTech for a substantial loan.

Negotiations ensued between GrafTech, Seadrift, and Milikowsky, culminating in GrafTech purchasing the remaining Seadrift shares (along with another company owned by Milikowski)[108] and Milikowsky received cash, five-year bonds totaling $150 million, and shares in GrafTech, making him GrafTech's major shareholder.[109] On November 30, 2010—the day before the deal was due to close, and by which time Netanyahu

---

106. Indirectly, whereas Netanyahu purchased shares in private company owned by his cousin which owned 61% of Seadrift.

107. No evidence was introduced to prove that Netanyahu actually paid 600,000 USD.

108. Seadrift was valued under this merger for approximately 310 Million USD, more than 50% less than its valuation in the 2008 transaction.

109. Approximately 11% of the issued shareholdings.

was already serving as prime minister of Israel,[110]—there was a twist in the narrative. Milikowsky purchased all of Netanyahu's shares in NMSD for $4.4 million. In other words, he paid Netanyahu more than seven times the price Netanyahu had paid him just three years earlier. It should be noted that during this period, Seadrift was at a low point in its business cycle, and the deal to buy the remaining 81 percent of Seadrift's shares by GrafTech was at a much lower valuation than GrafTech's 2008 purchase of 19 percent of Seadrift's shares (approximately $310 million compared to $715 million in the first transaction). Meanwhile, Netanyahu sold his shares to Milikowsky at seven times the price at which he had purchased them.

This is an extremely rare occurrence in the business world. Indeed, when one examines this deal from the purchase stage to the date of sale, it can only be described as miraculous—the kind of deal that makes no economic, financial, or business sense. In 2015, Milikowsky sold all of his shares in Graphtec and his bonds, and it appears that he made hundreds of millions from the deal. In the meantime, Netanyahu, as prime minister, started working on the process of acquiring maritime vessels and submarines for the Israeli Navy—this time, from German conglomerate Thyssen-Krupp. In 2010, before he sold his shares to Milikowsky and while he was serving as prime minister, Netanyahu started to advance the purchase of submarines and other navy vessels from ThyssenKrupp. One of GrafTech's most important customers at that time was ThyssenKrupp. It was in GrafTech's interest to increase procurement of submarines and navy vessels from ThyssenKrupp since each such purchase would indirectly increase the sales of Graphtec's products to ThyssenKrupp. As mentioned, between 2010 and 2015, a significant shareholder in GrafTech was Mr. Milikowsky, Netanyahu's cousin. Later, between 2011 and 2015, Netanyahu promoted additional deals worth around $2 billion for security boats and three more submarines for the Israeli

---

110. Netanyahu returned to power on March 31, 2009.

Navy—all of them from ThyssenKrupp. Moreover, Netanyahu also helped ThyssenKrupp by selling "advanced submarines"[111] from ThyssenKrupp to Egypt. In so doing, he increased Thyssen-Krupp's sales. It is important to know that Germany—because of the Holocaust and the sense of responsibility it feels toward Israel—did not sell operational weapons to Arab countries without first allowing Israel to inspect the equipment being sold and approve the deal. This is part of the "special relationship" between the two countries.

Due to this relationship, Germany would not have allowed ThyssenKrupp to sell its advanced submarines to Egypt. And then, in 2016, the Israeli Defense Ministry found out that Egypt had purchased two advanced submarines from ThyssenKrupp at a value of more than $1 billion. Moshe Ya'alon, the former army chief of staff, who was serving by then as defense minister, was shocked. He did not remember ever having given the Germans approval for such a deal nor was there any internal discussion on this matter. He contacted Netanyahu and asked him straight out whether he was aware of any such request and whether Netanyahu, as prime minister, had approved it. Netanyahu vehemently denied any involvement in the approval and said he knew nothing about it. Later, Israel's then president, Mr. Reuven Rivlin, made a state visit to Germany where he met, among other, Chancellor Angela Merkel. Ahead of the presidential visit, Ya'alon asked Rivlin, when he met with Mrs. Merkel, to ask her whether the German government has sought permission from Israel to sell advanced submarines to Egypt. Rivlin did indeed ask the chancellor about the matter. Merkel was surprised by the question and asked Rivlin, "Do you not keep ordered records in Israel!?" She then asked the German cabinet secretary whether Israel had given its approval. He reported back to Merkel, who in turn informed Rivlin that Israel had, indeed, given its approval

---

111. The euphemistic way of referring to nonconventional capabilities on submarines.

and that the approval came from the prime minister. Rivlin was shocked. When he returned to Israel, he informed Ya'alon what he had discovered, and the defense minister once again sought clarifications from Netanyahu. And once again, the prime minister denied all involvement.

However, there were more surprises and discoveries to come. In 2018, during an election campaign, Netanyahu was on his way to the airport when he surprised the Channel 12 television station by agreeing to an interview. He did so because he had become hysterical during the campaign.[112] In the interview, it was Netanyahu's turn to be surprised when he was asked about the shares in Seadrift and the approval given to ThyssenKrupp to sell advanced submarines to Egypt. Then, for the first time, and apparently under extreme psychological pressure, Netanyahu admitted that he was the one who had approved the sale of the advanced submarines to Egypt—but insisted that there were two or three other people who knew about it, two of whom strenuously denied the claim. Everyone involved in the case was stunned, as this admission contradicted years of Netanyahu's vehement denials. Yet, disappointingly, the Israeli public was not infuriated or agitated. By this time, Netanyahu already controlled most of the media outlets in Israel—the mainstream television stations (thanks to local and foreign tycoons), the print media (with one exception)—and his systematic and continuous brainwashing of the public was in full force.

And so, an affair that many believe to be the most serious in Israel's history, involving severe elements of potential corruption and the undermining of the country's very security interests, was allowed to pass without a thorough investigation. As soon as the case was raised by the Israeli press in 2016, Mendelblit publicly announced—before any formal inquiry had taken place and without all the facts being brought to light—that the prime

---

112. Netanyahu, who is known to become hysterical and panic quickly and is unable to withstand real pressure. See Ariel Sharon's comments about him in a television interview.

minister was not a suspect in any of the incidents. In doing so, he effectively exonerated and cleared Netanyahu of all suspicions. Not only did Mendelblit abdicate his primary role, but he also granted Netanyahu de facto immunity from investigation.

One may assume that, for example, any potential witnesses against the prime minister—if they already existed—realized that there was no point in testifying or turning state's witness and cooperating with the prosecution, given that the attorney general had effectively declared Netanyahu immune from prosecution and not even a suspect in the case. As a result, the most egregious case of alleged government bribery in Israel's history was buried without investigation. This conduct had severe implications for the rule of law in Israel. A potentially explosive affair was simply buried and never thoroughly or properly investigated, allowing the main protagonists to evade responsibility and avoid explaining their actions.[113] This moment had dramatic ramifications for the erosion and destruction of the rule of law in Israel. At the same time, Netanyahu and many others internalized that threats, slander, and intimidation were enough to convey a clear message to those entrusted with preserving the rule of law—including the person in charge of

---

113. In 2022, during the time of the short-lived government that replaced Netanyahu, a commission of inquiry was appointed, headed by the former president of the Supreme Court, Dr. Grunis, and with the former governor of the Bank of Israel and other prominent individuals. The committee was authorized to investigate the procedures for purchasing naval vessels, submarines and anti-submarine ships from Thyssenkrupp, and the authorization of the sale of advanced submarines by the German government to Egypt. In June 2024, the committee issued initial warnings to several individuals, including Benjamin Netanyahu. The latter was suspected of, inter alia, pushing for the purchase of a sixth submarine "without proper groundwork and deviating from operational needs determined by the government." He also "promoted the purchase of two anti-submarine ships from Germany without reporting and documentation, and without the involvement of the defense establishment" (a move that was halted in the end) and "gave his permission to sell submarines to a third party (apparently Egypt) while concealing these consents from Israeli relevant state officers and not documenting meetings and creating parallel and contradictory channels of action, thereby endangering state national security and sabotaging the foreign relations and economic interests of the State of Israel."

the prosecution, Mendelblit. It was a dramatic defeat for Israeli law enforcement.[114]

Meanwhile, the other three affairs surfaced and continued to make headlines. For reasons of brevity, they were referred to as Case 1000 (the case involving billionaire Milchan), Case 2000 (the conspiracy between Netanyahu and Yedioth Ahronoth publisher Arnon Mozes regarding Israel Hayom), and Case 4000 (the Bezeq and Elovitch affair).

In these investigations as well, Mendelblit, who was responsible for overseeing law enforcement, worked to limit the scope of the probes and restricted police interrogations.

There were five meetings between Netanyahu, Mozes, and a prime ministerial adviser. All were recorded (one by Netanyahu himself). The recordings came to light during an investigation into Netanyahu's adviser, who handed them over to investigators. Mendelblit was only forced to dust off the recordings and order an investigation after a journalist revealed their existence.

The result of the investigations known as Case 1000, Case 2000, and Case 4000 was that the State Prosecutor's Office concluded there was sufficient evidence to convict Netanyahu in all of them, and that he should, therefore, be indicted on charges of bribery and breach of trust. Once again, Mendelblit dragged his feet and refused to decide for months. Eventually, he indicted Netanyahu on reduced charges. In Case 2000, for example, the bribery charge was dropped and replaced with acting in deceit and breach of trust by a government officer, even though all the attorneys who handled these cases—including the state prosecutor at the time—had favored bribery charges in these cases as well.

When the investigations began, and later when the decision was made to indict Netanyahu, the prime minister worked together with a team of public relations professionals—including his son, Yair Netanyahu—and in cooperation with members

---

114. In July 2021, the Supreme Court ruled that this conduct did indeed raise puzzling questions but decided not to intervene in the attorney general's decision not to launch a criminal investigation against Netanyahu.

of the media, public state-run outlets, television stations, the written press, and social networks, to launch a smear campaign of slander, lies, and threats. Initially, they targeted the police investigators, then the police commissioner, a religious right-winger and former senior Shin Bet officer, who fully backed the police investigators once he was exposed to the investigative materials against Netanyahu. All were accused of bias against the prime minister. Later in the campaign, the term "leftist" became the go-to label for calling Netanyahu's opponents traitors. Netanyahu and his team orchestrated everything, but the prime minister himself tried to do his part clandestinely. Once the investigations were completed and the decision was passed on to the State Prosecutor's Office and the attorney general, the smear campaign shifted from the police and its investigators to the State Prosecutor's Office and the chief prosecutor.

The entire campaign was orchestrated to attack specific prosecutors, including the prosecutor in charge of all those cases, Deputy State Prosecutor Liat Ben-Ari. The attorney general was also subjected to a campaign of threats and slander, with every incident from their past—real or fabricated—becoming the subject of defamatory articles and demonstrations outside their homes. The antagonistic atmosphere toward law enforcement, orchestrated by Netanyahu, became the norm. Aspersions were cast against every law-enforcement official, police officer, and prosecutor. The foundations of the rule of law, which are not exempt from legitimate criticism, were turned into enemies of the state. Those upholding the rule of law were disparaged as "leftists" or accused of fabricating false charges against Netanyahu. The general public was taken in by these campaigns—either due to a lack of understanding of the facts, insufficient education to form an independent and informed opinion, or because they belonged to social groups that already harbored resentment toward other groups in Israel. By this stage, the legal proceedings had reached the courtroom, and indictments had been filed. The panel of judges also became targets of lies and slander on social media. The head of the panel, an experienced judge, was labeled a "leftist," and the campaign even sought to dig up dirt on her son, who worked as an intern at a law firm. As a result, it was evident that the judicial system—including the court—was also influenced by fear and intimidation. The situation was so fraught that, on the day the indictments were read out in court, thousands of inflamed Netanyahu supporters gathered in the streets next to the courthouse. Lawmakers from the ruling Likud party openly shouted slogans of contempt and hatred at the State Prosecutor's Office, the state prosecutor, Mendelblit, and the court itself.

Netanyahu himself appeared in court and stood at the entrance to the courtroom, ensuring that the official emblems of the state were clearly visible in the background of his speech. He stood at the podium, flanked by many of his ministers standing silently behind him, and delivered an aggressive, violent, and threatening

speech. In it, he attacked police investigators, the State Prosecu-tor's Office, and the attorney general, accusing them all of involve-ment in a conspiracy and of fabricating suspicions and baseless indictments against him. To see Netanyahu inciting against Isra-el's law enforcement authorities was both insane and terrifying. Yet, the Israeli public, for the most part, accepted this with under-standing. A combination of a failed education system, social polarization, and various societal divisions in Israel allowed this extreme and destructive spectacle to take place. The erosion of the rule of law and legal institutions was in full swing. Netanyahu led a campaign to dismantle and crush the institutions of law in Israel. And Netanyahu, it must be said, is exceptionally skilled at spreading incitement and lies with resolute pathos. A broad swathe of the public buys into these words of incitement.

Now, Netanyahu embarked on a prolonged campaign to safe-guard his grip on power, even at the cost of crushing the institu-tions of law and order in Israel. As a result, the smear campaign and incitement turned against the few journalists who remained committed to reality and reporting the truth. At the same time, he launched an unrestrained attack on the Supreme Court, portray-ing it as an elitist, "leftist" institution that rules according to its own interests and worldview. This campaign of incitement significantly undermined the standing of the Supreme Court in public opinion. As already mentioned, the foundations of civics education in Israel are limited to certain social groups. Signifi-cant segments of the population lack the ability and knowledge to understand facts and processes on their own. The education system is weak, investment in education is low relative to other OECD countries, and large parts of the public study in non-state educational frameworks where subjects such as history, civics, mathematics, science, and English are not taught. As a result, a lack of respect for the courts—and the Supreme Court in particu-lar—began to permeate the public. It was increasingly viewed as a "liberal" stronghold and became increasingly isolated. This was despite the fact that, in reality, the Supreme Court in Israel had not been truly "liberal" for many years. It was not groundbreaking and was composed largely of conservative justices, most of whom held centrist and right-wing views. Some were even settlers in the West Bank.[115] However, none of this deterred those behind the campaign of slander and incitement. Indeed, the campaign proved enormously beneficial for Netanyahu. In the 2020 election campaign—the fourth election in just 30 months—a petition was filed with the Supreme Court arguing that, according to Basic Law: The Government, Netanyahu could not run for prime minister while facing three indictments for serious corruption offenses. The Supreme Court, in a special enlarged panel of 11 judges, issued a unanimous ruling (!) determining that the Basic Law did not bar Netanyahu from running. This astonishing legal ruling marked a historic milestone in the history of the Supreme Court and contributed to the erosion of Israeli democracy. Every reasonable person understands that this was an unreasonable, immoral, and unethical ruling. A prime minister facing indictments for bribery and breach of trust is an intolerable phenomenon by any standard.

Even more astonishing is the fact that the same Supreme Court, some 30 years earlier, had ruled that an individual facing an identical indictment could not serve as a minister. And yet now, under this ruling, he could nevertheless serve as prime minister. The Supreme Court was fully aware of this glaring inconsistency but still ruled unanimously. A unanimous ruling—without a single dissenting voice—proves that the campaign of intimidation and threats against Supreme Court justices and the chief justice had borne fruit. How else can we explain such an unequivocal ruling without even one dissenting opinion? Now, of course, a person facing indictments for extremely serious offenses can serve as the prime minister of Israel and run for re-election. He can hold meetings with the justice minister, influence the selection of members

---

115. At the time of writing, there are two Supreme Court justices who lives in Judea and Samaria. Another justice is a member of the national-religious camp and was active in the settlement movement in her youth.

of the Judicial Appointments Committee, and contribute to the decision over the next attorney general, who is also responsible for the public prosecution. This is an utterly chaotic situation, one in which the foundations of proper governance and the principle of setting a moral example for the public are being systematically destroyed.[116] There are In democratic countries, even the suspicion of minor offenses has led prime ministers to resign. Meanwhile, in Israel, the Supreme Court and public opinion enabled a prime minister facing bribery indictments to remain in power. It is little wonder that Israel has dropped in the global corruption index—from a respectable 14th place just 27 years ago to an undignified 36th place today.

From time to time, however, history presents a critical and challenging test. The Supreme Court faced one such fateful decision—and failed. The consequences of this failure and the fear that gripped Israel's Supreme Court were encapsulated in a historic statement made by Chief Justice Esther Hayut during the hearing: "The fortress does not fall," she said, referring to the last bastion of the rule of law. But the fortress did fall. And, tragically, the Supreme Court played a role in its collapse.

The ruling was a major boost for Netanyahu and all his supporters. They understood that the campaigns of incitement, lies, and threats to the legal system—the Supreme Court included—had produced the desired results. This gave them the green light to ramp up incitement, violence, lies, and threats across all traditional and social media. Netanyahu became more confident in his ability to prevent the course of justice and make the institutions of law and justice ineffectual. From that moment on, Netanyahu and his natural partners—United Torah Judaism and Shas, the Ashkenazi and Sephardic ultra-Orthodox parties—along with the settlers who came to prominence in Otzma Yehudit and Habayit Hayehudi, recognized that the rule of law, the police, the prosecutor's office, the court system, and the Supreme Court

---

116. Netanyahu undertook to preserve non involvement in any actions which has relevance or effect on the proceedings.

itself could be manipulated and that the latter could be brought to the point of complete submission. Indeed, this process has been unfolding ever since. Aryeh Deri, a Knesset member, minister, and head of the Shas movement, which is mainly supported by immigrants from North Africa with basic religious tendencies (see Chapter 4), has served in the past as interior minister. During his term of office, he was indicted for fraud and stealing money from the coffers of public associations. Deri was convicted, his appeal to the Supreme Court was rejected, and he was sentenced to three years in prison. Seven years after his conviction and after completing his sentence, he returned to political activity and the chairmanship of Shas. Deri has been Netanyahu's political partner for many years; together, they allegedly have plotted and conspired in cases that verged on criminality.[117] Their political partnership dates back to 1996. Between 2009 and 2021, when Netanyahu served uninterrupted as prime minister, Deri was the interior minister in his government.

Once again, there were allegations that Deri evaded paying taxes on various incomes. By virtue of his position as attorney general, Dr. Mendelblit was required to make a decision in this matter. Instead of conducting the investigation efficiently and decisively, Dr. Mendelblit stalled for five long years. In the end, Deri was indicted on two charges of concealing income and evading taxes. In one instance, Deri sold his brother a real estate property and reduced the value of the sale by $400,000 to lower taxes. In the other, he failed to report real estate transactions totaling $500,000. These are severe offenses by any standard, and the usual punishment for them in Israel is up to two years behind bars. Mendelblit was dramatically lenient with the accused. First, instead of charging him with offenses under the Penal Code—concealment of income and tax evasion, both of which are serious offenses punishable by hefty jail terms—Deri was indicted under technical sections of the Penal Code, such as

---

117. The so-called "Bar-On-Hebron affair" in the 1990s, when Netanyahu was serving as prime minister.

the sale of real estate at a reduced price, which is nothing more than the offense of inaccurate or false reporting. Second, on the basis of technical provisions of the Penal Code, he reached an agreement whereby Deri would pay a fine of $45,000 (despite evading taxes to the tune of over $500,000) and call an end to his political career. This, at least, was the agreement as presented to the court by the State Attorney's Office representative and as noted by the judge in his ruling when he approved the arrangement between the prosecution (headed by Mendelblit) and Deri. Not a week passed, however, before Deri returned to political life and the helm of Shas. He continued to run the Shas political party in the run-up to the fifth election on November 1, 2022, and even served as a minister in Netanyahu's government. Later, following a petition filed, the Supreme Court ruled that Deri could not serve as a government minister because of his previous convictions and for misleading the Magistrate Court judge who handed down the sentence on the latest charges. After a week of delays, Netanyahu finally upheld the ruling, and Deri resigned from his position as interior minister and health minister.[118]

Mendelblit's handling of allegations against Netanyahu and Deri was repeated when it came to another of the prime minister's political partners—former Knesset member and health minister Mr. Yaakov Litzman, who was a representative of the ultra-Orthodox United Torah Judaism Party (see Chapter 4). As health minister and one of the most senior members of UTJ, Litzman was involved in the unsavory case of Ms. Malka Leifer, a Jewish citizen of Australia who ran an ultra-Orthodox school in Melbourne. Authorities in Australia accused her of sexually assaulting and raping eight schoolgirls and of abusing her position. She fled from Australia to Israel, where she claimed that she was unfit to stand trial and, therefore, could not be extradited to Australia. Psychiatric opinions, however, determined that she was competent to stand trial and could be extradited. Since Litzman

---

118. In practice, however, he still meets with civil servants from both ministries.

and Leifer were from the same stream of ultra-Orthodox Judaism, he came to her aid and sought to pressure the psychiatrist who determined that she was competent to stand trial and could, therefore, be extradited, in the hope that a dissenting opinion would emerge.[119] The police recommended that Litzman be criminally charged with fraud and breach of trust. Under Mendelblit's stewardship, the investigation lasted for three whole years, and when it was completed—just before the end of his term as attorney general—Mendelblit reached an agreement with Litzman and his lawyers, whereby the ultra-Orthodox former politician would be convicted of a criminal offense and pay a fine of $1,100. He simply turned a serious incident into a minor case. This is how the concepts of the rule of law and equality before the law gradually collapsed.

Under this civic atmosphere, the state prosecutor, who recommended indicting Netanyahu, found it difficult to find a new place of employment after the end of his term. His appointment to the Supreme Court, an appointment that would have been fitting for a man of his stature and qualifications under regular conditions, was completely unthinkable. He eventually found a job as a rector of the Israeli National Library. Deputy State Prosecutor Liat Ben-Ari, who managed the investigations against Netanyahu and the process of preparing and filing indictments against the prime minister, was threatened so often that she needed a bodyguard for several weeks. Even her son was threatened. Her house was targeted by violent and noisy protesters. She was vilified on social media, where slurs, curses, and insults were hurled at her. Her home also came under close inspection, and there were allegations that part of it had been constructed without a lawful building permit. They did everything they could to break her spirit and make her resign. The machine that produced the toxic defamation and threats was run entirely by many voices in the media and social networks. The trial itself is taking place in

---

119. Leifer was eventually extradited to Australia, where she was found guilty and sentenced to 15 years behind bars.

a Jerusalem courtroom. The panel of judges, who have also been subjected to threats, is operating slowly and cumbersomely. The hearings have been dragging on for almost four years, and the end of the trial is nowhere in sight. In the meantime, Israel held its fifth election in three-and-a-half years in November 2022. When the votes were counted, Netanyahu succeeded yet again in establishing the government, thanks to his coalition partners: Shas (headed by Deri); the ultra-Orthodox United Torah Judaism party; Habayit Hayehudi and Otzma Yehudit, both headed by religious, nationalist, messianic, extremist settlers (see Chapter 5). One of the issues Netanyahu and his partners intend to raise is changes to the way criminal proceedings can be brought against a sitting prime minister, as well as the option of "freezing" them as long as he remains in office. There have also been proposals to change the method of selecting judges, including, of course, Supreme Court justices, so that politicians control the process and can appoint judges of whom they approve. As part of the campaign to crush the rule of law and the status of law-enforcement authorities in Israel, there have also been calls for legislation that would prevent the Supreme Court from overturning laws that violate the basic rights of citizens. This is known as the Override Clause—which would allow a simple majority of Knesset members (61 out of 120) to annul any Supreme Court ruling that nullifies any provision of any law.

This is how Netanyahu hopes to neutralize the Supreme Court, turning it into a weak and ineffectual body. These processes are all part of other profound changes unfolding in Israeli society, including attempts to crush the independent media and to turn news outlets on mainstream television channels into mouthpieces for the Netanyahu regime. As a result, destructive processes are unfolding to crush and weaken fundamental elements of Israeli democracy. This includes weakening the Supreme Court, an override clause that would neuter its power, a "French law" that would prevent criminal proceedings against a sitting prime minister, and control over the judicial appointment process. In this way, and with the support of significant parts of the Israeli public, Israeli democracy is being emptied of its most basic characteristics; the rule of law and institutions that maintain it are being trampled, and democracy may turn into an empty vessel. These processes are part of an ever-intensifying internal struggle in Israeli society over the very character of Israel. Liberal, democratic Israel is slowly disappearing. Institutions and authorities whose role was to protect the rights of minorities (the LGBTQ community, Arabs, Reform Jews, and others) have seen their power weakened through attrition, threats, and legislative processes designed to crush their authority. When the Supreme Court faced its greatest test—when it was asked to rule on whether someone could run for prime minister while facing indictments for serious crimes— it ruled that this was permissible.

When put to the test, it was too weak to vigilantly defend the democratic nature of Israel's system of government. As a result, for a short period and during its most important challenge, the gatekeeper failed to stand up forcefully to defend the rule of law and was, so it seems, intimidated by Netanyahu and his large camp of supporters. The consequence of this failure is that Israel's fragile democracy is now on the verge of being shattered. Large segments of Israeli society lack education and understanding about the essence of the democratic system, its significance, and the importance of different groups in society being able to exchange opinions with a basic level of mutual respect. Under these circumstances, public figures who possess strong powers of manipulation and persuasion can influence and mislead public opinion.

Chapter 8

Crushing the institutions and rule of law

Benjamin Netanyahu is not the first Israeli prime minister to face criminal charges while in office. The first was Yitzhak Rabin, during his first term as prime minister. At that time, Prof. Aharon Barak, who would later be appointed president of the Supreme Court, was attorney general. During Rabin's term, it was revealed that while serving as Israel's ambassador to the United States, he had held a relatively modest sum of $20,000 in a foreign bank account. While he was legally entitled to have this money, Israel's foreign currency laws at the time prohibited citizens from holding accounts in foreign banks. The attorney general threatened to charge Rabin's wife, Leah, with illegally holding foreign currency in an overseas bank. As a result, Rabin resigned as prime minister. Indeed, there was a time, just four decades ago, when the Israeli government and its leaders respected the law, the attorney general, and his decisions. Compared to today's Israel, that feels like something from a different world. This was Israel in 1977. Later, during Ariel Sharon's tenure as prime minister, suspicions arose that his son had accepted between $2–3 million from a real estate developer, supposedly for "consultation on a realty project" in Greece—which never came to fruition. The suspicions led to a criminal investigation, but the probe was abruptly closed when Attorney General Menachem Mazuz, who would later become a Supreme Court justice, published a comprehensive report just four months after his appointment. The report ultimately concluded that there were no grounds for criminal proceedings against Sharon and his son.[120] However, the report raised difficult questions, and even a basic analysis of its facts—such as the payment of $640,000 for "surfing the internet for several months" and "searching for information about tourism in the proposed region for the project"—only intensified question marks s about the decision reached by the attorney general at the time. Nonetheless, the matter passed without criminal proceedings.

Later still, criminal investigations were launched against Ehud Olmert while he was serving as prime minister. Mazuz was still attorney general, and the state prosecutor was Moshe Lador, a diligent and determined man. They decided to conduct a preliminary investigation into Morris Talansky, a wealthy Jewish-American businessman who had allegedly paid Olmert tens of thousands of dollars over the years, which were suspected to be bribes. The investigation took place while Olmert—then the prime minister—waged an often-ugly battle against the State Prosecutor's Office, aided by his allies in various media outlets. Crude allegations were leveled against members of the prosecution and the state attorney in particular. However, in the end, Olmert accepted the judgment. He resigned as prime minister and continued to fight his case as a private citizen. The District Court eventually convicted him of accepting bribes and sentenced him to six years in prison. The High Court later reduced his sentence to 18 months after convicting him on one count of corruption, which he ultimately served. In Netanyahu's case, however, things unfolded very differently. His response to the criminal investigations led to the dismantling of Israel's system of governance, the pulverization of the judicial system, and the introduction of corruption, governmental lawlessness, racism, and discrimination into the very heart of the Israeli government. The moment investigations were launched into what became known as *Case 1000, Case 2000,* and *Case 4000,* Netanyahu—along with television journalists,

---

120. See Attorney General Menachem Mazuz's report, June 2004.

public relations experts, lawyers, social media influencers, and Knesset members from his own party, began a campaign of slander, threats, intimidation, and lies about the investigations. Unlike Olmert and Sharon, who generally respected law enforcement, Netanyahu acted differently. He launched wild, unrestrained, and direct attacks on the police officers involved in his cases. Insinuations and lies were spread about the police team and their motives.

When the police reached a critical juncture in their decision on whether to recommend an indictment against Netanyahu, the police commissioner—a former deputy director of the Shin Bet and a staunch right-winger, appointed by Netanyahu himself—became the target of personal attacks. He was labeled a "leftist" (a word that, by then, had taken on a derogatory meaning, equivalent to being called a traitor) and was subjected to a campaign of slander, invective, and threats designed to deter him. This pressure campaign did not succeed. The police recommended that the State Prosecutor's Office indict Netanyahu for serious offenses, including bribery, in *Case 4000*. In retaliation, Netanyahu refused to extend the police commissioner's term for a fourth year, as is customary, and ensured his departure after three years. At this stage, the decision on whether to file indictments moved on to a team of attorneys in the State Prosecutor's Office, headed by Attorney General Avichai Mendelblit—a former Military Advocate General who had also served as cabinet secretary under Netanyahu. From this point onward, the threats, lies, bullying, aggression, and intimidation campaigns escalated into a coordinated assault. The media and social networks became flooded with fabricated stories, conspiracy theories, and baseless claims that the State Prosecutor's Office was attempting a coup d'état. Members of Netanyahu's inner circle accused prosecutors of being "leftists" and launched a smear campaign against Mendelblit himself.

Facing pressure, Mendelblit, who did everything in his power not to indict the prime minister, convened former attorneys general, including former Supreme Court President Meir Shamgar and Professor Aharon Barak, for a two-day discussion. At this gathering, Mendelblit was given unequivocal support to file indictments. Under public scrutiny and internal pressure from members of the State Prosecutor's Office, including the state prosecutor, Mendelblit was forced to decide to file indictments in three different cases: Case 1000, Case 2000, and Case 4000 (the Bezeq affair). However, he moved to lower the severity of the charges; in two cases, he erased the bribery offenses and even removed Netanyahu's wife from the Case 4000 indictment—contrary to a sweeping recommendation by most members of the State Attorney's Office and state prosecution. Moreover, because of his fears—or perhaps for some other reason—Mendelblit even went to the trouble of convening a press conference, at which he apologized and tried to explain why he was "forced" to file the indictments. The moment the decision was made, Mendelblit and all the other attorneys involved became targets for threats, demonstrations, and hate speech on television and social networks. An ugly campaign, full of invective, lies, verbal violence, and sometimes the threat of physical violence, ensued—the kind of scenes usually witnessed in the Third World. Public opinion was immediately incited against the prosecution, and the Police Investigations Department and the Special Investigations Unit that dealt with such offenses (Lahav 433) were subjected to a similar campaign.

The general public, whose knowledge of the details of the charges comes from the mass media, was incited against the country's legal institutions. Incredibly, Netanyahu's popularity and standing among significant parts of the Israeli public were not harmed. Many other Israelis came to the painful realization that bribery is not viewed as a serious offense and does not disqualify an individual from serving as prime minister. It was a badge of shame for large parts of Israeli society. The process of moral erosion and the lack of respect for the truth became publicly visible. It is not by chance that between 1996, when

Israel was first included in Transparency International's Corruption Perceptions Index, and 2021, Israel fell from a respectable 14th place in the index to 36th. Netanyahu's keen senses helped him identify jealousy, grudges, and even hatred between different parts of Israeli society, among other things, on sectarian grounds, primarily among Jews from Arab countries toward Ashkenazi Jews and the "elite."[121]

This jealousy and resentment have existed in Israeli society since the 1970s, and various political leaders have used it to forge political careers (such as the late Menachem Begin and Aharon Abuhatzira, the founder of the "Tami" party). Netanyahu, however, exploited it in the most blatant, effective, and unrestrained way. Netanyahu has also turned the basic dispute between the so-called "right" and "left" in Israel (which are extremely vague concepts primarily based on attitudes toward the West Bank and the Palestinians) into a means of intensifying conflicts and disagreements—not by addressing the issues and substance of the debate, but by increasing hostility and hatred between different parts of Jewish society. As a result of a lengthy process—accompanied by the media, journalists who support Netanyahu on television networks and in the press, and a prolonged campaign on social networks—Netanyahu managed to deepen the animosity between the "right" and "left." So much so, in fact, that "leftist" became a derogatory word, equivalent to "traitor." Gradually, banners and slogans declaring that "Leftists are traitors" began to appear in the Israeli public sphere and on social networks, and in many parts of the public, the belief took root that leftists were treasonous to their country and supported the Arabs. This simplistic and empty-headed approach found fertile ground among significant segments of the Jewish public, whether due to ignorance and lack of education, resentment or grudge toward Ashkenazim, or due to the longstanding conflict

---

121. For that matter 'the elite" are mostly Ashkenazim, but not only, and their main feature is that they are educated, oppose Netanyahu and may have some "liberal" opinions.

between Israel and the Palestinians in Gaza and the West Bank, which engendered deep-held animosity among parts of the Jewish public toward them. Netanyahu, the masterful inciter and populist, instilled in public opinion the link between "leftists" and "supporters of Arabs." From there, it was a short path to calling them "traitors." Slowly but surely, proposals for dialogue and coexistence with the Palestinians, a political settlement in the West Bank, the suggestion that Israel return land in the West Bank, and any kind of solution to Jerusalem became minority opinions. No one in Israel could espouse such views without encountering extreme responses, including shouts, curses, threats, insults, and even physical violence. Thanks to Netanyahu, many parts of the Israeli population internalized that "leftists are traitors." At a later stage, anyone who did not support Netanyahu was subjected to such treatment. For example, Mr. Avigdor Lieberman, who for years was Netanyahu's political partner, distanced himself from him in 2015. The moment that Lieberman severed his political ties with Netanyahu, he found himself branded a "leftist." The great irony is that Lieberman lives in the West Bank settlement of Nokdim and is clearly part of the right-wing camp and has been since he was a youth. His father was a Beitar activist in Romania, and Lieberman continued that tradition when he immigrated to Israel from Moldova. But, as we have already established, anyone who is not a political ally of Netanyahu becomes an extremist and is immediately branded a "leftist" and, of course, a "traitor" by Netanyahu and his supporters.

As criminal proceedings and investigations against Netanyahu intensified in 2015 and 2016, so too did the incitement, combined with the takeover of traditional media outlets, including the embedding of journalists and media personalities who supported Netanyahu. Initially, he tried to pass legislation that would allow the newspaper *Israel Hayom*—which, at that time, was still blatantly and unilaterally supportive of Netanyahu[122]—to

---

122. "Israel Hayom" has since changed its tone in relation to Benjamin Netanyahu.

continue operating as a free newspaper, in order to crush the rest of the independent press (primarily *Yedioth Ahronoth*) and to allow Netanyahu indirect control over a media outlet with a large readership, which he believed would enable him to shape public opinion.

For a variety of reasons, these efforts were not successfully accomplished. However, in the 2015 elections, Netanyahu chose to weaponize fear—especially the fear felt among some parts of the Jewish public toward Israeli Arab citizens, who make up 21 percent of the overall population. Thus, on election day itself, in order to motivate and energize his supporters to go to the polls, Netanyahu embarked on a systematic campaign of disseminating news in various media outlets and social networks that "Arab voters are heading to the polling stations in droves." This slogan of intimidation was designed to mobilize his supporters to get out and vote. Netanyahu once again used his considerable capabilities to divide and incite against parts of Israeli society and to sow hatred and division—this time against Arab citizens, and on other occasions between left and right, settlers versus leftists, messianic national religious groups versus secular Israelis, and immigrants from Arab countries against Ashkenazim.[123]

Moreover, when the result of that election meant that he could not cobble together a coalition without partnering with an Arab party, he very quickly changed his tune. He began to passionately court sectors of Arab society. He started by visiting the Bedouin in the Negev—something he had not done since 2009, the start of his term as prime minister—and he visited Arab communities, where he declared that there were "good Arabs" who were equal partners in Jewish society. He even courted and conducted lengthy negotiations with Dr. Mansour Abbas, chairman of the United Arab List, which was founded by Sheikh Abdullah Nimar Darwish and advocates for the full integration of Arabs into the State of

---

123. Even though Netanyahu himself is Ashkenazi on both sides: his mother, Tzila, was born in Petah Tikvah during the time of the Ottoman Empire and his father was Warsaw-born. Prof. Benzion Netanyahu (né Milikowsky).

Israel as a Jewish state. Abbas himself, a dentist by training, was brave, sharp, and a devout Muslim. During these campaigns of incitement, Netanyahu continued his efforts to undermine and weaken the country's law-enforcement authorities. His conduct was far from that of a statesman, who would have managed the affairs of the State of Israel from a broad perspective, considering all parts of Israel's diverse society and caring about its future. Statesmanship was the cornerstone of the ideology of David Ben-Gurion, who is considered the founder of the State of Israel and who also struggled with members of his own camp over it. For example, when he sought to dismantle *Palmach*, the paramilitary organization, immediately after Israel's Declaration of Independence, or when he wanted to transform the IDF into the only military body in Israel and to unequivocally subordinate it to the sovereign civil authority of the Israeli government.

Although this attitude toward the formal institutions of the State of Israel was continued by his adversary Menachem Begin when he was leader of the right-wing Likud party, it has become obsolete under Netanyahu. The pursuit, assumption, and preservation of power—and, since 2016, attempts to eliminate criminal investigations against him, followed by efforts to dismiss the indictments filed against him—became the very heart and center of Netanyahu's attention. As far as he is concerned, this goal justifies all means, and he believes that everything is permitted to achieve it. Of course, Netanyahu—a skilled, educated man who reads voraciously and has impressive rhetorical capabilities—would never admit this about himself and continues to talk about statesmanship and the general good. But there is nothing behind this rhetoric. There are many similarities between Netanyahu's conduct and that of other world leaders—such as Mussolini in the 20th century, as well as other world leaders.[124]

---

124. In his book "Eternal Fascism," famed Italian writer Umberto Eco described how fascists take hold of power and the characteristics of a rule in a fascist regime. See also Denis Mack Smith, *Mussolini, published by Oxford University Press.*

Anyone who examines the political reality in Israel in recent years under Netanyahu's rule will find many common characteristics. The next six years, from 2015 to June 2021, saw Netanyahu remain in power and dedicate himself entirely to implementing the aforementioned characteristics—incitement against law-enforcement bodies and the complete discrediting of lawyers from the State Prosecutor's Office in general, particularly the team in charge of legal proceedings against the prime minister. There was a verbally violent campaign, including threats of physical harm, against the head of the prosecution team, Liat Ben Ari. Along with her family, including her son, who serves in the IDF, Ben Ari was subjected to such constant threats that the State Prosecutor's Office was forced to apply to the court for a restraining order against a pro-Netanyahu activist to prevent further incitement on social media.

In addition, Netanyahu and his allies continued their campaign of threats and slander against the state prosecutor—until the state prosecutor was replaced by someone who was not known to be particularly intrepid. The police commissioner, who gave his backing to the team of officers who investigated Netanyahu (and his wife), had his term ended early, after just three years. Then, for more than two years, the Israel Police did not have a commissioner, thereby achieving excessive obedience from the interim commissioner. Only after a petition was filed with the Supreme Court and vocal public outcry did Netanyahu, via his police minister at the time, name a new police commissioner. He appointed a police commissioner who would clearly not dare to behave in the same way as his predecessor. Netanyahu worked vigorously to silence criticism of him in other areas as well. For the position of State Comptroller—a role that, in the past, was able to publish personal criticism against Israeli leaders (for example, the criminal proceedings and suspicions against former Prime Minister Ehud Olmert were initiated and advanced by the then-State Comptroller, the late retired judge Micha Lindenstrauss)—he appointed an accountant from the national-religious camp. Immediately upon beginning his term, Netanyahu's newly appointed State Comptroller ruled that he would stop investigating criminal suspicions and potential corruption. Indeed, the office patently failed to provide protection to whistleblowers, something it has the authority to do under Clause 45 of the State Comptroller Law. The courts and the judicial system in general, and the Supreme Court in particular, also became targets for incitement and campaigns aimed at crushing public trust in them. Generally speaking, the court system relies entirely on public trust.

Courts have no authority to allocate budgets, hand out grants, or give jobs. All their power, therefore, in a proper and functioning democracy, derives from a minimum level of public trust that allows them to function properly. It is also clear that an efficient, substantive legal system, free of influence from politicians or tycoons, is essential in an active democracy, alongside a free, diverse, and independent press and media. The Supreme Court was subjected to a campaign of smears and threats. There was even a move to stack the court with more right-wing justices. Between 2016 and 2021, three new justices (including one female judge) were appointed to the Supreme Court—all of them very clearly identified with the national-religious camp; two of them are residents of West Bank settlements, and the third was active in *Gush Emunim*, a civil movement advocating for settlements in the West Bank, in her youth. Other right-wing or conservative judges, particularly those with an inclination toward the national-religious camp, were also appointed. Despite this significant change in its composition—and as part of a campaign to undermine the credibility and authority of the Supreme Court in public opinion, using the same pro-Netanyahu media outlets and journalists—the Supreme Court and its justices were repeatedly portrayed as "leftist," especially whenever a certain ruling did not fully align with Netanyahu's public stance. As a result, as far back as 2015, there has been a noticeable tendency on the part of Supreme Court justices to avoid friction with the government and to refrain from making decisive rulings against the government or the West Bank settlement enterprise. Even rulings ordering the evacuation of settlements built on privately owned Palestinian land have become nothing more than a tailwind for the settlers' continued activities. Between 2020 and 2022, for example, the Supreme Court heard the case of Mitzpe Kramim, a Jewish outpost near Kochav Hashahar in the West Bank. The outpost was established on private land owned by Palestinians (some of the land in the West Bank is privately owned, while substantial parts are owned by the state, which, before the Israeli occupation, belonged to the Hashemite Kingdom of Jordan).

According to the government's Property Order issued by the Israeli government after the Six-Day War, if the conditions stipulated in the order are met, the state can recognize the validity of land transactions with the Custodian of Absentee Property, provided that they were made in good faith. In other words, the Custodian of Absentee Property thought they were state-owned properties, even though it later turned out that he was wrong. In this case, a group of Jewish settlers purchased land from the Custodian, built a settlement there, and some 45 families started living there. Later, a group of Palestinians petitioned the Supreme Court, arguing that since the land was privately owned, it should be returned to its rightful owners. The settlers who bought the land claimed that they did so from the Custodian, who also believed in good faith that the land was not privately owned. In 2020, a panel of three Supreme Court judges ruled, in a majority two-to-one opinion, that the Custodian had not acted in good faith and that there were many warnings over the years casting doubt on the true ownership of the land. The Supreme Court therefore ordered the cessation of all construction activity in the area, barred the erection of illegal structures, and ordered the removal of existing buildings. However, since the justices apportioned most of the responsibility for the situation to the Custodian and not the settlers, they gave the government three years to find a new home for the settlers on state-owned land before they would have to leave the current site.

As a result of its ruling, the Supreme Court was subjected to more threats and slander. Ayelet Shaked, a former Justice Minister, described it as "an accursed ruling" and said, "There is no justice here." The attacks on the Supreme Court continued, and a motion was filed for a second hearing on the case. Unsurprisingly, the charged public atmosphere, the incitement against Supreme Court justices and branding them as "leftists"—a dog whistle term for "traitors" or "Arab supporters"—bore fruit. In July 2022, an expanded panel of Supreme Court justices handed down a second ruling on the same matter. This time, by a majority opinion, the previous ruling was reversed. The honorable panel found that the Custodian of Absentee Property had acted in good faith and, therefore, overturned the previous ruling. The court's ruling meant that settlers were entitled to continue living in the existing buildings and that there was no impediment to further construction in the disputed area.

This decision, of course, delighted the settlers and was another nail in the coffin of Palestinians' faith in the Supreme Court. It was one example among many of the successes of the campaign of intimidation, threats, and incitement against the Supreme Court, which was ordered to toe the government line. This pressure evidently bore fruit, and subsequent Supreme Court rulings showed that the justices had internalized the message and accepted the idea that they must act "cautiously" in rulings that may not please Netanyahu or his coalition colleagues (the settlers, the religious nationalists, and the ultra-Orthodox). Without any legislative change, the Supreme Court changed. Between 1980 and 2014, the Supreme Court was not hesitant to make courageous and bold rulings on controversial matters; after 2014, however, there was a gradual process of decline in the "courage level." From 2015 onwards, the process was gradually and systematically completed. Netanyahu was indicted on three counts. Despite the criminal proceedings, he continued to serve as prime minister. An unimaginable situation came to pass: a serving prime minister facing severe criminal proceedings, including on charges of bribery. The outcome, needless to say, was utter collapse of the whole system. The prime minister and the ministers in the coalition—some of whom are responsible for appointing judges (the justice minister and Knesset members from the ruling party), the appointment of the police chief (as well as police investigators), the appointment of a state prosecutor—continued to function notwithstanding the accusation of bribery, deceit, and breach of trust. The judges in his criminal proceedings, incidentally, took the unusual decision to exempt Netanyahu from appearing personally at hearings during his trial, thus allowing him to be absent from the courtroom for most of the process. Between 2016 and 2021, there were five parliamentary elections in Israel. Each campaign involved physical and verbal violence, incitement on social media, and pro-Netanyahu content on enlisted media outlets. Every television channel was staffed by journalists who, whether for ideological reasons or self-interest, leaned toward Netanyahu and his right-wing coalition. But each time he managed to forge a coalition, it was short-lived. In June 2021, in the fifth of these elections, after a fraught campaign and extremely complicated and complex negotiations, no fewer than eight different parties—from completely different sides of the political spectrum: national-religious, Arab, right-wing, center, and left-wing—succeeded in forming a coalition without Netanyahu. To most observers, this was nothing short of a miracle. The chances of it happening were supposed to be nil. And yet, that is exactly what happened.

The establishment of a new government, however, also created a forceful, brutal, and violent backlash from the new opposition, headed by Netanyahu. When Netanyahu handed over power to his successor, MP Naftali Bennett, for example, he did so in a meeting that lasted less than 20 minutes. In a country as complex as Israel, it takes far longer for the transition of power to go smoothly. Netanyahu even refused to hold a ceremonial handover of power. From the outset, the Netanyahu-led opposition claimed that the new government was illegitimate and illegal, that

Bennett was a "traitor" who had abandoned his principles just to be prime minister. In his speeches in parliament, Netanyahu never addressed Bennett as the prime minister of Israel. There were shameful scenes in parliament when the new government was sworn in at the Knesset. During Bennett's inaugural speech, opposition members hurled insults and curses at the new prime minister, who is an honorable man, an unambiguous rightist, and a member of the national-religious camp who served for years as the director of *Gush Emunim*. Those disgraceful scenes made it clear to everyone that Netanyahu and his fellow opposition members were not planning on remaining in opposition for very long. Indeed, immediately upon the formation of the new government in June 2021, Netanyahu spearheaded a campaign to crush it. In the Knesset, the opposition refused to establish several parliamentary committees, and sessions in the plenum were constantly interrupted by shouting, abuse, and the kind of cacophony that would not be out of place in a rowdy dive bar. Legislation that would unquestionably have benefited the Israeli public—such as formalizing visa-free travel to the United States, something that Washington was helping with—was stymied solely because the opposition did not want to give the incumbent government any "achievement" that it could present to the public. Exactly the same thing happened with an extensive infrastructure and railways plan and even legislation for the benefit of Jewish residents of the West Bank, where the Israeli legal system applies only to Jewish residents and the relevant administrative order must be extended every five years. (The Palestinians, of course, have a different legal system). Moreover, opposition forces launched behind-the-scenes activities and public protests designed to crack the coalition.

These protests particularly targeted the homes of Knesset members from the coalition, especially those from the prime minister's right-wing party. They did so because they recognized that the people who vote for them and those who often attend the same synagogue gatherings as they do might add their voices to those calling on them to quit the coalition. The demonstrations also targeted Knesset members and their children in raucous protests where offensive slogans were chanted. As a result, and gradually, two members of Bennett's party withdrew their support for the government, along with one Arab Knesset member from the Labor Party and one member from the Arab party that had been part of the coalition. So, after just 14 months, the "miracle" disappeared.

The short-lived government was a bright spot during a difficult time for Israel, with parties from different political corners coming together to try and rectify some of the problems that occurred during Netanyahu's rule. The fact that this coalition included an Arab party for the first time was refreshing and auspicious. But this novel situation infuriated significant parts of the Israeli public—and Netanyahu made cynical but effective use of this fact. He managed, for example, to convince significant segments that Israel was being governed by a "pro-Arab government" and falsely claimed the government allocated 54 billion shekels (about $15 billion) for investments in the Arab sector. Netanyahu would later admit that the sum was much lower: around 2 billion shekels. This exacerbated the tense atmosphere of incitement, the hatred between sectors of Israeli society, and intolerance toward differing opinions. The media discourse became violent, aggressive, and narrow-minded. The treatment of law enforcement authorities also became violent, disdainful, and distrustful. Under these circumstances, it is very easy to manipulate the public's anger in the direction of the judicial system in general and the Supreme Court in particular. It is no wonder, given this atmosphere, that a panel of 11 Supreme Court justices—hearing a petition that argued that Netanyahu cannot serve as prime minister while criminal proceedings are pending against him in three serious cases, including charges of bribery—ruled unanimously that there is nothing in Israeli law to prevent Netanyahu from running for and serving as prime minister, despite the indictments and criminal proceedings being conducted against him in court. There were strong legal arguments for and against the petition, in legislation and in case law. Therefore, the unanimous ruling—which did untold damage to the very foundations of the struggle against public corruption and basic governmental norms—raises the reasonable assumption that the justices of the Supreme Court have been influenced, consciously or unconsciously, by the campaign of terror and incitement against them.

And so, with a blitz of threats and slander the new government fell. Once again, Israel was going to the polls—for the sixth time in four years! What an achievement. In the sixth election, Netanyahu's party won 32 seats, more than a quarter of the 120 seats in parliament. Along with the ultra-Orthodox parties (Sephardic and Ashkenazi, national religious and messianic), he had a 64-seat majority in parliament and was able to form a new coalition.

Chapter 9

The Collapse of Democratic Systems and Netanyahu's Total Surrender to Extremist Groups

After forming his sixth government, Netanyahu was seen by his coalition partners—the religious, Sephardic, and Ashkenazi ultra-Orthodox parties (see Chapters 4) and the Messianic, ultra-nationalist religious parties (see Chapter 5)—as a weak, hesitant, and indecisive political figure whose personal future, including evading his criminal trials and their potential outcome, depended on their cooperation. Thus, a Middle East-style bazaar ensued, with each party representing a different sector of Israeli society. A frenzied campaign of "grabbing as much as you can" began, with each party in the coalition reaching into the public coffers and looking out exclusively for the interests of the sector it represented. Netanyahu had purged his Likud party of anyone with even a modicum of gravitas and replaced them with yes-men, transforming the party from a statesmanlike entity into one that was weak and dependent on the goodwill of the coalition parties.

This was clearly evident in the composition of the new Israeli government and what each of the parties managed to obtain in their respective coalition agreements. To forge his government, Netanyahu was willing to concede to almost any demand by his coalition partners. Thus, he agreed to include in the coalition Mr. Ben Gvir, an ultra-racist and extreme right-wing politician who was for years a member of the Meir Kahane Group (until Kahane was assassinated in the United States). However, just weeks before the November 2023 election, in interviews, Netanyahu was asked whether Ben Gvir would be part of his coalition and serve as a minister in his future government if he were the winning candidate. Netanyahu firmly ruled out such.[125]

Take *Shas*, a Sephardic religious party that has been under the leadership of Aryeh Deri since 2010. Deri, a talented and capable man by all accounts, was convicted as far back as the 1990s of theft, bribery, and fraud while serving as Interior Minister. He was sentenced to three years in prison, and, after seven years had passed since he completed serving his sentence, he was once again named Interior Minister in a Netanyahu government. He later returned not only to that post but also served as Health Minister—despite having been convicted again in 2021 of additional tax offenses (evading capital gains tax and income tax). Although Deri seemed to suggest during court hearings in his most recent case that he would cease to serve in any public position, he was suddenly appointed to a senior position in Netanyahu's government. In its coalition agreement, *Shas* ensured that the new government would commit to promoting the ultra-Orthodox Mizrahi-Sephardic sector, which it represents. Among other things, the schools and kindergartens run by *Shas* that were supported by state funds received substantial financial returns, budgets for the construction of residential apartments for members of the sector were increased, and representation of members of the sector in local authorities, government-governed corporations, and government ministries was expanded. People who qualified as rabbis and religious court judges—occupations that are strictly religious—were granted the same rights as individuals with academic degrees when it came to government tenders and appointments. Of course, this policy encouraged

---

125. Soon after formation of the Government a petition was filed with Supreme Court asking to revoke the appointment of Ben Gvir as the minister of Internal Security. Inter alia, based on his ideology, criminal convictions (13), past membership in Kahane's group and incitement activity. On February 20, 2024 the Supreme Court rejected the application.

and supported those with a religious education who lack an academic or broad education. Instead of encouraging further education to expand knowledge in fields such as technology, research, and science, the Israeli government under Netanyahu provided increased economic and other assistance for an entire sector that rejects modern education and the kind of expertise required to cope in the 21st century. In Israel, the democratic system of government consists of different parties that represent different sectors of the population. Therefore, Netanyahu's partners in his new government signed, as is customary, coalition agreements with Netanyahu's Likud party. While we will not delve into all the details of these agreements, they contain several common threads that must be analyzed. Each party took care of its own sector. The most obvious result was that there was almost no concern for sectors that were not represented in the coalition parties. For example, the secular and even traditional sectors were not represented at all, and their interests were not addressed by the government.

In fact, there was no real concern for the State of Israel as a whole—for the development of comprehensive education, investment in state-run education, the Education Ministry itself, environmental development programs, and so on. Each group was solely interested in securing as large a portion of the budgetary pie as possible. Without a guiding hand to look after the general good, the welfare of the state, and the public that was not represented in the coalition, the government lacked balance. Additionally, there were a number of issues important to the coalition parties that also reflected the character of a significant part of Israeli society and the direction in which it was heading. The impact they would have on the future of the State of Israel and its relations with the Palestinians, the Arab world, the international community, the United States, and world Jewry—especially American Jewry—was enormous and should keep anyone concerned for the character and future of the State of Israel awake at night.

These issues can be broadly grouped into six main categories:

First issue: The West Bank/Judea and Samaria

In its agreements with the coalition parties, especially those not from the national-religious camp, the Likud party undertakes that "the people of Israel have a natural right to the Land of Israel. The Prime Minister and the Government of Israel will act to promote the application of sovereignty in the West Bank while choosing the timing in accordance with the national and international interests of the State of Israel" (coalition agreement with the Religious Zionist Party, Articles 118, 123, and others). The agreements also include specific references to investments for residents of the West Bank, expanding budgets for roads, infrastructure, and consolidating Jewish settlement, including a five-year plan for the expansion of West Bank settlements.

It is still unclear how and whether this will be implemented, but the very approach of the new government—and a significant part of the Jewish population, which has adopted a more extreme position vis-à-vis the West Bank and the Palestinians—leads to the continued erosion of the democratic character of the State of Israel. The occupation, with all it entails, creates an atmosphere and public consciousness that erodes the foundations of democracy, the need to be open to the exchange of different opinions, to accept disagreements as part of our way of life, and to resolve them through negotiations and compromises rather than by unilateral force (as is customary in the military regime that exists in the West Bank). Of course, this process is liable to cause severe damage to Israel's international standing, as many already view it as an occupying force enacting an apartheid regime. All of this endangers the State of Israel, its democratic nature, and its ties with the world, including American Jewry and international allies. Another issue is that nationalist-religious-messianic parties have gained power, securing budgets and control over governmental resources (funding and appointments to key positions) that can expand their public influence and push more sectors of Israeli society in a religious-messianic-ultra-Orthodox direction. For example, the *Otzma Yehudit* party is currently headed by Itamar Ben-Gvir, who serves as internal security minister in Netanyahu's government and, as such, is responsible for the Israel Police and Border Police. Ben-Gvir is a religious nationalist and holds racist views. In his youth—until just a few years ago—he was a supporter of the late Rabbi Meir Kahane. He lives with his family in Hebron. In his twenties, he was a staunch opponent of the Oslo Accords and of Yitzhak Rabin. There is an infamous video of him holding what he claimed was the hood ornament from Rabin's car, in which he says: "Just like we got to your car, we can get to you, too." This was an allusion to the possibility that someone could attack Rabin, which is exactly what happened just a few weeks later, when Yigal Amir shot and killed the prime minister. In later years, Ben-Gvir supported terrorist attacks against Palestinians and even had a portrait of Dr. Baruch Goldstein, who murdered 29 worshippers at the Cave of the Patriarchs. Before the Supreme Court eventually barred Kahane from running in elections, he briefly served in the Knesset. Every time he would address the chamber, then-Prime Minister Yitzhak Shamir—a former *Lehi*[126] commander and a staunch right-winger—would walk out in protest. Today, one of Kahane's disciples is among the leaders of the nationalist-religious settler camp—an extremist whose ideology mixes religion and racism, who is unwilling to compromise on the West Bank, and who has no desire to reach understandings or dialogue with the Palestinian Authority. Moreover, he has been indicted no fewer than 50 times and has been convicted at least eight times. The fact that his party won seven seats in the most recent elections testifies to the changes in Israeli society: increased radicalization to the right and a surge in nationalist religiosity. This is a dangerous and destructive process. But in Israel in 2024, rationality does not reign supreme.

---

126. Lehi is the abbreviation for a small insurgent group which during the 1940s fought against the British Mandate in Palestine.

The following are extracts from the coalition agreement between Likud party and Otzma Yehudit, under the leadership of Bezalel Smotrich:

- **Clause 118**—The People of Israel have a natural right to the Land of Israel. In light of the belief in this right, the Prime Minister will lead the formulation and promotion of a policy within which sovereignty will be applied in the West Bank, while choosing the timing and taking into account all the national and international interests of the State of Israel.

- **Clause 119**—Young Settlements: In accordance with notices previously given by the State to the Supreme Court with regard to the intention to regulate settlements, within 60 days of their establishment, the Government will pass a resolution regarding Young Settlements which were established prior to the decision of the ministerial team headed by the Prime Minister on February 28, 2011. As part of the arrangement, the government will take care of, among other things, humanitarian connection to water and electricity infrastructures, essential public buildings and other critical infrastructures, and the government will allocate the resources required for this purpose. During the first six months of the government's term, an additional resolution will be passed on regulating the unregulated neighborhoods in the old communities that were established prior to the decision of the aforementioned ministerial team. In the aforementioned government resolutions, it will be determined how the aforementioned localities will be treated during the interim period until the completion of the legislation. Should this be necessary, both for the young settlements and for the neighborhoods in the old settlements, legislation will be advanced to regulate the said settlements for the interim period.

- **Clause 123**—Within 60 days, the government will approve a five-year plan for the development and expansion of settlement in Judea and Samaria, which will be formulated by the Ministry of National Missions and the Settlement Administration. In order to implement the plan, the Finance Ministry will allocate, between 2023 and 2027, an amount as determined by the finance minister and approved in the state budget. In addition, in order to complete the team of directors general regarding Judea and Samaria payments, the relevant regional councils will be budgeted an amount to be agreed between the aforementioned regional councils and the Finance Ministry and the Interior, for the purpose of alternative sources of income.

- **Clause 129**—The government attaches strategic importance to the development of roads and infrastructure in Judea and Samaria for the benefit of Jews and Arabs who use the roads and for security and safety purposes, taking into account the large number of road accidents in Judea and Samaria and the infrastructure problems there. To this end, the Transport Ministry's five-year plan will include a designated budget of 1.6 billion shekels for each year allocated for the planning and implementation of roads in Judea and Samaria.

- **Clause 132**—Amendments to the security legislation shall be made by General Order in order to ensure equal and efficient arrangements regarding the execution and registration of real estate transactions.

- **Clause 135**—The Ministry of National Missions and the Settlement Administration shall prepare five-year plans for the development of areas in Judea and Samaria for the benefit of all residents of Judea and Samaria in accordance with a work plan formulated by the Ministry and in coordination with the Prime Minister and will submit them to the Cabinet for approval.

- **Clause 136**—From 2023, the anomaly regarding residents living in areas with a high security risk in Judea and Samaria (areas defined as 3-5 in the Central Command's threat classification) will be corrected so that they will be entitled to tax benefits, similar to residents of other threatened localities.

- **Clause 137**—As part of the balancing grants and special grants given to local authorities in Judea and Samaria, a full response will be provided to all the excess expenses of the authorities, first and foremost security, including a full response to the unique expenses of the Judea *and Samaria Regional Council.*"

Second issue: Religion and strengthening religious elements

Another process addressed in the coalition agreements is strengthening religious sectors in Israel, including increased budgeting for various religious purposes. What they all have in common is the strengthening of the religious aspect in Israel. And it is worth mentioning that in Israel there is no separation between religion and state. Religious leaders are involved in the government, leadership, political parties and the state budget. Strengthening religious elements today means strengthening the conservative side, which is alienated from the international community, shuts itself off from the rest of Israel, is not open to broad education and despises basic values such as equal rights and the status of women. LGBTQ groups are ostracized or subject to restrictions and, of course, Palestinians remain on the margins of society. This is a dangerous process that is changing the character of Israel— making it illiberal, hostile to different streams and opinions, not pluralistic and not open to the wider world. The coalition agreements also include a requirement that holders of the title Rabbi and Rabbinical judge be considered, for the purposes of tenders in local authorities and government ministries, as equivalent to holders of an academic degree. In addition, the ultra-Orthodox Sephardic and Ashkenazi streams have succeeded in dramatically increasing the education budgets for their institutions.

Today, the budget per student in both the Sephardic and Ashkenazi ultra-Orthodox education systems exceeds the budget per child in the state education system. Moreover, various budgetary constraints from the past that were intended to encourage the introduction of mathematics, English, physics and history studies (known as the "core curriculum") have been removed. From now on, there is no financial incentive to teach core studies. In so doing, Netanyahu, solely for the sake of keeping himself in power, gave the ultra-Orthodox (Sephardic and Ashkenazi alike) freedom to continue teaching religious studies in their educational institutions without mathematics, chemistry, physics, civics and English. Of course, without all this, these schools are producing a growing population that is ignorant in many areas that are vital to a modern economy in a state that seeks and strives to be democratic and modern. Clearly, this reinforces the process that has existed for years in these sectors, which, as it continues, is liable to add entire sectors that are uneducated, unable to work in modern or technological professions, unable to contribute significantly to the GDP and unable to reach reasonable levels of livelihood without dependence on government support and budgets. This, of course, means that huge number of people—and their children—remain financially dependent on their leaders, those politicians who serve leaders of Shas party or prominent rabbis from the ultra-Orthodox Ashkenazi sector. The severity and long-term damage and jeopardy to the State of Israel of this process far outweighs the danger posed by any foreign country.

Israel's strength comes from being a democratic society, with a plurality of streams, with open access to higher education, which enables the advancement of education and technology, science, research and development of science and industry, alongside prosperity-generating activity in various fields. All of these provide the foundations of Israel's strength and healthy and robust strong economy (see Chapter 2). However, providing massive budgets to the Ashkenazi and Sephardic ultra-Orthodox sectors, without conditioning it on the introduction of the core curriculum in their schools, is effectively eliminating Israel as a modern, democratic state. Unlike other countries that have experienced a similar process of deterioration, Israel cannot exist as such, since it still has external enemies seeking its destruction. For now, however, this destructive internal process is only being exacerbated and bolstered.

See, for example, the following clauses from the coalition agreement signed between Likud and Otzma Yehudit, under Smotrich's leadership:

- **Clause 103**—*The Ministry of National Missions, through the Jewish* Identity Administration, will formulate a national plan to deepen Jewish identity for a variety of populations (students, leaders in the humanities at universities, leaders in public service, etc.). As part of the program, centers for heritage, humanities and identity studies will be established, and funds will be established to encourage Jewish creativity in cinema, music and culture. The program will strengthen and cohere the family unit. In order to implement the plan, the government will allocate an appropriate incremental budget based on the budget as follows: In 2023 a total of 700 million shekels, in 2024 a total of 800 million shekels and starting in 2025 a total of 950 million shekels. If necessary, the plan will be submitted to the government for approval.

- **Clause 104**—The Ministry of National Missions will formulate a plan to encourage and strengthen community resilience as a means of increasing social cohesion in Israel. By empowering and consolidating the significant community enterprise as a means of increasing social cohesion and Jewish identity in Israel, the government will allocate an appropriate budget of 600 million shekels to the budget.

- **Clause 105**—The government will act to promote cultural institutions that operate according to a religious lifestyle and serve religious audiences and artists, will support festivals and vocational schools and art, in the fields of theater, music, etc.

- **Clause 106**—The government will not approve Israel's accession to the Istanbul Convention.[127]

---

127. Istanbul Convention—the first convention in Europe to set legally binding standards designed to protect gender based violence, especially women and girls.

- **Clause 107**—In order to encourage employment and integrate populations with low participation rates into the labor market, the government will appoint a professional team with the participation of representatives of the Civil Service Commission, the Ministry of Finance, the Ministry of Justice, the Ministry of Education, the Ministry of Religious Affairs, representatives of the Shas, Religious Zionism and United Torah Judaism factions, among other entities, which will examine: The recognition of professional certificates as equivalence for a general bachelor's degree, so that the Civil Service Commission will recognize certificates issued by the Chief Rabbinate, rabbinical judges, tour guide, a CPA certificate, a teaching certificate from seminaries, colleges and institutions of Torah study for women, and a B.A. equivalence degree as a general bachelor's degrees, for the purpose of qualification for tenders and appointments that require an academic degree, and for the purpose of salary ranking and seniority in the civil service. In addition, the Ministry of the Interior will recognize the above certificates for the purpose of eligibility to compete in local authority tenders.

- **Clause 109**—Granting independent status to the rabbinical courts in petitions to the court in such a way as to enable the legal advisor for rabbinical jurisdiction to appear independently in court in petitions filed against the rabbinical courts.

- **Clause 110**—The government will introduce legislation to restore the rabbinical courts' authority to hear arbitration proceedings in matters of monetary law with the consent of the parties, without the need a ruling from the District Court.[128]

- **Clause 114**—In order to strengthen religious Zionist enterprises, the Ministry of National Missions will allocate an addition to the budget in the amount of 174 million shekels,

---

128. This is a new step in extending the jurisdiction and authority of rabbinical courts to commercial and business disputes.

which will be earmarked, inter alia, for eliminating budgetary erosion related to national service in the education system, education in agricultural youth villages, strengthening various educational frameworks and empowering the heritage of religious Zionism and its activities, the Museum of Religious Zionism, the legacy of Rabbi Kook, the Gush Katif Heritage Center[129] and so on. In addition, beyond the basic budget, 110 million shekels will be allocated to Chabad activities, Zionist emissaries overseas, a heritage program, public institutions that lend medical equipment to the sick and handicapped, as well as one-time additions of 156 million shekels for development and construction activities.

- **Clause 117**—National religious Torah institutions: The budgeting model of yeshivas that encourage military service, Hesder yeshivas and girls' midrashim will be maintained, out of recognition of the value of Torah study. In midrashim, unique expenses related to the study agenda, manpower, etc., will be recognized, and the means test will be amended so that a point value will be added to the student studying in the various educational frameworks.

- **Clause 166**—The government will promote a plan to ease the burden of tuition fees in high school yeshivas and ulpanas. The budget allocated to this program will be anchored in the budget and will amount to no less than 100 million shekels per year. The plan will be based on a ceiling on expenditures for family education.

- **Clause 167**—The Ministry of Education will fund 75 percent of the budget of recognized non-official institutions and 55 percent of the budget of exempt institutions, as a proportion to the full budget allocated to these networks. Non-official institutions that teach core studies on a broader scale will receive an additional budget in accordance with the scope of the core curriculum and subject to compliance with the rules

---

129. Located in Jerusalem, with the goal of memorializing the Jewish settlements in the Gaza Strip that were evacuated in 2005.

of examination and evaluation, and that the curriculum at the institution does not contradict the educational goals specified in the State Education Law as well as the integrative framework of students.

- **Clause 168**—The State Education Law: The government will promote an amendment to the State Education Law in order to strengthen and stabilize the status and independence of the state-religious education. The amendment to the law will be discussed by a special committee in the Knesset, which will work in conjunction with the Education Committee and the Constitution Committee. An MK from the Religious Zionist Party will serve as Chairman of the Committee.

- **Clause 170**—After the establishment of the government, a government decision will be approved to strengthen state-religious education in Israel. As part of the program, budgets and solutions will be allocated to advance the characteristics of the State Education Law in the budget, according to the size and distribution of the institutions, religious lifestyle, the possibility of gender segregation, boarding schools, secondary education under bodies that are not local authorities, including supervision systems in the areas of mental health, immigrant absorption, social education and special-needs education. In addition, the program will be allocated in the budget the amount of 637 million shekels.

- **Clause 178**—Pre-Military Preparatory Programs—The Preparatory Program Law will be amended in such a way as to be consistent between the annual growth rate in the number of students approved by the IDF and the preparatory program budget.

Third issues: Conversion and the Law of Return

As part of the process of increasing religiosity in Israeli society, the coalition agreements dramatically strengthen the Orthodox side of Judaism. In global Judaism, there are different streams, including Conservative and Reform. Within the Orthodox stream, there are many subgroups (Hasidim, Misnagdim, Chabad, and so on). Around the world, and in the United States in particular, most of the Jewish community is not Orthodox; only about 10 percent are Orthodox, while the rest are divided between Conservative and Reform. However, what they all have in common, to varying degrees, is their connection to Israel. One of the central issues on the agenda is conversion. Each Jewish group has its own rules regarding conversion, and each of the coalition agreements addresses this issue. All of them emphasize that the only conversions that will be recognized in Israel are those endorsed by the state and the Chief Rabbinate—meaning only Orthodox conversions. This is a slap in the face to the Conservative and Reform movements. Moreover, some of the most welcome immigrants who arrived in Israel from 1991 onward came from the former Soviet Union (Ukraine, Russia, Moldova, Belarus, and other countries).

This wave of Aliyah was a major boost for Israel, contributing to its cultural diversity, impressive technological excellence, high levels of education, and vibrant artistic and musical scene. However, some of these immigrants were not Jewish according to Orthodox halacha. Some had Jewish mothers, while others had to go back to their grandparents' generation to trace their Jewish roots. According to the Law of Return of 1950, which is one of the Basic Laws of the State of Israel—established as the only national homeland for the Jewish people—anyone who is "a Jew, the child or grandchild of a Jew, the spouse of a Jew, or the spouse of a child or grandchild of a Jew" is entitled to citizenship and the rights of an immigrant. For this purpose, a "Jew" was defined as anyone "born to a Jewish mother or who converted." The recognition of the grandchild of a Jew as entitled to citizenship under the Law of Return enabled many immigrants from the former Soviet Union, Ukraine, and other countries—almost all of whom were secular Jews—to be absorbed into Israeli society. This rise in secular Jewish immigration is viewed as a threat by Netanyahu's coalition partners. They fear that an increase in the secular Jewish population will weaken the demographic dominance of religious, nationalist, messianic, and ultra-Orthodox Jews in Israel. Such a shift could increase the political and economic power of the secular population, influencing the image and character of the state and its institutions. Therefore, the coalition agreements include a provision stating that they will work to amend the Law of Return and remove recognition of the grandchild of a Jew. Netanyahu, whose sole concern is maintaining power, agreed to this demand.

Additionally, all coalition agreements now include a provision stating that only state-sanctioned conversions will be recognized—meaning conversions conducted exclusively by the Chief Rabbinate (i.e., only Orthodox conversions). If Reform or Conservative rabbis conduct conversion proceedings, their conversions will not be recognized in Israel, and those who convert through them will not be recognized as Jewish under the Law of Return. Once again, the struggle for Israel's identity is being shaped in accordance with Orthodox Judaism, ensuring that a majority of Israelis remain conservative, nationalist, alienated from broad education, and supportive of the continued occupation of the West Bank—with all the destructive consequences that entails.

See, for example, the following clauses from the coalition agreement signed between Likud and Otzma Yehudit, under Smotrich's leadership:

- **Clause 38**—The government will act to expand the state conversion system and make it accessible to the public interested in conversion, all subject to the position of the Chief Rabbis of Israel. In addition, the government will allocate budgets for living scholarships for students who undergo a conversion process in the state conversion system.

- **Clause 91**—In light of the need to realize the goal of the Law of Return and bring about Jewish immigration to Israel, in light of the distribution and characteristics of immigration in recent years, in light of the difficulties created by the grandchild clause in the Law of Return and the need to prevent assimilation in Israel and prevent abuse of the rights granted by the state to immigrants who return to their country of origin shortly after immigrating to Israel, by the time the 2023 state budget is passed, necessary legislative amendments will be made to support a suitable immigration policy. The text of the legislative amendments will be finalized within 60 days in a committee that will be established with the participation of representatives from all coalition parties.

- **Clause 94**—The government will advance a reform to promote conversion through a state body, alongside the necessary legislative amendment to determine that a conversion conducted in Israel will be recognized by law only if it was carried out through the state conversion system, which will be subject to the rulings of the Chief Rabbinate of Israel. This restores the status quo that existed on the eve of the formation of the 34th government.

- **Clause 96**—In light of the importance that the Jewish people have attached to Torah study throughout the generations, the enactment of the Basic Law: Torah Study, which states that Torah study is a fundamental value in the heritage of the Jewish people, will be completed by the time that the 2023 state budget is approved.

- **Clause 101**—The government will act to increase activity in the field of conversion by supporting public and state bodies operating in this field by intensifying various public relations activities.

Issue Four: Discrimination on grounds of religious belief

If all of the above were not enough, all the coalition agreements also stipulate that legislation will be passed allowing a business owner to refuse to provide a service or sell a product to customers (subject to a limited number of exceptions) on the grounds of "religious beliefs." In other words, a law that permits discrimination based on religious belief. This directly contradicts the principles of equal rights, respect for all human beings, and the basic tenets of any liberal, humanistic system. Such a law aligns with the ideological beliefs of the groups that make up the coalition—social groups that support discrimination based on religion or nationality. Just as discrimination against Arabs is not foreign to them, neither is discrimination on religious grounds. These and similar provisions throughout the coalition agreements reflect the growing process of religiosity in Israeli society. The number of religious Jews from all Orthodox streams is increasing, particularly due to the higher birth rates in these sectors compared to other segments of the population. Thus, for example, an ultra-Orthodox family has about seven children on average, a family from the national-religious camp has 4.3 children on average, and a secular family (including traditional Jews) has about three children on average. Over the years, these figures have had a dramatic effect and are already shaping the face of the State of Israel and its Jewish society.

Issue Five: The West Bank, Judea and Samaria and the Palestinians

Apart from the coalition agreements with the Ashkenazi ultra-Orthodox parties, Agudat Israel and UTJ (see Chapter 4), all of the other coalition agreements stipulate that Israel will continue to control the West Bank, that there will be additional budgets for settlement in the West Bank, more financial support for settlers, and the expansion of infrastructure and roads[130] in the West Bank. Moreover, Article 136 of the coalition agreement with Itamar Ben-Gvir's Otzma Yehudit party also includes a provision that "a law shall be passed to impose a tax on donations transferred from foreign governments to Israeli organizations." Of course, the new government is deepening and entrenching Israel's hold on the West Bank, and there is no plan to advance any effort to resolve the Israeli-Palestinian conflict. The opposite is true. This government will further entrench the lack of a solution and settlement

---

130. According to several reports the road's budget is 20% allocated for West Bank and there is a 1.50 Billion USD five years plan for additional roads (see "Tadmor" research, "Haaretz," November 29,2024).

expansion; investment in Judea and Samaria will create additional obstacles to finding a solution. Even the two-state solution, which was accepted by many groups in Israeli society and the West as a reasonable, equitable solution, becomes an increasingly remote possibility during the term of Netanyahu's sixth government. Netanyahu himself lacks the will, the desire, vision, and character to start working with the Palestinians, including due to his own views and because he has no desire to fight his coalition partners. His whole purpose is to seize and keep a grip on power. Therefore, it is safe to assume that only a dramatic external or internal event could force the sixth Netanyahu government to engage in any attempt to resolve the Palestinian conflict. History teaches us that traumatic events have occurred and will continue to occur— but, of course, there is no way of predicting when and how these events will evolve.

These coalition agreements (cited in summary) reflect Netanyahu's absolute capitulation to the other coalition parties, all for the sole cause, i.e., securing the formation of a government under his reign as Prime Minister. And this capitulation bears not only substance but is also attached with financial and budgetary resources, all to provide for the substance of the coalition agreements, all at the expense of the other sectors not represented in the government. Moreover, Netanyahu consented, for example, to the ultra-extremist and racist Mr. Ben-Gvir, a former supporter of Rabbi Meir Kahane, and one who for years hung at home the picture of Dr. Goldstein, who murdered 29 Palestinians during the Oslo Accord process, to be appointed as Minister of Internal Security (in charge, among others, of the police force).[131]

---

131. For several times before the election, when asked, Netanyahu dismissed firmly any option that Ben Gvir will serve as a minister in his future government. Last 24 months has shown that this appointment has had significant adverse effect on the police and Rule of Law.

Issue Six: Overhauling the essence of the Israeli regime—from democracy to hollow democracy

This book is not intended to deal with the concept of "democracy," which would require dozens of volumes.

There are different democratic regimes, in terms of the components of democracy, the electoral system, elected institutions, the judicial selection system, and the relations between the three branches: executive, legislative, and judicial. The drafters of the U.S. Constitution dealt with this extensively (see *The Federalist Papers*), as did France and the United Kingdom, but everyone agrees that a regime must include these elements in order to be called a democracy:

1. Free and confidential parliamentary elections at a predefined frequency (in the U.K., the United States, and Denmark, for example, a four- or five-year term is customary; in France, the term is five years for the president and National Assembly and six years for the Senate).

2. The candidate who wins a majority in the election forms the government, the executive branch (or, in presidential elections in places like France and the United States, becomes president).

3. There is a separation between the three main branches of government: the executive branch (the government), the legislature (occasionally in bicameral regimes, such as in the United States), and the judiciary.

4. The government is limited in its powers and may not unduly violate the rights of individuals and various minorities, including on the basis of gender, sexual preference, religion, nationality, faith, ideology, race, or skin color.

5. The government is prohibited from violating individual rights, private property, and freedom of movement. The same applies to freedom of assembly and freedom of expression for individuals and groups (except in rare and extreme cases).

6. A free and independent media is an essential part of the existence of democracy, allowing for the flow of information,

criticism of the government, the legislative body, and the judiciary, as well as the exchange of opinions and ideologies. Without a free and dynamic press and media, democracy becomes hollow.

As established in the previous chapters, significant parts of Israeli society shun a broad education and modern, advanced professions. In addition, significant parts of Israeli society focus exclusively on religious studies. These sections of society currently include ultra-Orthodox Jews, both Ashkenazi and Mizrahi communities, as well as some of the West Bank settlements. Despite this, Israel has recorded impressive scientific, technological, and economic achievements, as detailed in Chapter 2, due to, among other things, the success of safeguarding a liberal-democratic regime that aspires to have independent bodies of government, including an independent judiciary, freedom of speech and assembly, academic freedom for education and research, and diverse cultural activity with few restrictions on freedom of expression. This more or less allowed various sections of Israeli society to coexist and enabled culture and education to flourish—which, in turn, yielded significant benefits for the economy. But none of these can survive and prosper in Israel under a dictatorial, autocratic, or authoritarian regime.

Such regimes strangle education and academia since educational and academic excellence threaten dictatorial rule. They are threatened by culture, theater, literature, music, and other components of a dynamic society. Since the establishment of Israel in 1948, for example, the media has been conscripted to the national cause and has been under the full or partial control of the government; independent media remained on the margins. However, democracy took root in Israel. The UN Resolution of November 29, 1947, recognizing both the State of Israel and the Palestinian state, stated in the appendix to the resolution that free elections would be held in both states within two months of the British Mandate military forces leaving Palestine, and that each parliament of these states would draft a constitution that would guarantee the rights of their inhabitants as recognized in democracies (see Sections 10–19 of the resolution, the text of which appears as Appendix 1 to this book). Indeed, on May 14, 1948, David Ben-Gurion, the first prime minister of Israel—considered the founder of the state—unveiled Israel's Declaration of Independence, which stipulated, among other things, that Israel would have a democratic government that would guarantee equal rights for all residents of the state and guarantee freedom of religion, freedom of assembly, and freedom of expression.

Over the years, however, and for various political reasons, Israel never adopted an official constitution. This was a mistake of historical proportions. As a result, Israel's legislative process included the passage of various laws and regulations, and, on occasion, important governmental matters were enshrined in what became known as Basic Laws (*Basic Law: Government, Basic Law: The Knesset, Basic Law: Judiciary,* and *Basic Law: The Army,* for example). But there was no enshrined constitution that was immune from amendment by a simple or minimal majority. So, Israel has no constitution. Fundamental rights are not protected in the constitution. Similarly, Israel's parliament does not have two houses (unlike, for example, the United States, which has the Senate and House of Representatives). There are no federations (like in Canada, Germany, and the U.S.). Israel does not have a long tradition or culture of democracy, like in the United Kingdom or France. Israel is not a member of any international organization that safeguards basic human rights, as European nations are. There are laws and there are Basic Laws.

Therefore, the Supreme Court's review of Knesset legislation is extremely important. In the absence of this authority, and since the Knesset in Israel is effectively controlled by the government, Israeli democracy has been transformed from a complex system that includes three basic institutions—a government that is the executive branch, a parliament that passes legislation, and courts that impose checks and balances on the government and the

Knesset—into one ruling, all-powerful institution: the government. Thus, without full independence of the court system, and especially the Supreme Court, Israel may transform from a democracy with institutions that exercise separation of powers and impose checks and balances into a hollow regime in which the last remaining vestige of democracy is elections every few years. Even these elections, however, will presumably produce skewed results, since the government wields all the power, is able to give out various incentives, and can influence public opinion, including via the media. In some countries, regulations have been passed ensuring that the courts are not authorized to exercise judicial review over a constitutional amendment. However, in these countries, there is a complex and rigid procedure for amending the constitution, requiring a supermajority in both houses of parliament (the U.S. Congress) and the approval of three-quarters of the states (in the United States). In France, the Constitutional Council has determined that it does not have the authority to review constitutional amendments, but the process of changing the constitution requires the approval of both houses of parliament by an ordinary majority or a majority of 60 percent in a joint special session of both houses of parliament and a referendum. In Ireland, a constitutional amendment requires a majority in both houses of parliament and a referendum. In Germany, two-thirds of both houses of parliament must approve changes to the constitution,[132] and the same applies in France and Norway. [133]

In 1992, in a vote in Parliament, and with just 38 of the 120 members of the Knesset taking part, Israel passed *Basic Law: Human Dignity and Freedom.* This law introduced, *inter alia,* the protection and safeguarding of basic rights for citizens and residents, including protection of property, human dignity and liberty, freedom of movement, protection of privacy, and individual privacy. In addition, Section 8 of the law stipulates that

---

132. See: Prof. Yaniv Roznai, "*Unconstitutional Constitutional Amendments: The Limits Of Amendment Powers,*" *(2017) Pages 204-206 (Henceforth: Roznai).*

133. As appears in Roznai, page 207.

these rights cannot be violated "save by means of a law that corresponds to the values of the State of Israel, which serves an appropriate purpose, and to an extent that does not exceed what is required." Citing this provision in the Basic Law, the Supreme Court, under Chief Justice Prof. Aharon Barak, ruled in 1995 that there had been a change in the country's legislative system and that Article 8 of the Basic Law also authorized the Supreme Court to invalidate laws that violate the basic rights set forth in the Basic Law (*Civil Appeals Authority 1908/94, United Mizrahi Bank Ltd. v. Migdal Cooperative Village, Ruling (4) 221*). In this ruling, there was one minority opinion (that of Justice Mishael Cheshin), who opined that the Knesset did not have the authority to enact a law that overrides other laws. In addition, there were those who argued that the Supreme Court had unlawfully and underhandedly assumed the authority to invalidate Knesset laws, and that the enactment of the Basic Law and the accompanying processes indicate that there was no intention at all to create a revolution. This controversy remains entrenched in the Israeli public sphere. However, it should be noted that since the *Bank Mizrahi* ruling, the Supreme Court has used its authority to strike down laws or provisions in laws only a total of 22 times. This is a small number, which indicates that the court is exercising a high level of restraint.

Netanyahu, however, had new plans.[134] He decided that a democratic regime with an independent judiciary threatened his rule and might even threaten his freedom because of the criminal proceedings being conducted against him. This unreasonable situation has led, since January 4, 2023—four days after the formation of the coalition government headed by Netanyahu—to a flood of directives and legislative proposals for significant regime change. These proposals included provisions stating that any part of a law overturned by the Supreme Court could

134. In all the coalition agreements there is a common article which refers generally to changes in Laws but the real intention and the excessiveness of the judicial reform contemplated were very much concealed. On purpose.

be re-enacted by a majority of 51 percent of the parliament (61 members out of 120), the goal of which was to neuter the Supreme Court and remove its authority to overturn laws and statutory provisions. In addition, it was proposed that the appointment of legal advisers in all government ministries would henceforth be made by the serving minister—as a "personal appointee." In other words, the minister would have the power to appoint or dismiss the legal advisor to his or her ministry. The proposal also included a substantial change in the composition of the judicial selection committee, which appoints judges, including those to the Supreme Court. Until now, the committee has been made up of nine members: three Supreme Court justices, three representatives selected by the government, and the remainder chosen by the Israel Bar Association. A majority of seven was required for a Supreme Court appointment, and a simple majority for a lower level of judicial office.

This meant that the government did not have an automatic majority on the committee. Now, however, the proposed rules would fundamentally change this system. According to the new proposal, the committee would be expanded to eleven members. Of these, eight would be appointed by the government and the political echelon, and only an ordinary majority would be required to appoint any judge. Thus, judicial appointments would become a tool for the government to determine the identity of judges serving in various courts—including the Supreme Court—as well as the promotion of judges in lower courts. The overall result of the new legislative system on the agenda (which was included in general terms in all coalition agreements, with all the coalition parties agreeing that it would be a top priority for the legislative process) was to render the Supreme Court unable to influence legislation that violates the rights of minorities, the LGBTQ community, Arabs, leftists, secular Jews, and Reform and Conservative Jews—essentially, anyone who does not have close ties with the ruling coalition parties. This would make judges subordinate to the executive branch, as politicians would control their appointment and subsequent promotion. It would deprive the judiciary and the Supreme Court of their independence. Judicial independence is a cornerstone of any democratic regime. Taken together, these proposals undermine the independence of the judicial system, intimidate the judiciary and its judges, and create a new reality in which a fundamental component of Israeli democracy would be erased. It would not be out of place here to quote statements made by Netanyahu himself on February 28, 2012, while he was serving as prime minister, before the serious indictments were filed against him:

"I believe that a strong, independent court allows for the existence of all other institutions in a democracy. I ask that you show me one dictatorship, one undemocratic society, where a strong independent court system exists. There's no such thing. In places with no strong and independent court system, rights cannot be protected. In fact, the difference between countries in which rights are only on paper and those in which there are actual rights—that difference is a strong, independent court. This is the reason that I am doing, and will continue to do, everything I can to protect the court system [so that it remains] strong and independent. Over the past few months alone, I have shelved every law that threatened to harm the independence of the system—from the attempt to hold hearings for judges in the Knesset, through limiting petitions to the court, to changing the composition of the committee for selecting judges. I will continue to operate this way."

Netanyahu was completely right. His comments were an accurate reflection of democracy. However, eleven years have passed since then, and, in the meantime, Netanyahu has been indicted on three serious charges, for which, if convicted, he could spend many years behind bars. Now, worried about his personal future, Netanyahu has completely changed his approach. He decided to ditch his democratic positions and his belief in the independence of the judiciary, transforming it into an enfeebled branch of government, subordinate to the rule of the executive branch. The result of these changes, which Netanyahu euphemistically calls "reform" in order to camouflage the real situation, is a dramatic transformation of Israel's governing mechanisms. He has done something similar to what President Recep Tayyip Erdoğan did to the judiciary in Turkey and what Prime Minister Viktor Orbán, the head of the Fidesz party, has done in Hungary. In addition to all of the above, Netanyahu's Minister of Justice also proposed changes to the way legal advisers in all government ministries are appointed and dismissed.

Every ministry in Israel has a legal department headed by a legal advisor. The role of the legal adviser is to provide the ministry and its minister with legal counsel, including outlining restrictions arising from the law. Until now, legal advisers were administratively subordinate to the director general of the ministry in which they worked, but in professional terms, they were all directly subordinate to the attorney general. They could not be dismissed except with the consent of the attorney general, and their legal opinions were binding. A Knesset research committee report from 2011 determined that this was the recommended structure in Israel to safeguard the independence of legal advisers in government ministries and strengthen their ability to ensure that ministries comply with the law. In Israel, where adherence to legal norms is not deeply entrenched, this system became even more crucial. The new proposal would fundamentally abolish this practice, replacing it with a system whereby the minister could appoint and dismiss his or her ministry's legal adviser, whose opinion would no longer be binding. This, of course, not only turns the position of legal advisers in government ministries into a political appointment—meaning that experienced professionals would be rejected in favor of individuals who share the minister's ideology—but also opens the door to increased nepotism and governmental corruption. Israel has already fallen in the global corruption index, dropping from a respectable 14th place in 1995 to 36th place in 2021. It is safe to assume that if these changes are implemented, Israel's ranking will continue to decline—perhaps even accelerating. The total effect of the judicial "reform" introduced by Netanyahu's sixth government—a coalition of religious, ultra-Orthodox, and nationalist parties, some of which also have messianic and racist beliefs and treat the principles and foundations of democracy with indifference (or even contempt)—provides Netanyahu with the necessary tailwind in his effort to crush and enfeeble the Supreme Court as the gatekeeper of legislation and weaken the judicial system as a whole. Instead of a "strong and independent" judicial system, as he put it in 2012, he is now urgently pushing for legislation that would fundamentally change the status of the judicial system—weakening it, politicizing it, making it subordinate to the executive branch, and stripping it of real power over the government or the ability to protect the rights of minorities, Arabs, women, the LGBTQ community, and anyone not connected to the coalition parties. Of course, as part of this process, the essence of the Declaration of Independence, written when the State of Israel was established in 1948—and considered the equivalent of the U.S. Declaration of Independence—becomes a dead letter. More on this in the next chapter.

The implications of the proposed legislation

The proposed legislation is a package through which a common thread runs: turning the government of Israel into the exclusive decision-making body, which determines and directs the legislative process without restrictions or scrutiny, with complete control over the selection of judges in all Israeli courts, including the Supreme Court. It makes legal advisers in government ministries personal appointees of the minister, effectively turning them into his henchmen, and reduces the ability of the Israeli government, its ministers, and elected representatives to audit unreasonable decisions. This is a real regime coup.

The basic systems of democracy, the idea of checks and balances between authorities, and the concept of an independent judicial system will all be abolished. Instead, there will be a single authority that wields unlimited control over the legislative system, and a judicial system stripped of the authority to annul legislation that violates basic values and the fundamental rights of citizens and minorities. There will be judges whose appointment and promotion depend on the government. This kind of change would transform the State of Israel from a democratic state, with liberal elements, into a state that is no longer democratic—one that only technically holds periodic elections. Needless to say, if all these changes are implemented, there will be no impediment to legislation revoking the so-called "grandfather clause," stripping Conservative or Reform Jews of their rights, imposing restrictions on their ability to hold prayer ceremonies at the Western Wall, introducing dress code regulations for women in the public sphere, enforcing physical and other forms of separation between men and women in all public spaces, and passing other legislation that aligns with the ideological spirit of the current government.

The current legislative initiatives serve all the partners in this government. Every party in this coalition sees these legal changes as advantageous. Since none of them view democracy, judicial independence, or the Supreme Court's authority to overturn legislation that violates basic rights under the Basic Law: Human Dignity and Liberty as essential or desirable, they therefore do not consider the issue of judicial independence to be of paramount importance. Netanyahu, whose only concern for many years has been seizing and holding onto power at any cost, sees this as an opportunity to control the judicial system—including the judges appointed to the Supreme Court, who will ultimately hear an appeal on his criminal charges. Moreover, some of the judges currently presiding over his criminal case in the District Court already exhibit signs of weakness and fear in handling Netanyahu's trial. After all, the prime minister's criminal trial has been dragging on for over four years and has only just reached the end of its first stage—the prosecution phase.[135]

---

135. The defense was set to start summoning it witnesses by December 2024 and still dragged on and on according to the whims of Netanyahu.

It is possible that Netanyahu is even planning, as part of the second phase of this dramatic legislative process, to split the role of attorney general into two roles, one of which is responsible for the whole of the state prosecution system. This would allow him to appoint a "sympathetic" prosecutor general and perhaps negotiated a deal whereby Netanyahu is allowed to remain prime minister. The ministers from Netanyahu's own party are all afraid of the prime minister and the apparatuses of slander, threats and lies that he employs, so they remain silent and carry out his every directive. Most of them are also lower-quality people, who owe their entire political careers to Netanyahu, because in any other reality they would not have been able to serve as ministers or Knesset members.

The ultra-Orthodox party will benefit from abolishing the court's authority to annul legislation. This party, as mentioned, is fighting against the military draft for its young men. In the past, the Supreme Court intervened in this situation, albeit very gently, being highly considerate of the ultra-Orthodox public and handing down weak and cowardly rulings—but it could still be seen as an obstacle. It is no coincidence that in a meeting with yeshiva students, Yitzhak Pindrus, a Knesset member from the ultra-Orthodox Degel Hatorah party, said in May 2022 that his "dream is to blow up the Supreme Court." Now, according to the new legislation, the court's powers will be stripped and it will become powerless within the governmental sphere. Of course, Sephardic Haredi party Shas, headed by Aryeh Deri, is also delighted with this legislation.

Deri held a grudge against the Supreme Court, which years ago convicted him of bribery and theft and sentenced him to three years in prison. More recently, shortly after the 2022 election, the court ruled that Deri cannot serve as a minister in the Israeli government because, when he was convicted of tax evasion, he vowed never to return to public life. This paved the way for a more lenient sentence, since the judge took his promise into account. Deri reneged on his promise and sought to serve as a minister in the new Netanyahu government. Netanyahu agreed—but the Supreme Court heard a petition against the appointment in 2023 and ruled that, since Deri had promised the Magistrate's Court that he would no longer participate in public life, he was therefore ineligible to serve as a minister. This infuriated him. He therefore pressured Netanyahu to ensure that the Knesset—which, as previously noted, has become an enfeebled body in Israeli politics, serving only the government and doing the prime minister's bidding—enacts a special law stipulating that the Supreme Court does not have the authority to disqualify a ministerial appointment.

It is clear from this that Deri also wants to deny the Supreme Court the authority to overturn laws. If, therefore, a special law is enacted that prevents the Supreme Court from overturning the appointment of a minister, the Supreme Court itself would not be able to overturn that law. And Deri, despite his criminal convictions for tax evasion and despite the previous Supreme Court ruling, would once again be eligible to serve as a minister in the Israeli government. This, incidentally, is yet another example of the moral and educational corruption that Netanyahu has introduced into Israeli public and political life. A minister who has twice been convicted of bribery and tax evasion is able to serve as interior minister. And, of course, the nationalist and messianic-religious parties also support the new legislative system. As far as they are concerned, the Supreme Court's power to intervene in legislation and the independence of legal advisers in government ministries are nothing but an obstacle to achieving their goals. As previously mentioned, their main plan is a change in the very nature of the Israeli judiciary, by establishing a state run according to Torah law, by curtailing individual rights for the LGBTQ community, increasing religious education and the vigorous expansion of infrastructure and construction in Judea and Samaria for settlers while increasing the burden on Palestinians and encouraging them to leave the West Bank. An independent Supreme Court with powers to intervene in legislation and legislative proceedings, like independent legal advisors, is nothing but an obstacle.

Indeed, even before the abovementioned legislation came into force, there was evidence of the judicial coup ahead. On February 22, 2023, a bill was submitted to the government of Israel which had not, as is customary, been approved by the Justice Ministry, had not undergone internal review, and was not brought to the attention of the attorney general. The bill was drafted entirely by Israel's current education minister and proved by Netanyahu. The bill deals with the 2007 law regulating the operations of Israel's National Library, which was established in 1892, many years before the establishment of the state. The purpose of the law was to preserve Jewish cultural, scientific, and literary assets, and among its treasures are the writings of Albert Einstein, Maimonides, Nobel Prize winner in literature Shmuel Yosef Agnon, and Franz Kafka. Following an agreement between the Hebrew University of Jerusalem and the Israeli government, and in accordance with the findings of a report compiled by a public committee, the law was passed, transferring responsibility for the property and assets of the National Library to a public council, which was supposed to be completely independent. Its independence was ensured by having a board of directors on which there was a majority (six out of 11 members) from the Israel Academy of Sciences and Humanities.

This law worked exceptionally well; among the members of the council were scientists and academics, and financial donations and acquisitions of cultural assets flourished. In February 2023, a bill was hastily presented to the government for approval, without prior scrutiny or preparation, and without the customary approval of the Justice Ministry. The bill was approved by the government and was due to be included in a more comprehensive bill for parliamentary approval. The new bill proposed amending the 2007 law so that a majority of the members of the National Library Council would be appointed by the minister of education, and the appointees would no longer have to meet any conditions or criteria to be considered qualified. This would give the government control over the aforementioned cultural assets and, at the same time, would be sweet revenge on Shai Nitzan. Because the same Shai Nitzan who served as state prosecutor and backed the State Attorney's Office investigations, which led to three criminal indictments against Netanyahu, is now chairman of the National Library Council. So, there's an element of personal revenge in this move, too. This is the new face of the State of Israel, according to the new legislation and the government—a clear and obvious example of how the character of the country is being altered beyond recognition.

This proposed legislation did not pass, but the trend remained the same. The current sequence of legislative processes began with one major move, which included: eliminating the intervention of the Supreme Court in legislation; taking control of the Judicial Appointments Committee, including the president of the Supreme Court; appointing legal advisors to government ministries; and eliminating justices' power to intervene in decisions by the government or by any elected officials, no matter how unreasonable and bizarre. Taken together, these changes, if they were enacted and in effect, would have effectively removed Israel from the group of democratic countries and given the government a free hand to make decisions without oversight and take control of the state's assets and economy. This group of proposals stirred the Israeli public from its slumber, especially secular Israelis and LGBTQ groups, as well as those parts of the national-religious community which have a more democratic worldview. There were widespread demonstrations and protests across the country and overseas against Israeli ministers and Knesset members. Given this outpouring of opposition, the government adopted the so-called "salami system," trying to pass anti-democratic legislation in separate measures, each of which was portrayed as undramatic. For example, there was an effort to include representatives of the government on Israel's Council for Higher Education, as well as legislation to abolish the authority of the courts to overturn manifestly unreasonable decisions by government ministers, elected public officials, and the government itself. These are all steps in a series of legislative initiatives that will end with the elimination of the very foundations of democracy in Israel and will transform it into a regime ruled by a populist-nationalist-messianic government—with the support of the ultra-Orthodox sector, which gets all its funding from the state coffers and benefits from the contribution of other sectors. This is indeed a dramatic process that has led, from January 2023 until October 7, to fierce opposition from democratic forces in Israel. The struggle is ongoing. How it ends will determine the character of the State of Israel for a long time. Here, too, Netanyahu has made a huge contribution to the destruction and enfeebling of Israeli democracy, to the undermining of governmental apparatus and institutions designed to preserve individual liberty, governmental checks and balances, and preventing infringement of freedom of speech, including, of course, demonstrations.

Democracy is delicate and fragile; it requires a basic cultural and educational infrastructure and a deep social consensus regarding its importance. It also requires basic values to be accepted in society, such as equality for all, the understanding that disputes must be resolved through dialogue and peaceful means, without violence, and basic respect for minorities, as well as the understanding that those with different opinions must be respected. These and other basic elements do not exist in Israeli society today. There has been an increase in the proportion of the ultra-Orthodox population, which does not believe in democratic education, combined with the nationalist-messianic-religious camp, which grew as a result of the occupation and the expansion of messianic-nationalist views supported by yeshivas and rabbis who raised generations of students on extremist religiosity—a nationalist approach that advocates Jewish supremacy over Arabs, Palestinians, and foreigners in general. Many groups whose educational foundations are flawed, to whom basic democratic values are unclear and sometimes even pointless, have also contributed to this shift. All of this has turned the majority of Israelis into people who place no importance on the foundations of democracy, equality, individual and minority rights, equal status for women, and, of course, recognition of the curse of the occupation. Sometimes, these values are met with disgust and outright opposition. Against this backdrop, it is easy for inciteful and populist leaders like Netanyahu and Ben-Gvir to rile up public feelings of anger and to shatter trust in the judicial system, the High Court of Justice, the State Prosecutor's Office, and the police. As a result, Israel now faces the danger of serious domestic struggles that could even claim lives. Among the devastating effects of this would be a substantial decline in GDP and massive damage in the fields of education, science, research, and the academy.

The liberal-democratic camp, the High Court and a government acting against the rule of law

Netanyahu decided that, during the course of 2023, he would take control of every part of the Israeli institutions of state, especially the judiciary. This would allow him to maintain a complete grip on power, scupper his criminal trial and perhaps even thwart investigations into the submarine affair. He was joined in this effort by the other parties in his coalition, all of which have nothing but resentment and contempt towards the Supreme Court and everything it represents. From their perspective, democracy is completely unimportant (as per the ultra-Orthodox parties) or is nothing more than a quadrennial election ceremony that has no real content. For the latter group, as represented by the extreme right-wing religious parties headed by Finance Minister Bezalel Smotrich and National Security Minister Itamar Ben-Gvir, who is responsible, under the current government, for the police and Border Police, democracy is merely procedural.[136] According to their ideologies, the content should be taken from Torah law from the time of King David. In other words, the status of women

---

136. See comments from MK Simcha Rotman, from Smotrich's party.

would be greatly eroded, they would be excluded from academic studies and professional advancement, and they would be relegated to domestic positions. The LGBTQ community would also, of course, be denied equal rights since they are seen as an "abomination." The same would also apply to the Arab and Christian minorities in Israel.

These processes are not only a putsch, turning a democratic state into a dictatorial regime with messianic-nationalist-religious elements, but also a dramatic change in the nature and character of the State of Israel. From a state that aspired to be a liberal democracy, it will become a religious, nationalist state that embraces Jewish supremacy. Under these conditions, the more respectable and capable segments of Israeli society will begin to look for ways to leave the country and to build their future elsewhere. The fact that these bills are not only a change in the system of government but that they also herald a fundamental struggle for the character of the state slowly began to dawn on significant parts of Israeli society—and not only among secular Jews. Even some national-religious Jews, who used to support the old National Religious Party or Hapoel Hamizrachi, were horrified to realize that the government's goal was to change the character of the state and abolish all elements of liberal democracy. Realization that the danger was real began to sink in. Since January 2023, gradually, demonstrations broke out across Israel against the entire government and against the legislation aimed at weakening the power of the Supreme Court and changes to the system whereby judges and legal advisors in government ministries are appointed. There have been many different kinds of demonstrations, and the number of people attending protests in a single day has reached the hundreds of thousands; for the sake of comparison, that would be like tens of millions of people demonstrating across the United States.

The demonstrations lasted for more than 30 consecutive weeks and included midweek rallies and marches to Jerusalem. The demonstrators came from those camps that value democracy and understood that without democracy, the State of Israel would not only change its very nature but would also gradually lose its strength and educated forces, on whose shoulders Israel's economy and security rest. The opposition movement organized spontaneously and from different sections of society. Massive numbers of people—initially mainly the secular, liberal public, both rightist and leftist—took the helm of protests against the judicial coup. These were the people who effectively carried the State of Israel in its liberal, democratic form, enabling the country to enjoy a relatively high GDP, and also indirectly, through their paid taxes, facilitating the financing of the many educational institutions in the ultra-Orthodox sector, along with economic benefits for members of the ultra-Orthodox community, as well as massive investments in Judea and Samaria, including settlement construction, paving roads and other infrastructure projects, such as electricity, irrigation, sewage, and public buildings. Protests were held in various public arenas. It started with mass demonstrations, beginning with protests attended on Shabbat evening by 50,000 people throughout the rainy winter season. The number of participants continued to swell, however, and in March 2023, some 300,000 people attended a rally in Tel Aviv, and a similar number attended other protests across Israel. That would be equivalent to some 20 million Americans taking to the streets.

The demonstrations gradually evolved, and protest leaders began to emerge. The opposition parties were weak and unwilling to stand up to an aggressive, belligerent regime that does not shy away from even the most brazen measures. As protests against the proposed legislation that began piling up in parliament intensified, it became apparent to the general public that they were facing not only a plan for a regime coup that would lead to the appointment of judges by a committee composed of a majority of government representatives, thereby imposing political control over the judiciary and making it subservient and obligated to the government, but that this was a larger, comprehensive coup plan. When data regarding Israel's national budget for 2023 and 2024 was published, it suddenly became clear to the public that the abovementioned coalition agreements, which the general public did not make an effort to read or understand, were actually being implemented—firstly through the state budget. It became known that the ultra-Orthodox sector was given an additional 14 billion shekels (approximately 4 billion USD) for educational institutions for two years—which is half of Israel's entire budget for its academic institutions, the latter being the cornerstone of the Israeli economy and strength. Substantial sums were also allocated to increase investments in the West Bank, for educational institutions belonging to the Shas party, for substantial investments in the religious sector and for additional budgets for various activities in the West Bank. On the other hand, the budget for the Innovation Authority, whose role is to encourage start-up companies and scientific entrepreneurship activities, for example, was reduced—as were the budgets of other institutions of higher education.

Of course, these actions harmed the Israeli economy, research, and education, and incentivized the growth of the ultra-Orthodox strata, which was not interested in comprehensive education. This posed a genuine strategic threat to Israel. The coalition parties only cared about the sectors they represented. As for Netanyahu, his interests were exclusively self-serving—staying in power and safeguarding the coalition so that he could take control of the judicial system and void his criminal trial, while bolstering his government and his grip on power. All at the expense of the State of Israel. Following this catastrophic budget, top Israeli and international economists published a statement warning that the new budget and the judicial coup would severely damage the Israeli economy and the status of research and education in Israel, thereby causing a brain drain and a dramatic decline in research and development activity and the establishment of new startups in Israel. In addition, Israelis who volunteer for reserve duty in the IDF, beyond their obligatory reserve duty, began to organize; they announced, together or individually, that they would stop volunteering for the army units in which they served. This was especially evident in the Air Force, special commando units, and the Israeli Cyber and Intelligence Directorate. The protests gained momentum until, in March 2023, Defense Minister Yoav Gallant publicly declared that the regime coup legislation must be stopped in order to avoid dramatically harming the IDF's preparedness for war. Netanyahu was infuriated by Gallant's comments, and the prime minister announced the dismissal of the defense minister—effectively firing him just for telling the truth and warning that the process entailed huge security risks to Israel. Netanyahu's decision sparked a massive outburst of public fury. Within hours of the prime minister's statement, tens of thousands of Israelis—some estimates say 150,000 people—took to the streets of Tel Aviv late at night, in protest, blocking roads and starting bonfires in opposition to Netanyahu's unreasonable decision. This time, a forceful response from the liberal-democratic camp, combined with pressure, both overt and covert, from the White House and its representatives (including the renowned journalist Tom Friedman of *The New York Times* and the U.S. ambassador to Israel, Tom Nides), forced Netanyahu to back down from firing Gallant. In his customary opaque manner, the prime minister announced that he was "suspending Gallant's dismissal"—an appropriately vague quasi-decision from Netanyahu, who is known for his hesitation and inability to make significant decisions.

Thereafter, there was a two-month period, until the end of May 2023, when the coalition parties engaged in doomed negotiations, spearheaded by the Israeli president, aimed at reaching an agreement on the legislation that made up the judicial overhaul. Even though Herzog is an affable, educated, and cultured president, he lacked the strength of personality required in such critical and conflict-filled days; his mediation efforts failed. The coalition used this period to fine-tune the tactics they would use to implement their regime coup. Instead of the legislative blitz that they tried to introduce in January 2023, they apparently identified a change in the liberal-democratic camp, which had for many years quietly accepted the worrying phenomena in Israeli society and submissively tolerated these new anti-democratic measures as well. The coalition came to the conclusion that the regime coup could be achieved gradually, using the so-called "salami method," segment by segment. In the meantime, more bills were being introduced, all of them intended not only to serve Netanyahu and his goal of eliminating the independent judiciary but also to satisfy the demands of the other coalition parties, including legislation on religious and minority matters.

During this period, for example, no fewer than 225 (!) bills were brought before the Knesset. For example, bills were introduced to expand the powers of the rabbinical courts and allow them to base their rulings on halacha and Torah law. There were bills to ensure gender segregation at public beaches and swimming pools. Other proposals included recognizing anyone with rabbinical qualifications as equivalent to an academic degree for the purposes of being appointed to a government position or participating in government tenders. There were even bills to curtail the rights of the LGBTQ community. Moreover, there were systematic moves to take control of institutions of higher education and install representatives who would work on behalf of the government. There were similar bills aimed at imposing government control over television networks, including the power to oversee broadcasts and their content, as well as control over government financial support for television networks that coincidentally support the current government and its goals. Later, there was even a brazen attempt to fire the chairman of Yad Vashem, Israel's official memorial to the six million victims of the Holocaust. His sin was that, even though he himself is a rightist and a settler, he was appointed to the position by the previous government and is considered close to MK Gideon Sa'ar, who once dared to challenge Netanyahu for leadership of Likud. Now, settling scores also became part of Netanyahu's drive to take total control of the institutions of state.[137]

These measures prompted the national-religious democratic camp—people who once voted for the original National Religious Party and Hapoel Mizrachi—to join the protest against the regime coup, since they recognized that Israeli democracy was in real danger and that the State of Israel could soon become a very different state: dictatorial, nationalist, discriminatory, racist, and trampling on the rights of minorities. Moreover, an ever-growing group of military reservists, especially from the Israeli Air Force and from elite units (including commando and intelligence), publicly declared that they would not serve in military reserve duty while there was an ongoing political campaign aimed at destroying the democratic institutions, separation of powers between government bodies, and the basic system of checks and balances. This trend posed, on the one hand, a serious alarm regarding the preparedness of the IDF in case of military conflict—a threat which Netanyahu played down in public,[138]—and on the other hand, was met with a huge wave of hatred, curses, and smears across all forms of media, led by government ministers, coalition MKs, and their supporters. But the government did not back down from its intentions and plan. The coalition, faced with all this outrage and resistance, decided to introduce the regime coup slice by slice. The first piece of legislation that was advanced, therefore, was the amendment to the "reasonableness clause." What is this clause all about? Over the years, the Supreme Court has developed a thesis stating that if administrative decisions, including those of government ministers, are found to be "extremely unreasonable"—and it is important to note that the alleged "unreasonableness" must be extreme—the Supreme Court and the administrative court are empowered to intervene, even to the point of annulling them.

---

137. This maneuver was stalled eventually.

138. Netanyahu once said that "the country can manage without several squadrons of the Air Force but cannot without government."

This power infuriated the current coalition, since, among other things, it could delay or even prevent extremely unreasonable decisions. For example, it could block the appointment of incompetent people solely on the basis of their ties to the parties forming the government. Experience shows that, in most cases, any extremely unreasonable government decision conceals murky motives, often related to quid pro quo arrangements and the like. To this end, the coalition launched a smear campaign against the Supreme Court and its justices for "unlawfully" assuming the authority to invalidate ministerial and government decisions on the grounds of "unreasonableness."

Under the current Israeli government, it is common for facts to be distorted, twisted, and manipulated. Therefore, even on this matter, the government did not explain that the High Court's authority to intervene in government decisions applies only in cases of "extreme unreasonableness" and that such interventions, in reality, were rare and only in extreme cases. However, the government's propaganda machine, which includes the whole social media network, television channels, newspapers, and certain radio and TV reporters, launched an orchestrated and organized campaign to persuade the people that the court has the authority to intervene in any decision it deems "unreasonable," and that "unreasonableness" is a subjective and unmeasurable matter, and therefore, the court has assumed the authority to "run the state." The government, according to this propaganda, was merely trying to correct this serious anomaly. So, by means of a systematic—and false—campaign of propaganda, the government launched an effort to pass a new Basic Law,[139] stating

139. The State of Israel does not have a constitution, unlike the United States. Israel does not have a legislative system to protects human and individual rights. Basic Laws were intended to be the basis for a future constitution, but there is no provision in Israeli legislation that determines the status of a Basic Law and how it differs or is superior to a regular law. Therefore, it is possible to enact a law by a majority of even two MKs in favor and one against and call it a Basic Law. This, of course, makes a pathetic joke of the concept of Basic Laws, which is how the Israeli government and its leader, Benjamin Netanyahu, acted in this case.

that the court cannot overturn a decision passed by "the Israeli government or ministers on grounds of reasonableness." The goal of this legislation is to allow the coalition to pass resolutions without the threat of "extreme reasonableness" hanging over them. This paves the way for corrupt decisions and those that are motivated by behind-the-scenes deals. It may pave the way for a decline in the quality of government and for a multitude of acts of corruption.

This legislative blitz revived the popular opposition. By this time, the democratic-liberal camp had internalized the magnitude of the danger and the fact that the regime coup and the enfeebling of the independent judiciary were just one link in a chain of planned measures to deliver religious, national, and racist blows and to undermine the rights of minorities (Arabs and the LGBTQ community), as well as women. The opposition forces intensified their struggle, and more and more volunteers from special units in the IDF, the Air Force, Military Intelligence, and cyber units announced that they would no longer volunteer for additional reserve duty. This, needless to say, had far-reaching implications for the IDF's military capability and preparedness. However, even this very real danger, which was alarmed by the IDF chief of staff and other ex-military figures, did not deter Netanyahu from realizing his goal at this time—taking control of the Israeli judiciary and the media to establish an autocratic and authoritarian regime in collaboration with his coalition partners. Why did Prime Minister Netanyahu choose the "reasonableness clause" as the first slice in his "salami" legislation? The answer is clear: because it opens the door to appointing people connected to the government and the coalition to key positions in the civil service and will also enable them to favor their cronies—through jobs with hefty salaries and excellent social conditions. It will give them more control over the decision-making process, including advancing the economic interests of tycoons and media companies loyal to these politicians. The obvious outcome is that the governmental system is crushed and made unprofessional. Israeli institutions will be filled with functionaries, not based on their skills, executive ability, and professionalism, but according to personal, political, or business ties with the current government and the coalition parties. This will inevitably dismantle the institutions of government. The consequences for the Israeli economy and society are certainly devastating.

However, there is an additional reason why Netanyahu and his party decided that this would be their starting point: there is some "ideological" support for the move. It may be portrayed and marketed to the public as not particularly harmful to the independence of the judiciary. Moreover, it also appears not to be hugely significant and, therefore, does not generate strong opposition. The "ideological" support was disseminated via a government propaganda campaign, supported by pro-government (and government-supported) media outlets. According to these media propagandists (at TV Channel 14 and radio station *Galei Yisrael*, as well as some reporters from other channels, such as Channel 12 and Channel 13), the chief justice of the Supreme Court used the "reasonableness clause" to "interfere" with the government's ability to implement its plans and to hinder or nix government decisions. This is far from the truth and reality, however. As already mentioned, the Supreme Court and lower courts only used the "reasonableness clause" on rare occasions. There have been just a few dozen cases over many years, while hundreds of thousands of government decisions have been approved during those decades. Moreover, whatever intervention there was only happened when there was "extreme unreasonableness." Hence, interference in government decisions on these grounds has been rare.

In September 2023, the Supreme Court heard petitions arguing that the amendment to the *Basic Law: The Judiciary*, which revokes the court's authority to oversee government and ministerial decisions that are unreasonable (or even extremely unreasonable), including cases of omission to act, is illegal. The attorney general submitted her opinion, which starkly contrasted with that of the government itself.[140] While the AG argued that the legislation would affect the nature of the Israeli system of government, disrupt the balance between the judiciary and the government and its ministers, and may lead to the corruption of the civil service and undue influence in the selection process of civil servants, the government argued that not passing the amendment would lead to anarchy and that the Supreme Court does not have the authority to overturn the passage of a clause within a *Basic Law* (as opposed to a regular law). As already mentioned, Israel has no legislation to stipulate the difference between a "law" and a "Basic Law," and therefore, any amendment can be called a "Basic Law," even though its passage process is identical to that of a regular law.

All these questions were addressed by the High Court. Before the hearing, the government launched yet another campaign via social media outlets and TV channels indirectly controlled by the government and through journalists and online personalities working in quasi-service of Netanyahu, arguing that the Supreme Court does not have the authority to cancel the amendment to the *Basic Law* since it is, in titular terms, a "Basic Law" and not a "simple law." Knesset members started to threaten the Supreme Court justices, warning them not to dare rule on the annulment of the legislation. It was explicitly argued that the Supreme Court would create a state of anarchy in Israel. Smotrich, a religious-messianic-nationalist, far-right extremist who serves as Minister of Finance, warned the Supreme Court that its ruling to "cancel the Basic Law would bring about the end of democracy in Israel." The Speaker of the Knesset, a member of the prime minister's party, delivered what was supposed to be a statesmanlike speech a week before the Supreme Court hearing, in which he argued that the court does not have the authority to annul a *Basic Law*. He quickly moved on to explicit threats against the justices,

---

140. During the last two years, there have been many cases where the AG refused to represent the government in the Supreme Court due to total disagreement on the legal aspects of the matters at hand.

telling them that annulling the legislation would be tantamount to "trampling the Knesset." He did so with crude and threatening language. This, of course, was a baseless claim, but there is no room in Israel today for methodical and serious discussions. These are dark times. Everything is being done to serve the decision to appoint the leaders of messianic, extremist, nationalist and religious groups to key positions in government, to give them enormous powers and authority, and a public platform to disseminate their ideology in every media outlet. There is nothing more dangerous than this process of internal destruction.[141]

For Netanyahu's current coalition, reality, facts, and a desire to serve the public in general are not significant considerations. What matters are the partners' interests, which are the sole basis for the accompanying propaganda, disinformation, and justifications. In practice, the government is misleading and misinforming public opinion, riding roughshod over the facts and reality; it denies and avoids the fundamental principles of responsibility as well as its duty to accuracy. Opponents of the government's plans, which currently consist of organizations actively involved in promoting democracy—rather than just the empty shell of quadrennial elections (which is what the current coalition wants)—are protesting in various ways. Indeed, at the time, it was a protest movement that was greatly admired in democratic Western states. Even reports issued by international rating agencies like Fitch and Moody's about the state of the Israeli economy and Israel's ability to repay its debts referenced these protests positively, arguing that they balanced out the serious dangers posed by the legislation being advanced by the Israeli government. In a certain sense, the protests even contributed to the fact

---

141. On January 1, 2024, the Supreme Court issued its ruling. A majority of 12 out of the 15 justices ruled that the Supreme Court has the authority to criticize and even cancel legislation, including Basic Laws. By a majority of eight justices to seven, also it ruled that the Knesset's amendment to the Basic Law regarding "reasonableness," that is, its effort to void the court's authority to cancel unreasonable decisions by the government, is null and void. In so doing, it gave the foundations of democratic governance in Israel a major boost.

that Israel's credit rating remained unchanged until October 7, 2023. Having said all that, the battle over the character and future of the State of Israel is still being waged. Decades of under-the-surface processes—which the State of Israel and Israeli society tried to deny and which various groups suffered in silence while swallowing their anger—erupted. In 2023, Netanyahu's ability to incite and spread hatred, lies, and conflict between different parts of Israeli society managed to anger and agitate the "democratic public," which includes secular and national-religious members of the now-defunct National Religious Party, immigrants from both Mizrahi and Ashkenazi communities (despite Netanyahu's long-term and by no means unsuccessful efforts to incite conflict between these groups).

This camp suddenly understood that the foundations of the State of Israel's existence, which they mistakenly believed to be stable and solid—namely, a democratic state with stable governmental institutions, separation of powers, an independent judiciary, systems of government with oversight and criticism, an independent media, and institutions of higher education free from government intervention—had been nullified. This camp gradually realized that the so-called "judicial overhaul" would not only affect Israel's judicial system but was, in fact, part of a broader attempt by the current government, with its constituent parties, to change the very foundations, values, and basis of the state. Instead of upholding Israel's Declaration of Independence of May 1948—which determined that the new state would be democratic, would protect the rights of residents irrespective of religion, gender, or race, and would preserve a system of government based on the principles of justice and honesty in the spirit of the Jewish prophets—this government is engaged in a budgetary and legislative blitz designed not only to crush the judicial system, especially the Supreme Court, but also to impose legislation based on a bigoted, religious, nationalist, and racist agenda. This agenda aims to annul freedom of opinion, academic freedom, and the rights of the Arab minority in Israel while bolstering

Israel's religious camp and continuing to expand Israeli control over the West Bank. The same is true in the realm of higher education, where the education minister—a member of Netanyahu's party—is working vigorously to change the composition of the committee responsible for budgeting institutions of higher education in Israel and weaken its influence among the various institutions. This process started soon after the formation of the government and has been advancing systematically. Among the new appointees to the committee are individuals who cannot be considered the elite of Israeli academia; rather, they are people with no significant academic achievements, whose primary "advantage" is their support for the current government. Concern for the future of higher education in Israel has never been greater. The importance of higher education in general cannot be overstated, especially given its contribution to the Israeli economy, Israeli society, and culture. Israel's advantage over its neighbors is that it is a democratic society with freedom of opinion, freedom of demonstration, free education, encouragement of research and development, a free and independent press, and an independent judiciary. Without these, all of Israel's advantages will disappear, and the devastating ramifications will be imminent.

Deterioration of the rule of law, public order and the economy

In the meantime, during the nine months between January 2023 and that fateful day on October 7, Netanyahu and his government proved to be not only radically nationalist, messianic, and religious but also lacking real executive capabilities. There has been a dramatic deterioration in life in Israel—in every conceivable sphere. For example, in 2023, there were 233 murder cases in the Arab sector, compared to 109 in 2022. In the Jewish sector, there were 66 murders in 2023, compared to 38 in 2022. Until 2015, the ratio of homicide cases between the Jewish and Arab sectors was 1:4, whereas in 2023, it was 1:13. The deterioration in 2024 continued. By December 31, 2024, 220 homicide cases had already occurred in the Arab sector—all under Ben-Gvir's tenure as Minister of National Security (which oversees the Israel Police).[142]

The incompetence of the current Israeli government under Netanyahu is evident not only in its handling of crime in Arab society under the racist police minister Itamar Ben-Gvir but also in the economic sphere. There has been a worrying decline in Israel's once-thriving technological sector. Previously, Israel held the highest rate in the world for the establishment of new technology start-ups. However, 80 percent of new Israeli companies are now being registered in the State of Delaware rather than in Israel. This shift will have dramatic implications for Israel's future tax revenues. Moreover, foreign investment in Israel has dropped by a staggering 60 percent. Foreign investment in high-tech companies specifically has declined by 68 percent[143] and since. Since Israeli high-tech accounts for about 50 percent of the country's total exports and 25 percent of its tax revenues, the extent of the economic damage is clearly severe. Under Netanyahu's leadership, the continuation of these trends will only increase the scale of economic harm. The foreign exchange rate has also reacted accordingly. Until late 2022, the Israeli shekel was considered a strong and stable currency. However, since January 2023, the shekel has depreciated by approximately 13 percent, dropping from 3.25 shekels per U.S. dollar to 3.76 shekels per U.S. dollar. State revenues have also plummeted during this period. While there was a budget surplus at the end of 2022, by August 2023, Netanyahu and his government had turned it into a budget deficit.[144]

---

142. See "Taub Center," report published February 10, 2025.

143. Source: IVC, second-quarter report, 2023.

144. The events of October 7 and the subsequent year of war have only exacerbated Israel's economic downturn.

Chapter 10

October 7, 2023:
The Black Saturday and the aftermath

During the writing of this book, Israel was struck by the dramatic and horrific events of October 7, 2023. This was a Shabbat (Sabbath), and it fell during the Simhat Torah Jewish holiday. At 6:29 A.M., while most Israelis were still asleep, approximately 3,500 well-trained Hamas terrorists launched a surprise attack, which was made possible by failings within the IDF's intelligence establishment. Having broken through the perimeter fence between Israel and Gaza, they entered the kibbutzim adjacent to the border unimpeded, as well as the more distant communities of Ofakim and Sderot. In addition, they also stumbled upon the Nova music festival, attended by some 4,000 people, which was taking place at Kibbutz Re'im. During their attack, Hamas terrorists murdered, abused, looted, and burned homes. Some of their victims, including women and children, were beheaded or burned alive. The bodies of the victims were mutilated, and there was widespread use of sexual violence. They committed unspeakable and unimaginable atrocities. It was the greatest disaster to befall the State of Israel in its existence and the worst attack on Jews since the Holocaust. This horrific, brutal attack most probably would not have happened if, during 2023, another government and another prime minister, instead of Netanyahu and his ministers, had been in place. A standard and careful government, which paid attention to ongoing security threats and properly managed defense alarms[145] and taking care of security

---

145. Throughout 2023, many alarm signals warned that a potential military attack may occur imminently.

procedures[146] instead of the Government in place during 2023, could have prevented the October 7 massacre and its horrific consequences. The IDF, which permanently deploys two-thirds of its troops in the West Bank, increased its presence in the occupied territories under the Netanyahu-Ben-Gvir-Smotrich government. In the weeks before the Hamas attack, half of the three battalions stationed on the Gaza border were redeployed to the West Bank to protect settlers' celebrations at Hawara, an Arab village in the West Bank, and at Joseph's Tomb. This is another aspect of the occupation and the heavy price that the State of Israel pays for it: it forces the IDF to deploy a large number of infantry troops for policing and supervision. As a result, there were too few troops deployed on Israel's borders, including along the Gaza Strip.[147]

The devastating outcome was a combination of utter surprise,[148] a lack of military preparedness on Israel's part, minimal military presence along the border, and horrific acts of murder and massacre. It took between six and eight hours for the IDF to deploy a significant number of troops to the area. For those hours, Hamas terrorists were left to carry out their atrocities unimpeded. Netanyahu himself was dumbstruck, panicked, and utterly paralyzed. During those critical hours, he did not function at all. It was only at 12:30 P.M., six hours after the murderous attack began, that Netanyahu convened the first cabinet meeting. By then, hundreds of people had been murdered, butchered, and abused in nearby moshavim, kibbutzim, and at the music festival—children and adults alike. In any other country, the prime

---

146. PM meets the IDF's head of the Intelligence branch twice a month. From January of 2023 until October 7 –Netanyahu only met with him twice.

147. On that day, the same was true on the northern border with Lebanon, where the Iranian-backed and Iranian-funded Shiite terror organization Hezbollah was deployed.

148. The fact that Israeli forces, as well as statesmen, were taken by surprise is very intriguing. Since 2014, Israel knew that Hamas planned to attack Israeli civilian villages and kibbutzim near the border, taking hostages and killing as many civilians as possible. Netanyahu, in his book "BiBi-Story of My Life," page 464, describes the plan in specifics.

minister would have resigned immediately after such an incident. Netanyahu, however, has never taken responsibility for failures. He denies responsibility and finds others to blame. That's
what he did this time, too.

It is worth remembering that Netanyahu is a leader who
panics easily—something Ariel Sharon, under whom Netanyahu
served as finance minister, famously said of him. On October 7,
these characteristics were patently evident. When Hamas terrorists from the Nukhba unit broke through the border fence and
attacked Israeli communities at 6:29 A.M., Netanyahu was at
home in Caesarea, having returned the day before from a vacation. He left his home in Caesarea for the Prime Minister's Office
at 8 A.M.—but only convened the cabinet at 12:30 P.M., six hours
after the attack began and while Israeli citizens were being
massacred almost unimpeded.

Netanyahu has marketed himself to the Israeli people as "Mr.
Security" and "the Protector of Israel." In practice, he has been
anything but. While news of the disaster unfolded, Netanyahu
was, for several hours, totally out of control. He was paralyzed.
U.S. President Joe Biden probably saw what kind of mental state
the Israeli prime minister was in and immediately dispatched
the USS Gerald R. Ford to the Mediterranean. Secretary of State
Antony Blinken also rushed to Israel, accompanied by a group of
senior U.S. military commanders. In a rare move, he even participated in an Israeli cabinet meeting the week after the attack in
an attempt to stabilize the situation and keep everything under
control. It took Netanyahu several weeks to return to his char-
acteristic behavior, once the situation became more stable and
his panic and paralysis passed. Then he started behaving as he
always has—putting his personal interests and the preservation of his regime ahead of the interests of the State of Israel. The
Gaza war is still ongoing, and it is too soon to try and summarize
it.[149] However, in the context of the Israeli-Palestinian conflict,

---

149. Fighting has expanded to include Hezbollah on the northern front and
there was also, for the first time, a direct military confrontation with Iran.

the West Bank, Gaza, and the settlers, it is worth examining an additional element. Hamas is the political rival of the Palestinian movement headed by the PLO, which is currently represented by the Palestinian Authority in the West Bank. Hamas is a popular movement within Palestinian society. It is a religious, militant, and extremist organization. It is a movement that, in its charter, calls for the destruction of the State of Israel and the establishment of a Muslim state in its place. Hamas took power in Gaza through a violent coup in 2007, one year after Israel withdrew all of its troops and approximately 8,000 settlers from the Strip. Immediately after the Israeli withdrawal, the Palestinian Authority controlled Gaza, but clashes quickly broke out between the PA and Hamas, culminating in the latter taking control in 2007. It is vitally important to differentiate between Hamas and the Palestinians in the West Bank.

Israel's ultimate interest is to bolster the standing of the secular nationalists in Palestinian society in the West Bank and to crush Hamas, which is not only a radical Muslim terrorist organization in the mold of the Muslim Brotherhood but also deeply corrupt. Hamas is funded by Qatar and Iran, as well as through financial exploitation of the people of the Gaza Strip. Between 2016 and 2023, the Israeli government, at Netanyahu's initiative, transferred between $1.2–1.5 billion from Qatar to Hamas.[150] By doing so, Israel actively strengthened Hamas and weakened the Palestinian Authority, all under Netanyahu's guidance. As far as Netanyahu was concerned, Hamas was an "asset" and the Palestinian Authority was a "burden," so he tried to create two separate Palestinian camps, undermining the camp that was willing to recognize the State of Israel in order to avoid being forced to discuss the two-state solution. After all, implementing the two-state solution would require leadership, vision, courage, and the ability to handle disagreements within Israeli society. It would be a major challenge. Hamas does not care about

---

150. Monthly deliveries started at $15 million and grew to $30 million.

the people of Gaza. While governing the Strip, the water system collapsed, leading to 12 percent of children in Gaza dying from contaminated water. The money sent to Hamas is primarily used to acquire weapons and fund Hamas' military forces—while its leadership continues to grow richer. Some Hamas leaders are believed to be multimillionaires. What little was left over was spent on development, healthcare, and education. From this perspective, Hamas is not only the enemy of the State of Israel, with which there can be no compromise, but also the enemy of the people of Gaza. Indeed, the ongoing conflict with Hamas once again highlights the urgent need for the State of Israel to reach an agreement with the Palestinians over the West Bank. Such an arrangement would, of course, require security agreements to prevent military buildup in the West Bank and to prevent Hamas and similar organizations from taking over a future Palestinian state. It would also require the integration of Israeli and foreign military forces along the Jordanian border. Israel must ensure that the eastern border with Jordan is not open to various types of military forces, including terrorist organizations, and that the West Bank remains fully demilitarized with no military forces that could pose a future threat to Israel.

This has always been the case, and the Hamas attack on October 7 has merely reinforced it. However, the establishment of a Palestinian state, the evacuation of isolated settlements, and an international plan to strengthen the Palestinian economy—including fundamentally changing school textbooks that incite violence among Palestinian children in the West Bank—are vital for the future of the State of Israel. This will be incredibly complex, take a long time, and encounter hurdles, obstacles, and opposition. It will require courageous, determined, and wise Israeli leadership—totally unlike the Israeli government of 2024—and equally courageous, determined, wise, and non-corrupt Palestinian leadership. The assistance and deep involvement of the United States, together with the oil-rich Gulf states, led by Saudi Arabia, are necessary and cumulative conditions for the success of such a historic move. It is in Israel's primary interest to remain a democratic state with a Jewish majority and to remain part of the international democratic community. The stain of the occupation, with all its terrible implications, must be removed so that Jews around the world—including and especially their younger generation—can identify wholeheartedly and fully with Israel. The importance of this support cannot be overstated. Will such leaders step up? Only time will tell. History teaches us that leaders often emerge during times of historical crisis. As of December 2024, Israel finds itself at just such a breaking point.

Shortly after October 7, President Biden launched the outline of a plan that included steps toward the establishment of a Palestinian state, strengthening the Palestinian Authority, and granting civilian governmental powers to the Palestinian Authority in the Gaza Strip instead of Hamas, in order to fill the post-war vacuum with a moderate body like the PA, rather than extremists like Hamas. Within this framework, massive reconstruction work would be carried out in the Gaza Strip after months of devastating war.[151] This would also allow for the possible integration of Saudi Arabia in the normalization process with Israel. This kind of plan is exactly what Israel should aspire to; it should be working toward this goal, which will contribute to the country's continued economic, scientific, and cultural prosperity. There are, of course, risks involved and a price to pay—namely, recognizing the need for a demilitarized Palestinian state in the West Bank, or substantial parts of it, and granting governmental powers to the Palestinian Authority in the Gaza Strip. Netanyahu, for his part, has already made his customary bombastic declarations, stating that he will not allow the PA—which he refers to as "an enemy of Israel"—to assume any such powers.[152]

---

151. Around 60 percent of homes in Gaza have been destroyed and much of the infrastructure has been damaged. The same is true of hospitals and other facilities.

152. Netanyahu, as usual, flip-flopped, according to what suits his interests at any given time. On Page 493 of his autobiography, for example, he states that

Under the Netanyahu-Ben-Gvir-Smotrich government, with its extremists, its messianic settlers, and its racists, such a move is impossible. Israel could, therefore, miss the historic opportunity created by the crisis in Gaza and could fail to take advantage of the willingness of the United States, the Gulf states, and Saudi Arabia to be part of an important process. Needless to say, Netanyahu is unwilling and incapable of conducting or initiating such a move, both because of his partners in the government, on whom his regime depends, and because of his personality, his lack of the requisite courage and leadership. Under current circumstances, Biden not only recognizes this reality but also understands the great power and influence the United States has over Israel. Precisely because of Netanyahu's 15 destructive years of rule, Israel's utter dependence on the United States has become an incontrovertible fact. Therefore, the United States has enormous leverage and influence over Israel. If it wants to, it could push the processes that the region so badly needs, even against the wishes of the Israeli prime minister and his coalition partners. With some profound thinking, these processes will serve both the interests of Israel, which wants to integrate into the region, and, of course, the United States, which seeks to maintain its regional influence, especially in the Gulf. As is the way of crises, the current conflict creates an opportunity of historic proportions—an opportunity that cannot be missed, even if it engenders the wrath of the current government. President Donald Trump, who initiated the *Peace to Prosperity* plan during his first term, will have an historic chance now to push forward a similar plan with the Israelis, Palestinians, and Saudi Arabian leaders.

---

in a meeting with Ex-President Obama he raised the idea of reaching border arrangements with Egypt over Gaza, whereby the Palestinian Authority would take control of the Strip. Just like that. Incredible! But, as already established, Netanyahu changes his positions according to the situation and according to what suits him personally. No wonder there are intellectuals who described him as "*a small man in big times.*"

Epilogue

In 2024, the State of Israel was facing a historic crossroads. The establishment of the State of Israel—after 2,000 years of exile, the destruction of the Second Temple, and the fundamentally unsuccessful Bar Kokhba revolt against the Romans—was an extraordinary event in world history. No other nation has returned to its land and established a modern state after 2,000 years of exile. From a historical perspective, during the First Zionist Congress in Basel, Switzerland, in 1897, the chances of success were close to zero. And now, despite all the doubts of the rationalists, it has become a reality. There is good reason that some of the Messianic streams in Judaism saw the establishment of Israel as the "hand of God." Others, like myself, see it as a rare combination of events, with leaders who had remarkable talent, intelligence, courage, and determination; a spirit of yearning among Jewish people to return to the Land of Israel; and the antisemitism that was an integral part of Jewish life in the European Diaspora for two millennia. And, of course, the Holocaust—one of the most dramatic events in the annals of human history and certainly the most dramatic in the history of the Jewish people.

All of this came together to create the wonder known as the establishment of the State of Israel. Since then, Israel has undergone extraordinary processes. It absorbed massive numbers of immigrants from Europe and Arab countries, who arrived penniless and made up 150 percent of the population of a country that had just emerged from a war of independence that claimed many victims. Israel then embarked on a path full of challenges, wars, and the need for massive spending on defense—yet it developed a strong economy, advanced high-tech industries, first-rate research-and-development centers, universities, and scientific institutes with exceptional scientists and researchers, including Nobel Prize laureates in various fields. During this period, however, Israel was dragged into destructive processes that could lead it down a perilous path, already endangering its image, democratic regime, future, and very existence. On the one hand, from 2009 to 2024 (except for one year), Israel was led by Benjamin Netanyahu—probably the worst prime minister in the country's history. Apart from a political talent for seizing power and the ability to influence public opinion with bombastic rhetoric and pathos, Netanyahu lacks leadership or management capability. He surrounded himself with people who were incompetent and unskilled, whose only advantage was absolute loyalty to Netanyahu.[153] Netanyahu's destructive power has left Israel in 2024 in the hands of a government of extremists, the messianic religious, and the ultra-Orthodox.

Netanyahu is incompetent and dangerous to Israel, and his ministers—most of whom are truly inept—exacerbate this crisis. After the horrors of October 7, Israel initially enjoyed worldwide sympathy and support. However, Netanyahu and his government launched a military operation in Gaza that lasted over a year, resulting in the deaths of more than 40,000 people[154] have been killed, including an estimated 12,000 children. Large areas of the Gaza Strip have been completely destroyed, and there is a real danger of famine and epidemics. The international community—including Israel's allies—is starting to distance itself from Israel. Countries that were once considered friendly toward Israel are becoming increasingly vexed by the Netanyahu government's violent behavior. These sentiments are exacerbated by the fact that the current Israeli government is not working toward a resolution of the Palestinian conflict and is offering the Palestinians

---

153. With a handful of exceptions.

154. Of whom, 15,000 are Hamas terrorists. These figures are estimations, not verified.

no horizon whatsoever. Given the composition of the current government, this process will only intensify and accelerate. For Israel to flourish and exist as a modern, developed country with advanced, productive, and successful educational, industrial, and cultural institutions, it must meet the following three criteria: A) A state with an active democratic system. B) Ending the occupation of the West Bank and reaching an agreement with a demilitarized Palestinian state while maintaining military control of the eastern border with Jordan. C) The support of and close coordination with the United States and American Jewry.

These three elements are necessary conditions for the continued prosperity and existence of the State of Israel. All three are intertwined, and a common thread runs between them. It is impossible to maintain an active democracy while being an occupying force. The occupation, by its very nature, contradicts a democratic regime—one that is based on the right to demonstrate, respects differing opinions, provides a public arena for disagreements and dissent, upholds a free and independent press, maintains a strong and independent judiciary, and ensures robust individual rights. The occupation is gradually eroding all the foundations of Israeli democracy. The introduction in 2023 of the regime coup by Netanyahu's Likud party and its coalition partners—the messianic, nationalist-settler parties and the hatefully racist party headed by Ben-Gvir—has proven that Israeli democracy is fragile and is not a fundamental value for significant segments of the population. Many in Israeli society want to crush and neuter Israeli democracy. As far as they are concerned, holding elections once in a while is enough—while the other foundations of democracy can simply disappear. This is the essence of the judicial coup. While it is true that, in 2023, the Israeli public took to the streets in massive numbers and slowed the judicial coup, the danger to Israeli democracy remains. The root cause of opposition to an active democracy and an independent judiciary appointed by independent bodies rather than politicians is the occupation. Messianic settlers, such as Finance Minister Bezalel

Smotrich, see an independent judicial authority as an obstacle to fulfilling their aspiration of denying civil rights to Palestinians in the West Bank and violating all their rights and property, with the aim of weakening them or forcing them to leave their homes. This is nothing short of ethnic cleansing. Despite all its weaknesses and flaws—of which there are many—democracy is the only viable system of governance in a socially diverse country like Israel. Democracy and its institutions enable the existence of an active, diverse society with many sectors and groups, making coexistence possible for all parts of Israeli society. The gradual degradation of democratic institutions and values, a process that has taken place over the last decade but accelerated in 2023, will lead to Israel's "Lebanonization" and the collapse of Israeli society and government. And, of course, only in an active and fully democratic regime can Israeli institutions of higher education, research, science, culture, and intellectual thought operate in a free, productive, and innovative manner. Democracy, with its institutions of checks and balances and free exchange of ideas, is the only system of government that allows creative, thinking, and innovative people the freedom to operate unfettered. Without it, talented Israelis will gradually leave and take their skills elsewhere.[155] And they are These individuals form the very framework on which Israel's economic, cultural, industrial, and technological strength is built. It is also clear that Israel owes its continued existence and prosperity to aid from and its alliance with the United States and American Jewry.

If anyone still doubted this undeniable fact, the events of October 7 and their aftermath should remove those doubts. Without the political and, of course, military assistance of the United States, Israel would be in a dire situation. Thanks to the United

---

155. Even before the events of October 7, more than 20 percent of Israeli doctoral students were working outside of Israel. In 2023, there was an increase of 45 percent in people leaving Israel. The proportion of academics among these people is higher than the rate in the general public. This phenomenon has continued in 2024.

States, the fear of a coordinated attack by Hezbollah from Lebanon was contained. It was also thanks to the U.S. that the IDF had a supply of ammunition essential for military operations in Gaza and in the fight against Hezbollah.[156] But U.S. support is not guaranteed if Israel ceases to be an active democracy. The shared values between the two countries strengthen the alliance and the bond between their people.

The occupation, with all that it entails, also generates anti-Israeli sentiment in the United States and will lead to the erosion of the administration's support for Israel. These gradual processes have been taking place in recent years and are, of course, intensifying at present. At their core, they stem from a reality in which Israel occupies the West Bank and does nothing to reach an agreement with the Palestinian Authority—whether in its current weak and corrupt form or in a different format under new leadership. American Jewry, which has traditionally supported Israel, is finding it increasingly difficult to do so—especially the younger generation—given that Israel has been an occupying force for years and that there are growing signs of apartheid in the West Bank. American Jews struggle to see Israel as "a light unto the nations" or as a country with which they can fully identify. The younger generation is the future of American Jewry, and their engagement is vital for continued U.S. support of Israel and for maintaining the critical connection between American and Israeli Jews.

Therefore, all of these components are essential for Israel's continued prosperity, and they are deeply connected: undermining one affects all the others. The events of October 7 have brought Israel to a historic crossroads. Hamas has proven itself to be an extremist Islamic organization in the style of the Muslim

---

156. And, at the current time, the same is true of Iran. Until October 7, incidentally, there were ministers in Netanyahu's government who had the brazen stupidity to argue that Israel is a superpower and does not need the United States. And when the Biden administration expressed its reservations about the judicial overhaul, there were those who complained about the United States interfering in domestic affairs – and Netanyahu did nothing to stop them.

Brotherhood. The elimination of the State of Israel is one of its core goals, and it has demonstrated contempt for women's rights, minorities, and the LGBTQ community. It is a violent, corrupt regime that has failed to protect the interests of the people of Gaza. It is certainly not a partner for negotiations with Israel. However, there is a substantial number of Palestinians who are interested in coexistence with Israel, and Israel must nurture and strengthen these voices. The current Israeli government, in its present composition, is not interested in any such process. It is actively working to thwart and sabotage any possibility of cooperation, thereby creating a racist regime based on Jewish supremacy over Palestinian residents of the West Bank. This government has dragged Israel into the greatest disaster to befall the Jewish people since the Holocaust. It continues to bring Israel down due to its extremism, its messianic and ultranationalist ministers who are incapable of running a modern state, and its leadership's lack of executive and managerial capabilities. They are unable to make important decisions and lack vision, strategy, and leadership. At the same time, the current situation presents Israel with an extraordinary historical opportunity.

Israel now has the possibility of engaging in a process of reconciliation with the Palestinian people. This process will be difficult and take years. It will require difficult decisions from both sides, with many obstacles along the way. But it is a necessary effort, as the benefits for both sides would be immense. In fact, Israel would stand to gain even more from such a new environment, as it is better positioned to continue advancing economically and scientifically. Such a process would enable Israel to finally be integrated into the Middle East, joining an alliance with the moderate Arab states and benefiting from the new geopolitical landscape. Furthermore, it would strengthen Israel's ties with the United States and American Jewry. This is a historic opportunity that must not be allowed to slip away. To seize this historic opportunity, Israel must replace its current government with one led by individuals of vision—real leaders, not opportunists. It must be led by people with solid strategy, decision-making abilities, and strong executive capabilities. Israel still has plenty of people who are up to this task. It is thanks to such people that the miracle of the State of Israel still exists.

Appendix A

A partial list of the "inaccuracies"[157] in Benjamin Netanyahu's autobiography 'Bibi: My Story'

Page 76: Ehud Barak. Netanyahu writes about Barak's role in "Sayeret Matkal," an elite commando unit, and downplays the medals of honor he received (5), implying that they were not awarded for bravery in the field but for intel-gathering operations "which became routine over time." Writing about Barak's role in the Sabena operation, Netanyahu claims that "Barak's only role was to stand on the asphalt and blow his whistle." This, of course, is a blatant attempt to minimize Barak, who would later go on to become one of Netanyahu's major political rivals. Barak was commander of the Sayeret Matkal at the time of the Sabena hijacking and was responsible for planning the operation and was in command of Netanyahu himself in this very operation.[158]

Page 85-90: The Yom Kippur War. Netanyahu writes about him rushing back to Israel to fight during the Yom Kippur War. But he omits that immediately after the war he returned to the United States to continue his studies. He left his military unit, unlike his

---

157. The manipulative use of "facts" takes on varied and various forms, including outright lies, misrepresentations, partial facts, distorted facts, ignored 'inconvenient' details and so on. The examples in this appendix are versions of this phenomenon.

158. Barak in his book *My Country: My life, fighting for Israel, searching for peace,* describes Netanyahu as acting recklessly by wearing paratroopers' red combat boots before the operation, while the rest of the assault force was disguised as technical personnel. According to Barak, this almost torpedoed the rescue operation.

comrades, who remained in the reserves for many more months. Evading reserve duty became a typical part of Netanyahu's behavior. He would later serve no more than 35 days of reserve duty by the time he was 32, compared to other reservists, who are called up for at least 30 days every year! Therefore, he stopped serving in the reserves altogether. According to his reserve duty commander, Netanyahu also evaded service during the first Lebanon War (1982) when he presented some kind of excuse and was exempted from any further reserve duty in perpetuity. See the letter dated April 11, 2023, by Lieutenant-Colonel Shlomo Raisman.

Page 110: The War of Independence. Netanyahu writes in detail about the exploits of his father, Prof. Benzion Netanyahu, in the United States between 1940 and 1948. He omits two significant facts, however. Firstly, in December 1947, he was one of the signatories of a full-page petition in the New York Times, arguing against the establishment of the State of Israel in the borders proposed by the UN resolution from November 29, 1947. This petition, which David Ben Gurion ignored, would have been a dramatic and historic mistake. Secondly, Netanyahu forgets to mention that his parents remained in the United States during the War of Independence until it was clear that Israel had won the 1948 War of Independence. The family returned from the United States in 1949, after the War of Independence was decided.

Pages 124-125: "Operation Entebbe." Netanyahu describes the major role played by Yoni Netanyahu, his late brother, in planning the operation and even quotes Muki Betser, Yoni's deputy during the operation. However, an examination of Betser's book ("Secret Warrior," Keter Press, Pages 288-313) reveals that most of the planning of the operation was carried out in Yoni Netanyahu's absence, since he was on operational duty in the Sinai peninsula at the time. Indeed, the alleged quote from Betser about Yoni's contribution to the operation does not appear anywhere in the book and was, it seems, at least partly, made by Netanyahu.

The 1996 assassination attempt against Hamas leader Khaled Mishal in Jordan. As prime minister, Netanyahu ordered the Mossad to launch an operation to assassinate Hamas leader Khaled Mishal in Jordan using poison. The assassination failed and the perpetrators were arrested. There was a major crisis between Israel and Jordan, under the late King Hussein. As prime minister, Netanyahu panicked and lost his head, as he does in times of crisis. He ordered the Mossad chief to fly to Jordan and take an antidote—a secret formula that no one else knew of—with him. He subsequently freed dozens of terrorists, including Hamas founder Sheikh Ahmed Yassin. He did so because he panicked and lost his head. In his book, Netanyahu portrays himself as having acted judiciously and wisely. There is no mention of the panic which led to his poor decisions.[159]

A small, effective government. On Page 237 of the book, Netanyahu boasts that in 1996 he formed a small government comprising of just 18 ministers, thereby making good on an election promise to replicate "what is customary in the United States." Almost 30 years later, his current government has 38 ministers.

The establishment of the Netanyahu government in 2009: In the 2009 election, Netanyahu's Likud won 27 seats while Kadima, headed by Tzipi Livni, won 28 seats. According to Israeli custom, therefore, the president asked the leader of the largest party to try and form a coalition government. Livni, however, failed to do so, and the president then asked Netanyahu to try and form a government. He managed to do so, but only because he offered the ultra-Orthodox parties substantial financial benefits, even while Livni was still negotiating with them. He promised the leaders of the ultra-Orthodox parties that he would "give them much more

---

159. Areil Sharon later described Netanyahu as he flaked out and collapsed as "totally broken," and therefore he took over to handle the crisis and negotiate the release of the two Mossad agents who were caught in Jordan. See N .Mishal, *Released for publishing (Hebrew), 2011.*

than her" (Page 360). He writes: "Our bloc won 65 seats, a clear and decisive victory, and within a few weeks I formed a government," as if it were a trivial matter, rather than the result of his willingness to give the ultra-Orthodox what they wanted—at the public's expense—in order to seize power.

The submarines and shares affair. This grave and scandalous affair, which has not been investigated at all, is only marginally mentioned in Netanyahu's book and he does not address the key issues. For example, there is no mention of his $600,000 purchase of shares in the family's NMSD company, which was owned by his uncle in the United States and which owns 61% of Seadrift, which he 3 years later sold to an entity owned by same uncle for $4.47 million in October 2010, when he was serving as prime minister. The same is true of the book's description of a tender for navy vessels to protect Israel's gas facilities in the Mediterranean. The tender was canceled at the last minute when Netanyahu was already prime minister, and instead, Thyssenkrupp was awarded it. To this end, it appears that the tender was also altered to meet the exact specifications of the ships that Thyssenkrupp produces.

On Page 497 of the book, Netanyahu claims that between 2015 and 2020, he worked to realize his goal of "turning Israel into a rising world power." Needless to say, he had no real, detailed or systematic plan—or even any professional team. In retrospect, this becomes even more bleak, given that in 2024, Netanyahu brought Israel to the lowest point in its history. It is internationally isolated, has profound disputes with the U.S. administration, is embroiled in the Gaza quagmire following a military surprise that stemmed from a combination of arrogance, baseless claims that "Hamas has been deterred," and governmental and military lawlessness and was already downgraded twice by global rating agencies. The first time since the State of Israel began grading.

Gas: Netanyahu is trying to take credit for anything positive that happens, including gas production off Israel's shores. The discovery and production of gas in the Mediterranean Sea are the work of entrepreneurs and experts with daring and vision, as well as a professional group from Israel and the United States. Netanyahu omits to remind his readers that he once promised the Israeli public that the public fund that is supposed to receive a percentage of the revenues from gas production would put hundreds of billions into the state's coffers. In practice, by 2022, the fund had just 4.5 billion shekels, according to *The Marker (January 24, 2023)*.

Hamas and the Gaza Strip: During the 2009 election, Netanyahu gave an unequivocal promise to the public, stating that, if elected, he would "eliminate Hamas." In practice, from the moment he came to power, he did nothing to fulfill this promise. There is no mention of this promise in his book. And certainly no mention of the fact that he did not lift a finger to make good on his hollow promise. In fact, exactly the opposite is true: he strengthened Hamas and ensured that huge sums, believed to be more than $1 billion, were transferred from Qatar to Gaza. He even refused to carry out several operations that top security officials recommended executing from time to time against Hamas leaders, including Yahya Sinwar, the man behind the October 7 massacre.

Appendix B

Israel's Declaration of Independence[160]

ERETZ-ISRAEL [(Hebrew)—the Land of Israel] was the birthplace of the Jewish people. Here their spiritual, religious and political identity was shaped. Here they first attained to statehood, created cultural values of national and universal significance and gave to the world the eternal Book of Books

After being forcibly exiled from their land, the people kept faith with it throughout their Dispersion and never ceased to pray and hope for their return to it and for the restoration in it of their political freedom.

Impelled by this historic and traditional attachment, Jews strove in every successive generation to re-establish themselves in their ancient homeland. In recent decades they returned in their masses. Pioneers, *ma'pilim* [(Hebrew)—immigrants coming to Eretz-Israel in defiance of restrictive legislation] and defenders, they made deserts bloom, revived the Hebrew language, built villages and towns, and created a thriving community controlling its own economy and culture, loving peace but knowing how to defend itself, bringing the blessings of progress to all the country's inhabitants, and aspiring towards independent nationhood.

In the year 5657 (1897), at the summons of the spiritual father of the Jewish State, Theodor Herzl, the First Zionist Congress convened and proclaimed the right of the Jewish people to national rebirth in its own country.

---

160. Taken from the official Knesset website.

This right was recognized in the Balfour Declaration of the 2nd November, 1917, and re-affirmed in the Mandate of the League of Nations which, in particular, gave international sanction to the historic connection between the Jewish people and Eretz-Israel and to the right of the Jewish people to rebuild its National Home.

The catastrophe which recently befell the Jewish people—the massacre of millions of Jews in Europe - was another clear demonstration of the urgency of solving the problem of its homelessness by re-establishing in Eretz-Israel the Jewish State, which would open the gates of the homeland wide to every Jew and confer upon the Jewish people the status of a fully privileged member of the comity of nations.

Survivors of the Nazi holocaust in Europe, as well as Jews from other parts of the world, continued to migrate to Eretz-Israel, undaunted by difficulties, restrictions and dangers, and never ceased to assert their right to a life of dignity, freedom and honest toil in their national homeland.

In the Second World War, the Jewish community of this country contributed its full share to the struggle of the freedom- and peace-loving nations against the forces of Nazi wickedness and, by the blood of its soldiers and its war effort, gained the right to be reckoned among the peoples who founded the United Nations.

On the 29th November, 1947, the United Nations General Assembly passed a resolution calling for the establishment of a Jewish State in Eretz-Israel; the General Assembly required the inhabitants of Eretz-Israel to take such steps as were necessary on their part for the implementation of that resolution. This recognition by the United Nations of the right of the Jewish people to establish their State is irrevocable.

This right is the natural right of the Jewish people to be masters of their own fate, like all other nations, in their own sovereign State.

ACCORDINGLY WE, MEMBERS OF THE PEOPLE'S COUNCIL, REPRESENTATIVES OF THE JEWISH COMMUNITY OF ERETZ-ISRAEL AND OF THE ZIONIST MOVEMENT, ARE HERE

ASSEMBLED ON THE DAY OF THE TERMINATION OF THE BRITISH MANDATE OVER ERETZ-ISRAEL AND, BY VIRTUE OF OUR NATURAL AND HISTORIC RIGHT AND ON THE STRENGTH OF THE RESOLUTION OF THE UNITED NATIONS GENERAL ASSEMBLY, HEREBY DECLARE THE ESTABLISHMENT OF A JEWISH STATE IN ERETZ-ISRAEL, TO BE KNOWN AS THE STATE OF ISRAEL.

WE DECLARE that, with effect from the moment of the termination of the Mandate being tonight, the eve of Sabbath, the 6th Iyar, 5708 (15th May, 1948), until the establishment of the elected, regular authorities of the State in accordance with the Constitution which shall be adopted by the Elected Constituent Assembly not later than the 1st October 1948, the People's Council shall act as a Provisional Council of State, and its executive organ, the People's Administration, shall be the Provisional Government of the Jewish State, to be called "Israel."

THE STATE OF ISRAEL will be open for Jewish immigration and for the Ingathering of the Exiles; it will foster the development of the country for the benefit of all its inhabitants; it will be based on freedom, justice and peace as envisaged by the prophets of Israel; it will ensure complete equality of social and political rights to all its inhabitants irrespective of religion, race or sex; it will guarantee freedom of religion, conscience, language, education and culture; it will safeguard the Holy Places of all religions; and it will be faithful to the principles of the Charter of the United Nations.

THE STATE OF ISRAEL is prepared to cooperate with the agencies and representatives of the United Nations in implementing the resolution of the General Assembly of the 29th November, 1947, and will take steps to bring about the economic union of the whole of Eretz-Israel.

WE APPEAL to the United Nations to assist the Jewish people in the building-up of its State and to receive the State of Israel into the comity of nations.

WE APPEAL—in the very midst of the onslaught launched against us now for months—to the Arab inhabitants of the State of Israel to preserve peace and participate in the upbuilding of the State on the basis of full and equal citizenship and due representation in all its provisional and permanent institutions.

WE EXTEND our hand to all neighboring states and their peoples in an offer of peace and good neighborliness, and appeal to them to establish bonds of cooperation and mutual help with the sovereign Jewish people settled in its own land. The State of Israel is prepared to do its share in a common effort for the advancement of the entire Middle East.

WE APPEAL to the Jewish people throughout the Diaspora to rally round the Jews of Eretz-Israel in the tasks of immigration and upbuilding and to stand by them in the great struggle for the realization of the age-old dream—the redemption of Israel.

PLACING OUR TRUST IN THE "ROCK OF ISRAEL," WE AFFIX OUR SIGNATURES TO THIS PROCLAMATION AT THIS SESSION OF THE PROVISIONAL COUNCIL OF STATE, ON THE SOIL OF THE HOMELAND, IN THE CITY OF TEL-AVIV, ON THIS SABBATH EVE, THE 5TH DAY OF IYAR, 5708 (14TH MAY,1948).

Printed in Dunstable, United Kingdom